For Denni With Love

IMAGES
of America

SEASIDE

Carol L M...
March 24, 2009

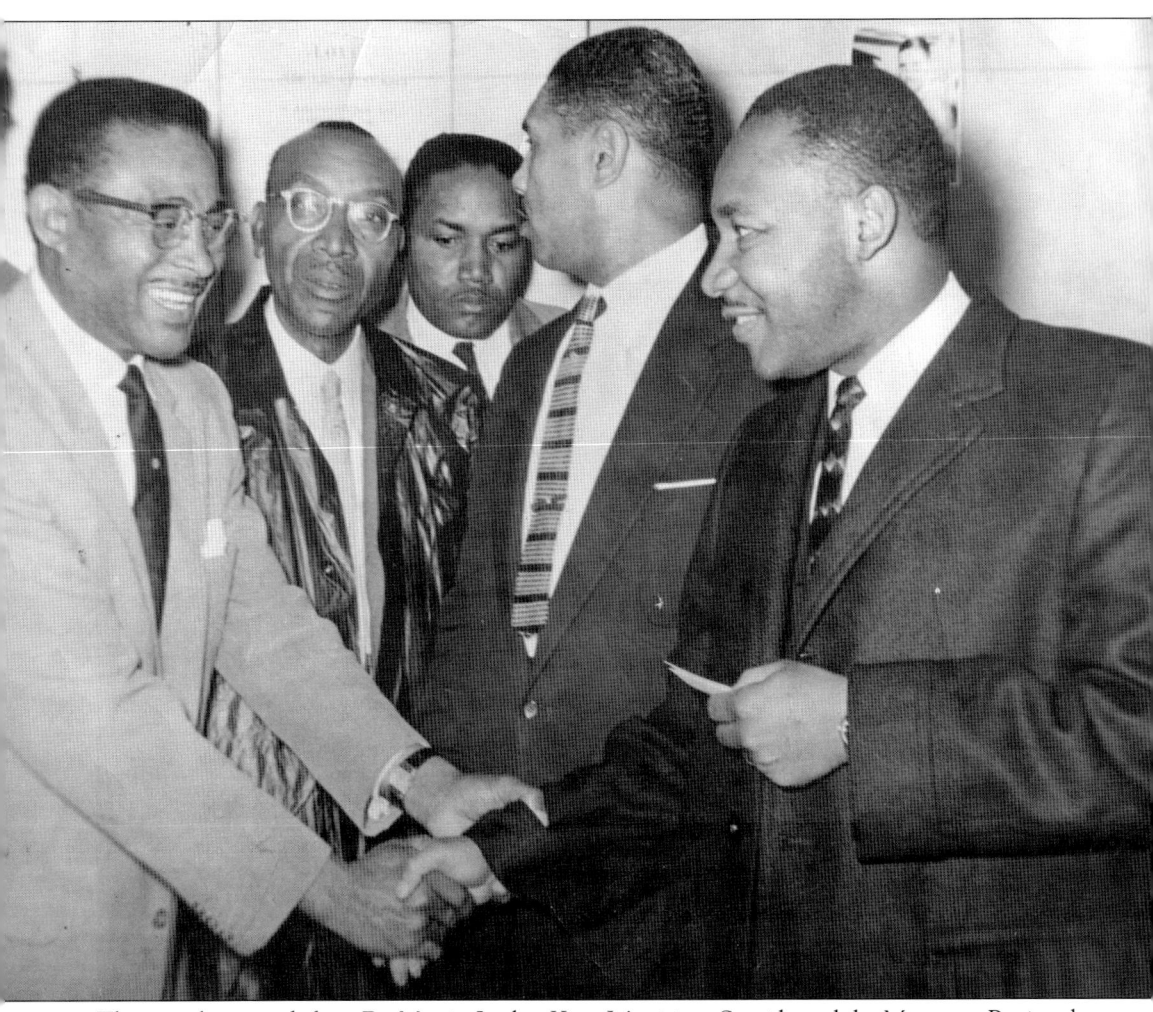

This is a photograph from Dr. Martin Luther King Jr.'s visit to Seaside and the Monterey Peninsula in 1962. From left to right are John Bean, Rev. G. E. Ellis, councilman Stephen Ross, Rev. C. Lewis McFadden, and Dr. Martin Luther King Jr. (Courtesy of the Lenora Bean Collection, City of Seaside Archive.)

ON THE COVER: Robert's Oak, considered the largest oak tree in the world, is pictured in 1890. (Courtesy of the City of Seaside Archive.)

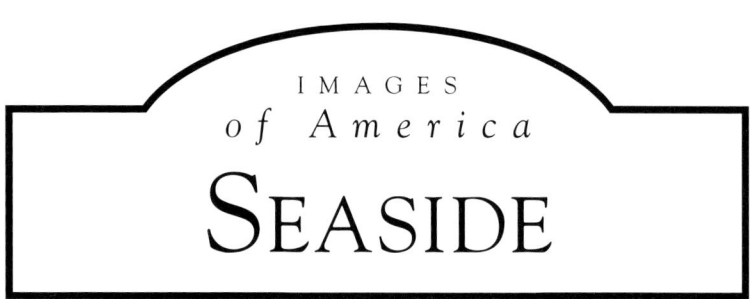

Carol Lynn McKibben and
the Seaside History Project

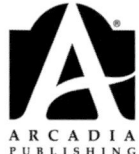

Copyright © 2009 by Carol Lynn McKibben and the Seaside History Project
ISBN 978-0-7385-6981-9

Published by Arcadia Publishing
Charleston SC, Chicago IL, Portsmouth NH, San Francisco CA

Printed in the United States of America

Library of Congress Catalog Card Number: 2008933393

For all general information contact Arcadia Publishing at:
Telephone 843-853-2070
Fax 843-853-0044
E-mail sales@arcadiapublishing.com
For customer service and orders:
Toll-Free 1-888-313-2665

Visit us on the Internet at www.arcadiapublishing.com

Contents

Acknowledgments		6
Introduction		7
1.	Resort Era and First Settlement	11
2.	Depression, War, and the Creation of a Community	25
3.	Revitalizing the Population in the Postwar Era	65
4.	Reinventing Seaside in the 1960s	81
5.	Civil Rights!	97
6.	From Military Town to Budding Resort	119

Acknowledgments

It is with great pleasure that we take the opportunity to thank the many individuals and organizations that made this project possible. First and foremost, we are grateful to the Seaside City Council—Mayor Ralph Rubio and council members Don Jordan, Tom Mancini, Steve Bloomer, and Dennis Alexander—whose continued support demonstrates their dedication to preserving the history of their city. City manager Ray Corpuz guided and championed us when we needed it most. This work could not have been completed without him. Dr. Albert M. Camarillo of Stanford University provided great insight, sustaining us with his enthusiastic commitment to the history of minority communities in California.

We are appreciative of the funding support we received from the California Council for the Humanities, the Community Foundation of Monterey County, the Monterey Peninsula Foundation, Clark Cares Realty, and Eric's Deli in Seaside. No project in historic preservation can possibly be accomplished without assistance, and we benefited enormously from their collective generosity.

John Castagna educated us with patience, kindness, and humor on the technical aspects of the work. Thank you for your encouragement, help, and cheerful collaboration.

Thanks to Kurt Kuss, California Archivist, Defense Lanuguage Institue, Foreign Language Center, Historic Research Collection, Chamberlin Library; and to Dennis Copeland, Archivist and Historian for the Monterey Public Library. Both were of immeasurable help in everything from finding photographs to advice on choice and quality. They are also great supporters and friends. We also thank Carolyn Plummer and Ibrahim Omer, former staff members of the Seaside History Project, for their contributions to this project.

The people of Seaside, to whom this book is dedicated, graciously opened family albums and allowed us access to priceless memories and moments in time. There are a few individuals who deserve special thanks: Ruthie Watts, Pearl Carey, Richard Joyce, Patricia Wasson Cal, Lenora Bean, Evangelina Perez, and Sherman and Elizabeth Smith.

Sarah Nicora would like to extend special thanks to her parents, Debbie and Charlie Nicora, and to Matt for his sweetness, support, and love.

I would like to thank Sarah (who became an overnight expert in scanning and layout) for her judgment, acumen, great work ethic, and can-do spirit. My incredible children, Andrew and Becky, and my daughter-in-law Diana once again provided welcome relief, joy, support, and love throughout this process. My greatest thanks and love are, as always, for Scott.

Introduction

Mention the locations Pebble Beach, Carmel, or Monterey and most Californians and perhaps most Americans will know you are talking about the Monterey Peninsula and its world-famous tourist attractions. But mention the city of Seaside outside of the immediate local area, and few, if any, know about this little city located adjacent to the well-known resort destinations. However, if you refer to Fort Ord, historically one of the largest military bases in western America, most people can quickly situate the relatively unknown city of Seaside as the military town that borders the base.

Seaside's history began in the 19th century. A Progressive Era subdivision of Monterey located only a mile from the famous Del Monte Hotel, Seaside was a tiny community of middle-class whites who envisioned the area as a resort destination in the 1880s when they first settled there. World War I and the establishment of Fort Ord in 1917 transformed the community into a training area for soldiers stationed in the nearby Presidio of Monterey, discouraging both development and infrastructure, which began Seaside's reputation as a community on the other side of the tracks from Monterey. The Depression of the 1930s reinforced that perception as migrants from the American Dust Bowl flocked into Monterey for work in the canneries. They quickly settled in Seaside, where property values were lowest, even free, if one simply claimed a piece of land and built a home. World War II brought expansion of the military base and another new population transformation as military families, many of whom were black, Asian, and mixed race, settled in Seaside.

When Pres. Harry Truman ordered full integration of the armed services by Executive Order 9381 in 1948, Seaside was a tiny subdivision of Monterey with a population of fewer than 10,000. The surge of black military personnel and their families, as well as soldiers of all races, doubled the population, so that by 1956, the number of Seaside residents had grown to 21,750. Incorporated in 1954, Seaside annexed parts of Fort Ord in 1968, which increased its population to 32,000. Seaside was, by 1970, the most populous city on the Monterey Peninsula and the second largest in the county. Between 1960 and 1970, the population of Seaside had more than doubled (the total population reached 35,940), as did the black population (7,341, or 20 percent of all city residents). A decade later, the changes were even greater. The black population in 1980 stood at 29 percent, about 13,000, while the white population decreased to 47 percent. By 1980, although no single group could claim majority status, Seaside became known as the center for black settlement and had the most concentrated population of African Americans in California between Oakland and Los Angeles.

Despite the adverse effects of being connected to the military base (crime, violence, and a transient population), and within an environment where racism, segregation, and resistance to African American residents were apparent, Seaside represented hope and opportunity for blacks. Richard Joyce described Seaside as a "utopia for black people" when he arrived in 1952. Unlike other cities in California or in the East or American South, he claimed, "everything was open in

Seaside for young, enterprising black people. Things weren't fixed. The city was unincorporated. There was tremendous opportunity for us to create something new."

The African Americans who came to Seaside between World War II and 1980 did just that. They were mostly military people, sophisticated travelers who had often served in Europe, the Far East, and throughout the United States. They were well educated, most were graduates of black colleges in the American South, and, most important, they were steeped in the civil rights movement led by Dr. Martin Luther King Jr., which was successfully changing the structure of American life. Almost everyone associated with civil rights and social justice who came to California, from Dr. Martin Luther King Jr., to Rosa Parks, to Dolores Huerta and many others, visited Seaside in the postwar era. Moreover, there was a unique gender component to civil rights in Seaside. Black women, many of them the wives of army officers, were able to engage the community politically in ways that their husbands, who were active-duty soldiers, could not (active-duty military personnel were forbidden to participate in local politics). This black demographic contrasted sharply with the white one. Whites in Seaside tended to be less welleducated migrants from the Dust Bowl or nearby communities who were small-business owners rather than professionals. Although whites were the first of Seaside's mayors and city councilmen, blacks, both women and men, quickly organized into a formidable political force. Their strategies were a middle way, a civil rights political activism that was different—both from the goals and strategies of Dr. Martin Luther King and also from the racially charged politics of the urban East and West in the 1960s and 1970s.

Black Seaside civil rights activists built coalitions with whites, Hispanics, and Asians to desegregate housing, create fair employment practices, desegregate school faculties, and, most importantly, elect blacks to political office. While Southern civil rights activists focused on voter registration and Northerners focused on busing, Seasiders were getting elected as mayors and members of the city council, being appointed to important city commissions, and working as city managers and high-level staffers in city government. While civil rights activists in Boston and Chicago were integrating schools, Seasiders integrated school faculties, the school board, and the highest levels of school administrations. When rioting broke out in Watts, Seasiders, who had always built coalitions and governed collectively with other groups, held forums discussing issues of fairness and social justice. Seaside black youth marched, too, but they also created an alternative to the racial identity politics of other cities during the 1960s through the 1980s, which makes their history truly central and unique in the history of the American civil rights movement.

Seaside's history has been intimately tied to Fort Ord, but it is far more than just another military town and African American settlement. Seaside's history reveals fundamental patterns that have shaped California and the West. The story of a multiracial population struggling to live together, first as a military town then in a post-military world, is a huge part of Seaside history as it has been and continues to be in metropolises such as Los Angeles, San Francisco, Oakland, and other large urban areas in California. Indeed, Seaside is one of dozens of California cities that now have majorities of minorities. Seaside is also reflective of so many California cities that during the civil rights movement were forced to grapple with issues of racial inclusion and social and economic justice, emerging by the 1980s as a municipality uniquely characterized by a politics of inclusion. It is also a city, like so many throughout the Southwest and the nation, that has been transformed demographically in the last 30 years by the mass immigration from Mexico.

The story of Seaside is a great deal more than the story of thousands of individual lives over time in a small, multicultural military community. This is a history that tells us much about race, ethnicity, class, gender, and military towns in California and the West. The history of Seaside is part and parcel of the larger forces that have shaped our society during the last century, and at the same time, it is a story all its own.

This book of photographs documents important aspects of Seaside history from its inception in 1880 to its 1980 transformation as the zenith of African American community life. Chapter one begins with Seaside's founding and development from a resort to a military town. Chapter two documents the subdivision from the Depression era through the World War II years and finally its process of incorporation into a suburban town separate from Monterey in 1954. Chapter three focuses on the first demographic transformation that turned a mostly white community into a city of color and, particularly, into the center of community life for African Americans on the Central Coast. Chapter four is the story of urban renewal, redevelopment, and the physical changes brought on by federal policies that allowed communities like Seaside to build new housing and infrastructure in the 1960s and 1970s. Chapter five is the culmination of identity for Seaside as it claims its place in American history as the site of one of the most important and unique centers for civil rights in California and the nation. The flowering of black culture in the form of black fraternities and sororities, and the myriad social events they sponsored to raise scholarship funds for Seaside youth, including the Blues Festival and Jazz Festival, is a testament to Seaside as a mecca for African American social and cultural life.

In the current day, Seaside is once again changing from a city dominated by black culture to one that increasingly represents Latino culture and history. As it has always been, Seaside's best example of the changeover is political. The first-ever Mexican American mayor of the city, Ralph Rubio, was elected in 2004 and is currently serving his second term.

One
RESORT ERA AND FIRST SETTLEMENT

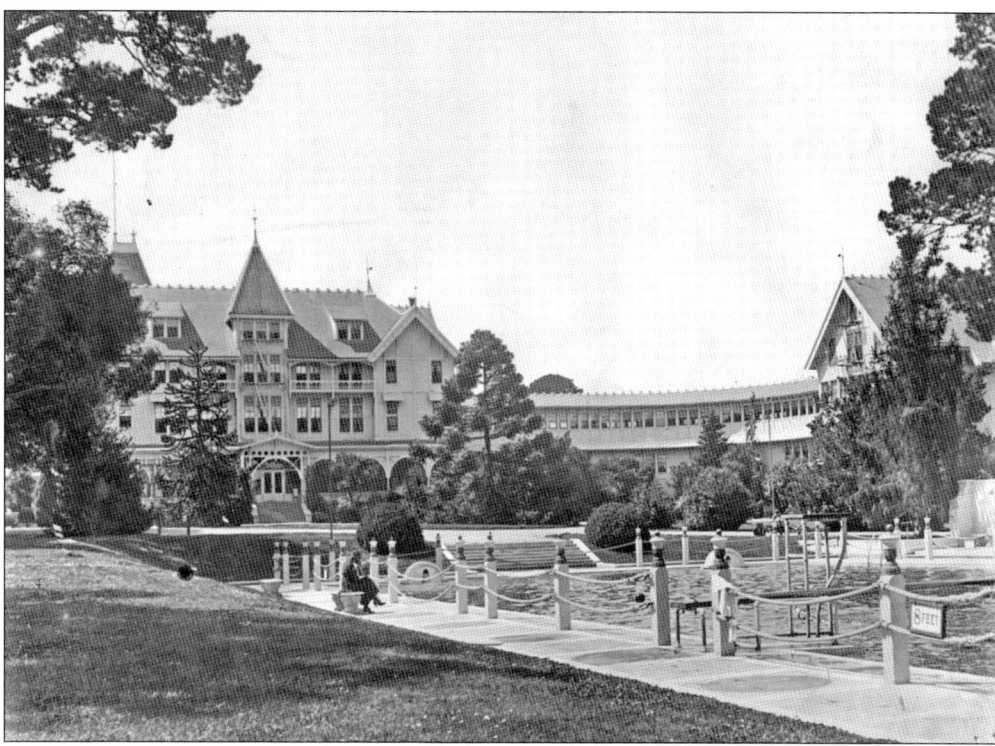

Seaside began the same way the Hotel Del Monte began, as a part of the city of Monterey. Because the subdivision of Seaside was located just a mile to the northwest of the hotel, it was initially conceived as an outgrowth of the resort community and was identified as a tourist destination for the middle classes, while the Del Monte catered to the elite. First built in 1880 by Charles Crocker, the hotel was destroyed by fire in 1887, rebuilt, and then destroyed by a second fire in 1924. The hotel was rebuilt for the third time in 1927, and at this point, the subdivision east of Monterey was already being transformed to reflect the military population associated with Fort Ord. The navy used the rebuilt hotel for training and instruction, and bought the property outright in 1947, utilizing it as the Navy Postgraduate School from 1951 through the present day. The history of the Hotel Del Monte–Naval Postgraduate School symbolizes the critical changes Seaside underwent in the late 19th century and early decades of the 20th century from resort to military town. This photograph of the Hotel Del Monte clearly shows it to be an elegant resort destination for elite vacationers. (Courtesy of the Monterey Public Library, California History Room.)

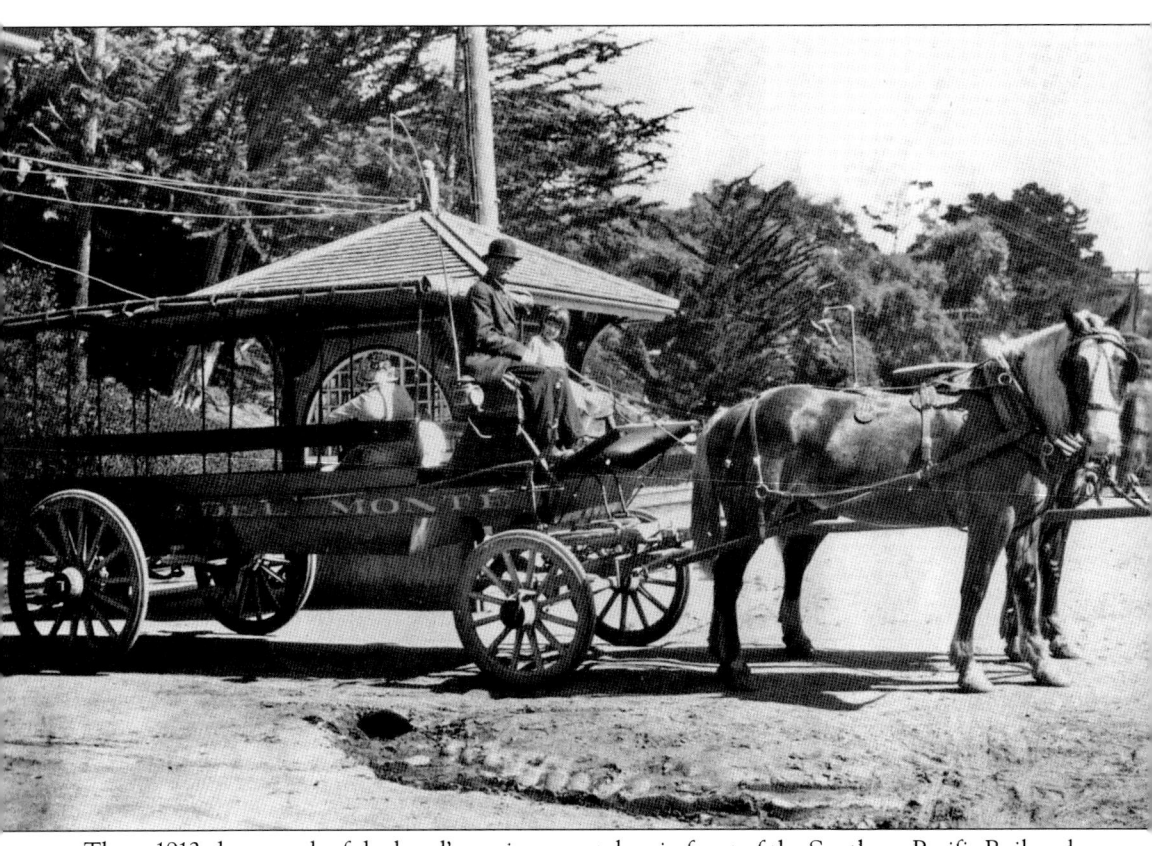

The c. 1912 photograph of the hotel's carriage was taken in front of the Southern Pacific Railroad depot across from the Hotel Del Monte. (Courtesy of the Monterey Public Library, California History Room.)

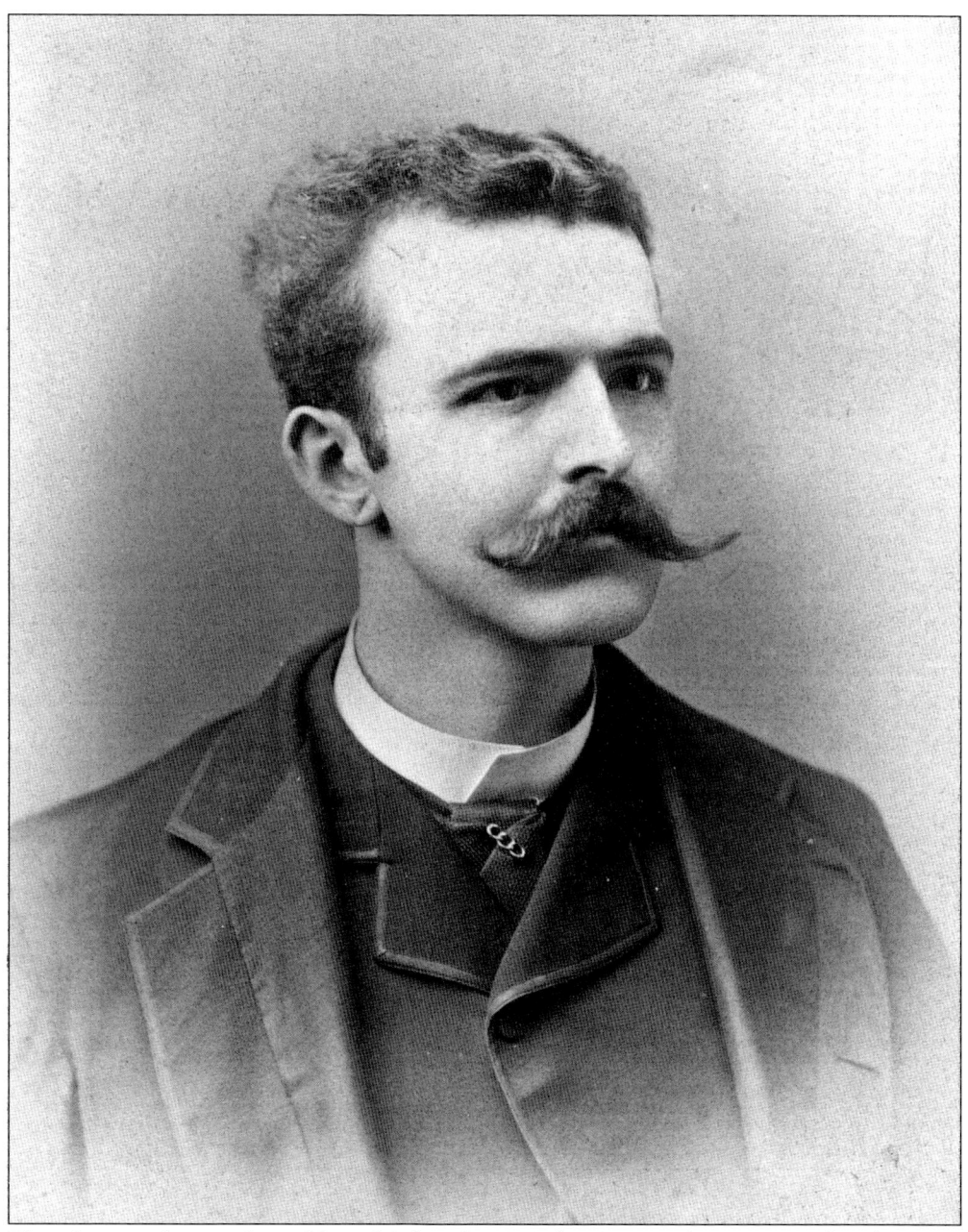

This photograph was taken of Seaside's founder, Dr. John "Doc" Roberts, pictured at the age of 24. Like so many other ambitious pioneers, Doc Roberts left New York in 1887 for California and settled near relatives in Pacific Grove. He and his uncle bought 160 acres from the David Jacks Corporation, which he divided into 1,000 lots for sale as vacation property. He also made his home in the new residential area that bordered Monterey and the hotel. (Courtesy of the City of Seaside Archive.)

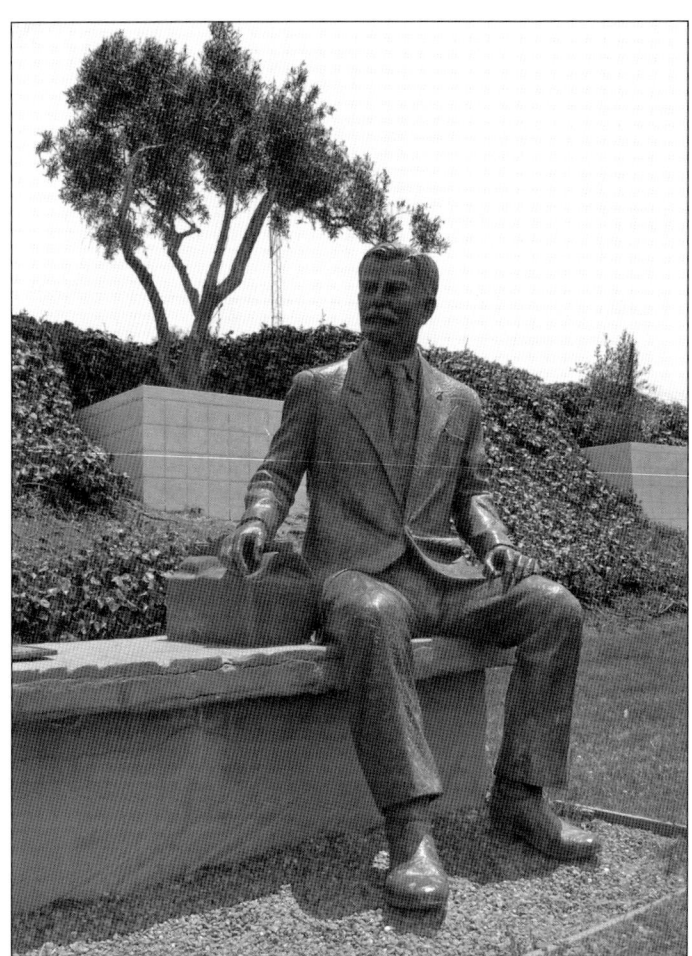

Two years later, Doc Roberts founded the Seaside Post Office, pictured below, and a school in the new Seaside district of Monterey. Roberts was known for successfully demanding road access from the new community of Seaside to the rest of the peninsula. Roberts was elected to the Monterey County Board of Supervisors in 1908 and is credited with establishing several important roadways, including the portion of Highway 1 that linked Monterey north to Castroville. This statue of Doc Roberts (at left) sits in front of Seaside City Hall today. (Both, courtesy of the City of Seaside Archive.)

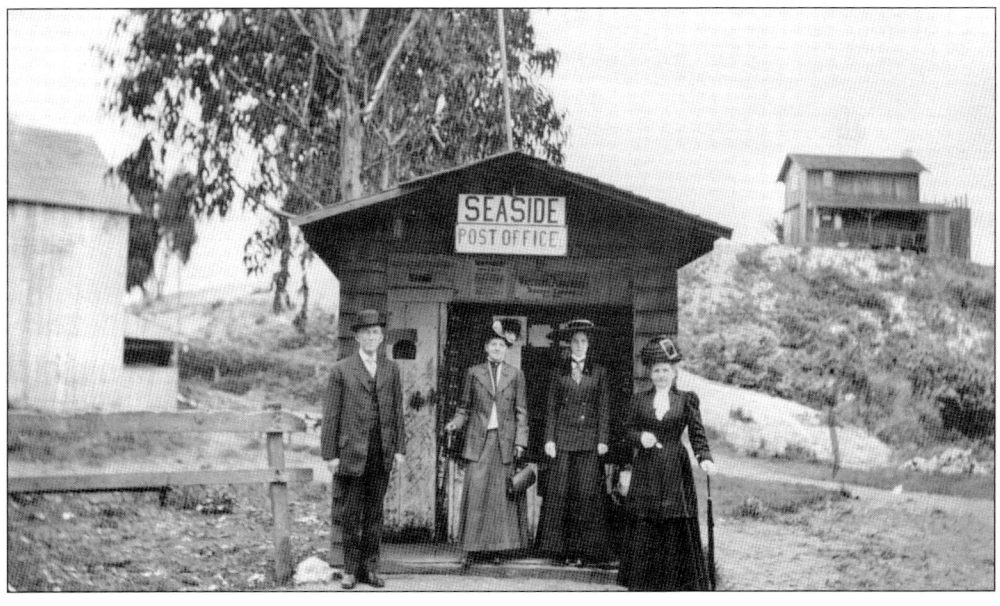

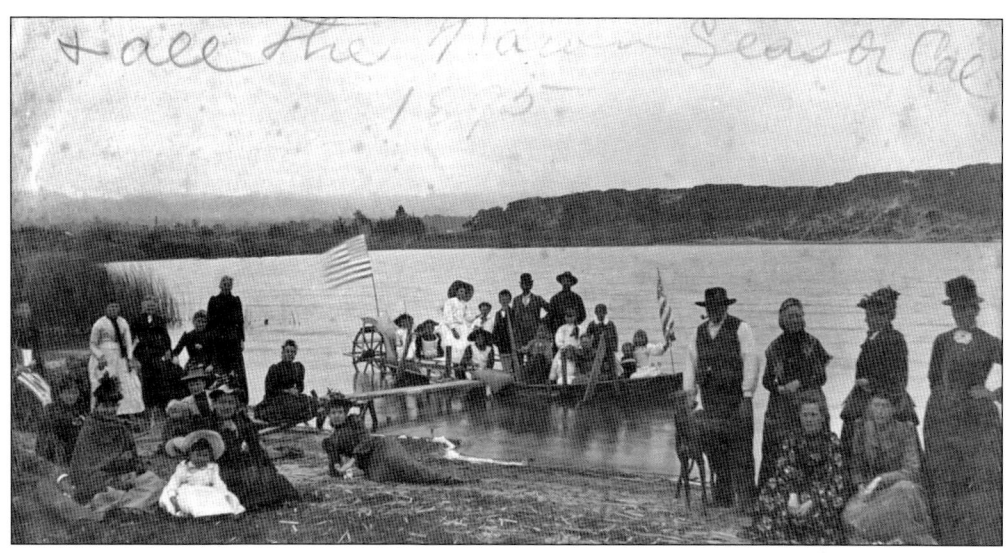

The above photograph of Seaside residents in front of Roberts Lake on the Fourth of July in 1895 shows the community as it first formed. The photograph below is the first house in Seaside, built by the Bayliss family. The two Bayliss sisters are shown here around 1888. The first settlers of Seaside were Caucasian migrants from the American South and Midwest who wanted to create a community in the new suburb of East Monterey similar to the suburban environments emerging in nearby Pacific Grove and Carmel. Like so many other Americans who came West during the Progressive Era, the first residents of Seaside were mostly farmers and ranchers, often veterans of the Civil War who aspired to the middle class. All found opportunity in the sparsely populated subdivision of East Monterey. Seaside, in its earliest years, gradually became a place for summer vacationers and farming folk. (Both, courtesy of the City of Seaside Archive.)

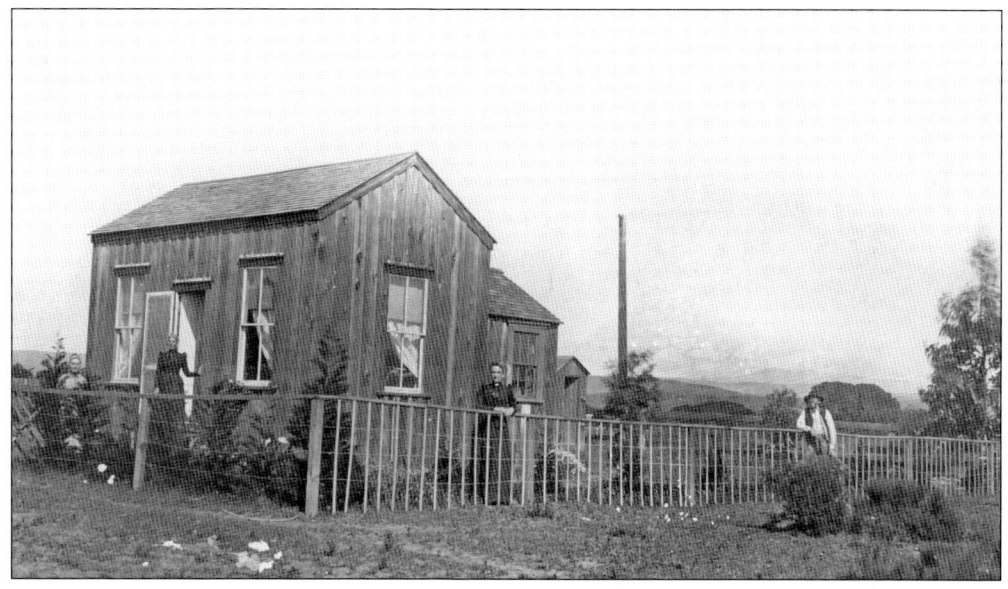

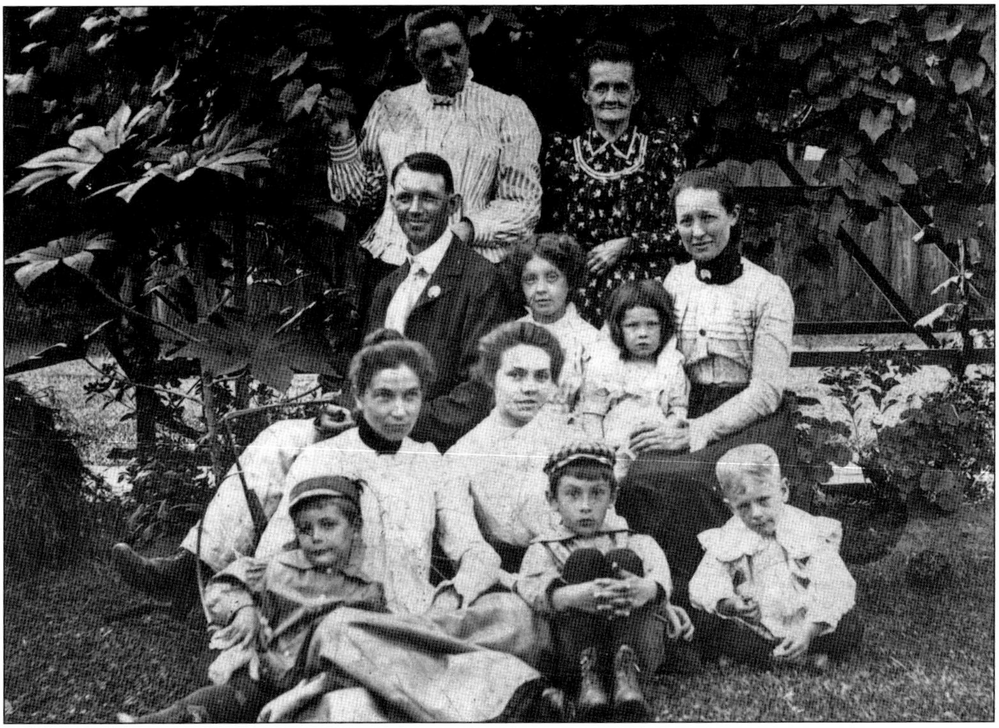

These photographs of the Wasson family typified the circuitous settlement patterns that marked late-19th- and early-20th-century American migration to California. The above image shows the Wassons, a farming family, in a family portrait in Illinois in 1900, and while the photograph below, taken 10 years later, shows the family in transit from Oklahoma to Seaside, where they established a home and where members of the family still reside today. (Both, courtesy of the Wasson Family Collection, City of Seaside Archive.)

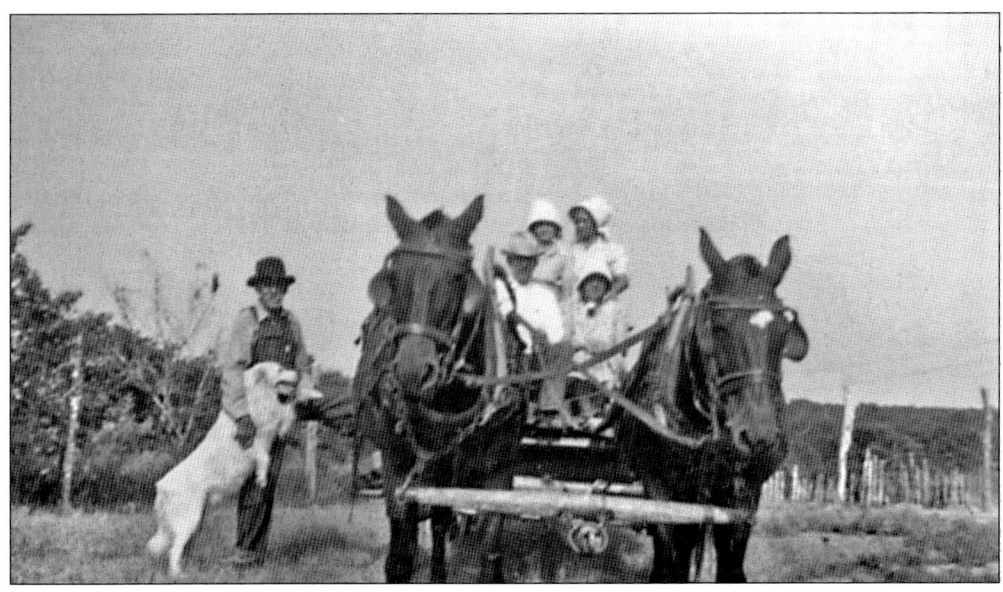

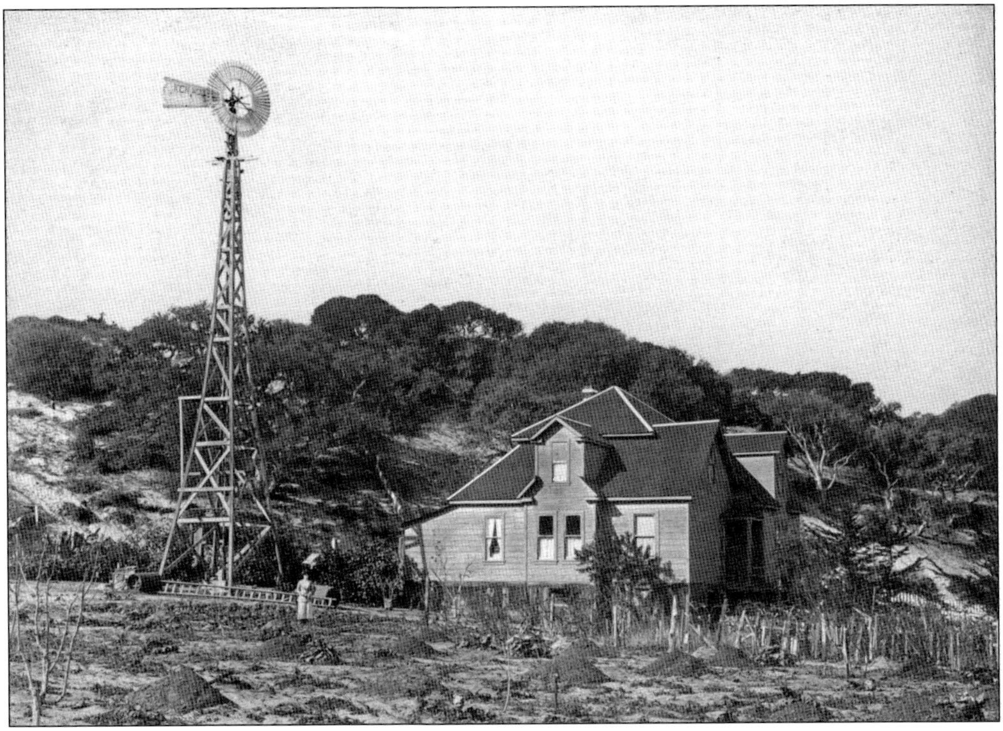

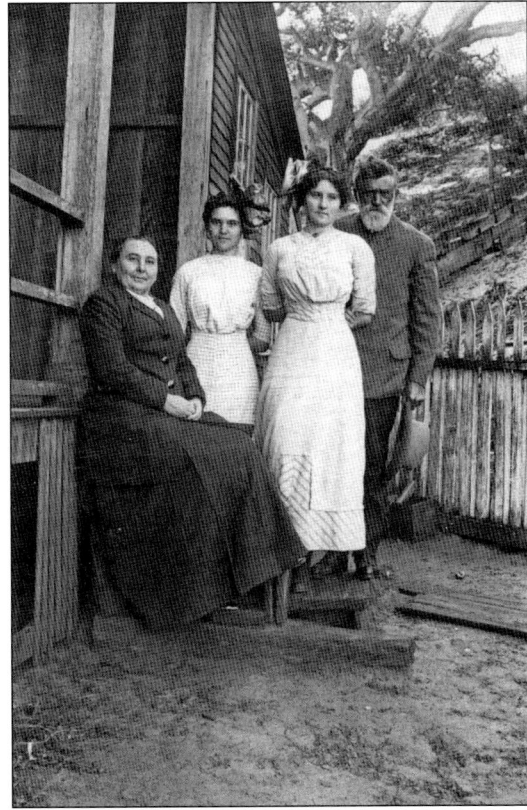

The Henneken family arrived on the Monterey Peninsula in 1859 and first settled on land in Carmel Valley, bought at auction from the City of Monterey. They and 12 other homesteader families subsequently lost their property in a nasty lawsuit with the David Jacks Corporation. The Hennekens then settled in Seaside in 1903, where they farmed and were also known as beekeepers. Above is a 1903 photograph of the family in front of their home, and at right is a close-up of the Henneken family on the front porch. From left to right are grandmother Mary Henneken, Marguerite, Dolores, and grandfather Kasper Henneken. One of the earliest to settle in Seaside, Kasper Henneken became county beekeeper and also established Seaside's first waterworks. (Both, courtesy of the City of Seaside Archive.)

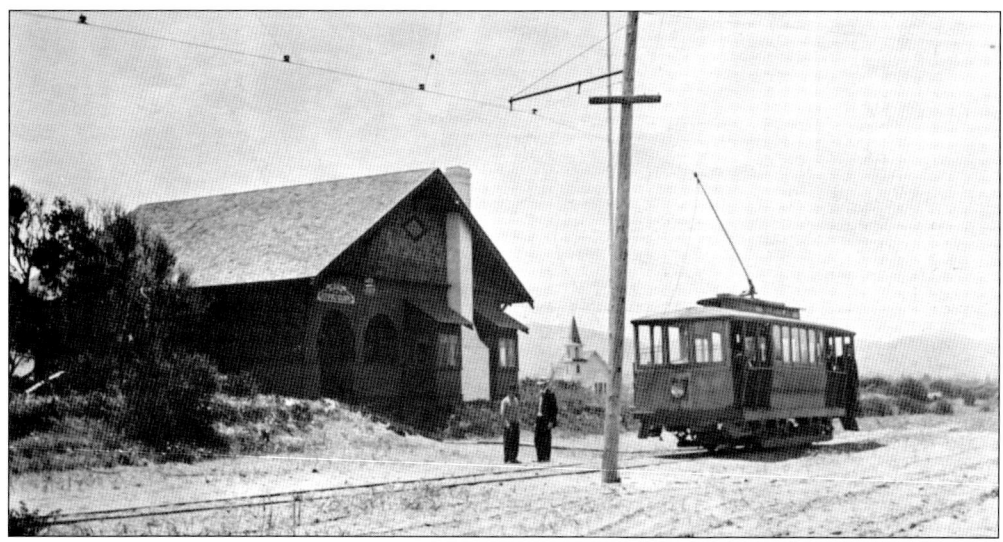

One of the most essential developments for any suburb in the late 19th century was transportation. The Southern Pacific Railroad gave Seaside easy transit to Monterey and San Francisco, and made settlement in Seaside attractive. Enthusiastic about establishing Seaside as a viable middle-class suburb, the first residents organized clubs, gathering together to celebrate holidays, birthdays, and other events. Pictured here is the c. 1912 Seaside Civic Club, located along the Southern Pacific Railway Depot. Below is a photograph of the entire town taken under the famous Robert's Oak tree, considered the largest oak tree in the world. (Both, courtesy of the City of Seaside Archive.)

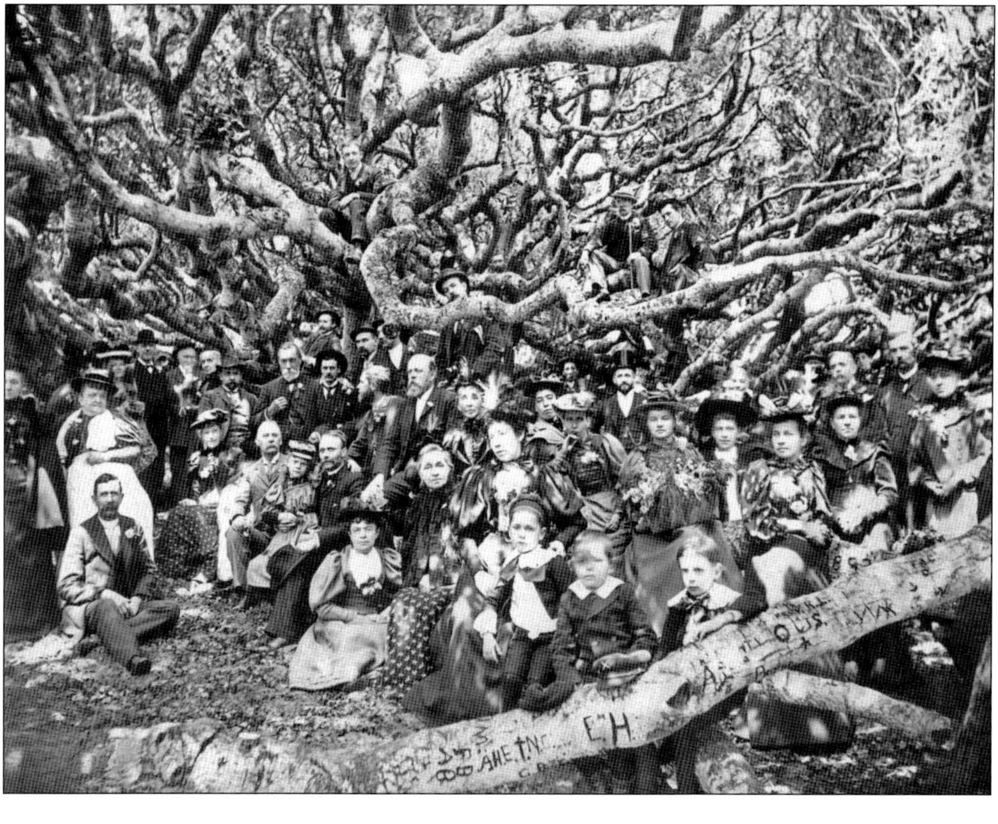

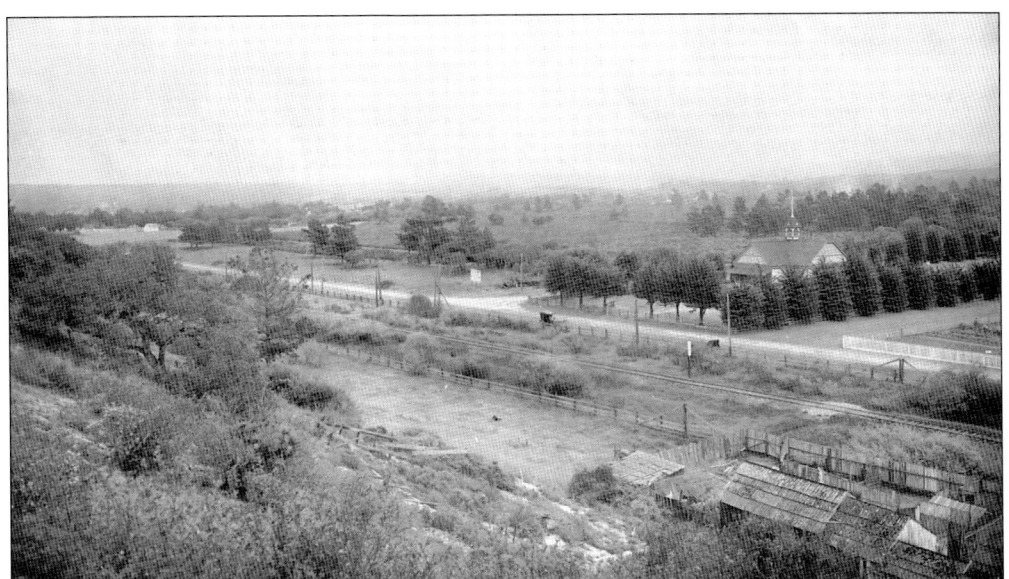

Del Monte Avenue became one of Seaside's most important main streets. Seaside built the Del Monte School, shown in the upper right of this photograph, which was taken around 1900. (Courtesy of the Monterey Public Library, California History Room.)

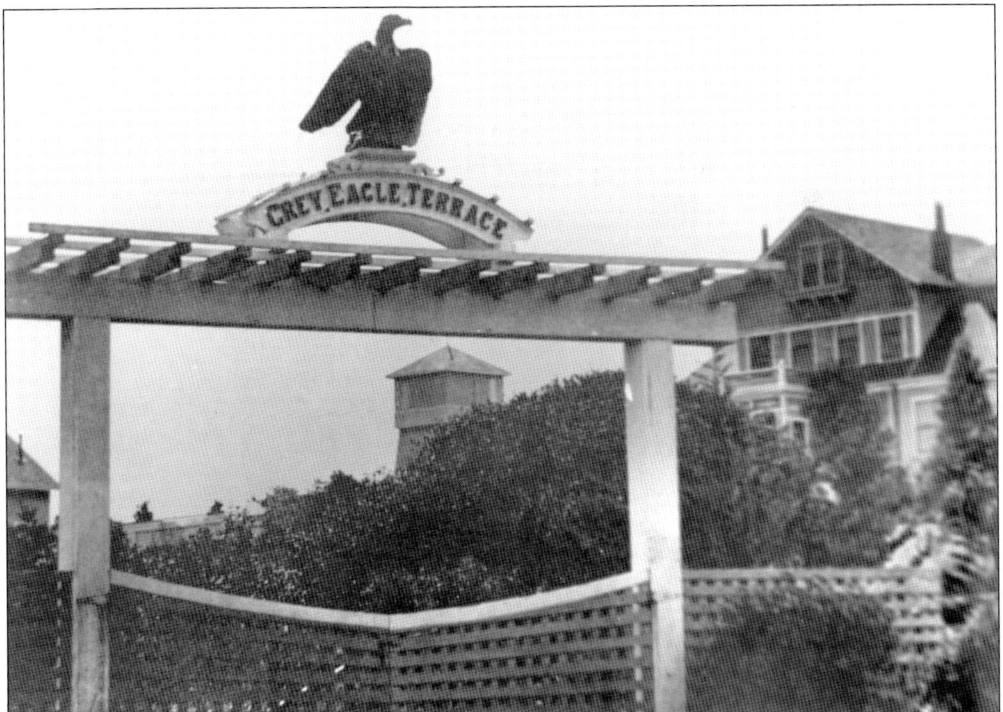

Dr. White Wolf, grandson of Grey Eagle, chief of the Choctaw Nation, took advantage of inexpensive land in Seaside and built a home there, called Grey Eagle Terrace. He had great difficulty finding a contractor who would agree to build such a mansion for a Native American. The mansion was destroyed in 1917 and the land subdivided into lots. The area is still known as Grey Eagle Terrace today. (Courtesy of the City of Seaside Archive.)

MONTEREY DEL MONTE GROVE

THREE HOURS FROM SAN FRANCISCO.
FIVE HUNDRED YARDS FROM THE GROUNDS OF THE HOTEL DEL MONTE.
ONE OF THE LARGEST SUMMER RESORTS IN THE WORLD.

We offer to the Public in the above Tract some very choice lots for from $30 to $70 each according to location; size of lots 25 x 110 feet.

Now is the time to secure for yourself a Summer Residence, the cost of which would be nominal.

No more liberal offer of land ever made to the Public.

TERMS -- One-half Cash, and balance in 6 months, with interest at 8 per cent. per annum.

DAVID STERN & SONS

Real Estate Agents and Auctioneers, 323 MONTGOMERY ST., S. F.

surveyed by W. G. Little
April, 1888

These lots will be very much sought after owing to: first their desirable and healthy location and second their close proximity to one of the world renowned hotels. The temperature varies but 6 degrees between summer and winter, making what is so much sought after, namely "Indian Summer." This places it ahead of all other summer resorts inasmuch as it omits the extreme heat and the extreme cold. "Del Monte" being visited both summer and winter by all who visit California and also by our own residents, would naturally give this tract superiority over any other part of the state, in never being dull or quiet.

Here everything is always life, and amusements of all kind can be found, such as surf-bathing, warm salt water bathing in the beautiful Bath House of the Hotel (the latter being open to the public), drives that cannot be excelled for most all the points in the vicinity are historical. Boating on a beautiful lake right on the tract, yachting in the Bay of Monterey, etc.

Everything conducive to both health and pleasure can be had here, leaving nothing to be desired and surely placing the locality far ahead of any competitor. Here for a small outlay, you can purchase a site for, and (lumber having to be freighted but a very short distance) on very advantageous terms, build yourself a summer residence to your own taste. And what can be more beautiful than having your own home to go to in the summer, and where your neighbor is your friend, as this place will undoubtedly be in the form of a colony.

There is a fine well with water on the tract and water can be found anywhere on the grounds at a depth of from 12 to 20 feet , besides which the water of the "Carmel Water Works" can be brought to the tract.

This tract can only improve both in beauty and value as the Pacific Improvement Company is spending large sums of money in tree planting and otherwise beautifying their possession.

DAVID STERN AND SONS,   WILLIAM HANNON,
323 MONTGOMERY ST., SAN FRANCISCO   MONTEREY

Developers eagerly promoted Seaside as a resort destination both for its environmental attributes and for its easy access by train and streetcar to Monterey and San Francisco. Pictured at left is a typical advertisement extolling Seaside's virtues as a vacation destination at the dawn of the 20th century. Below is a photograph of a crowd waiting to purchase land in Seaside at auction. (Left, courtesy of the Monterey Public Library, California History Room; below, courtesy of the City of Seaside Archive.)

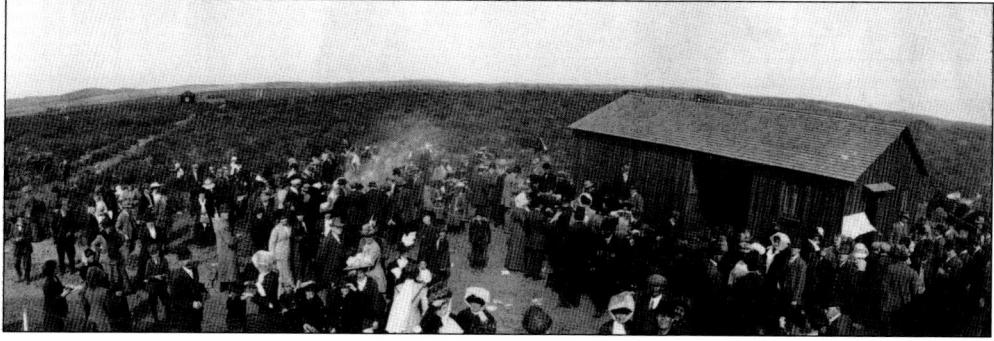

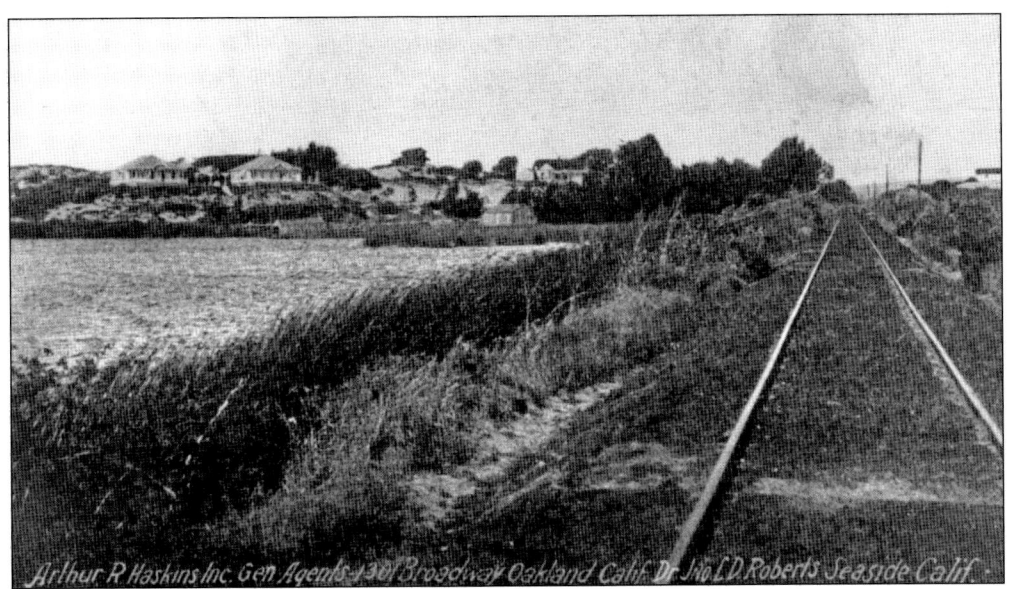

This view of Seaside from the Southern Pacific Railroad tracks and the 1917 map of the new subdivision pictured below show just how far Seaside had come since its founding in 1889. By 1920, Seaside was an example of Progressive Era suburban expansion that included transportation systems, housing, and community life. (Above, courtesy of the City of Seaside Archive; below, courtesy of the Monterey Public Library, California History Room.)

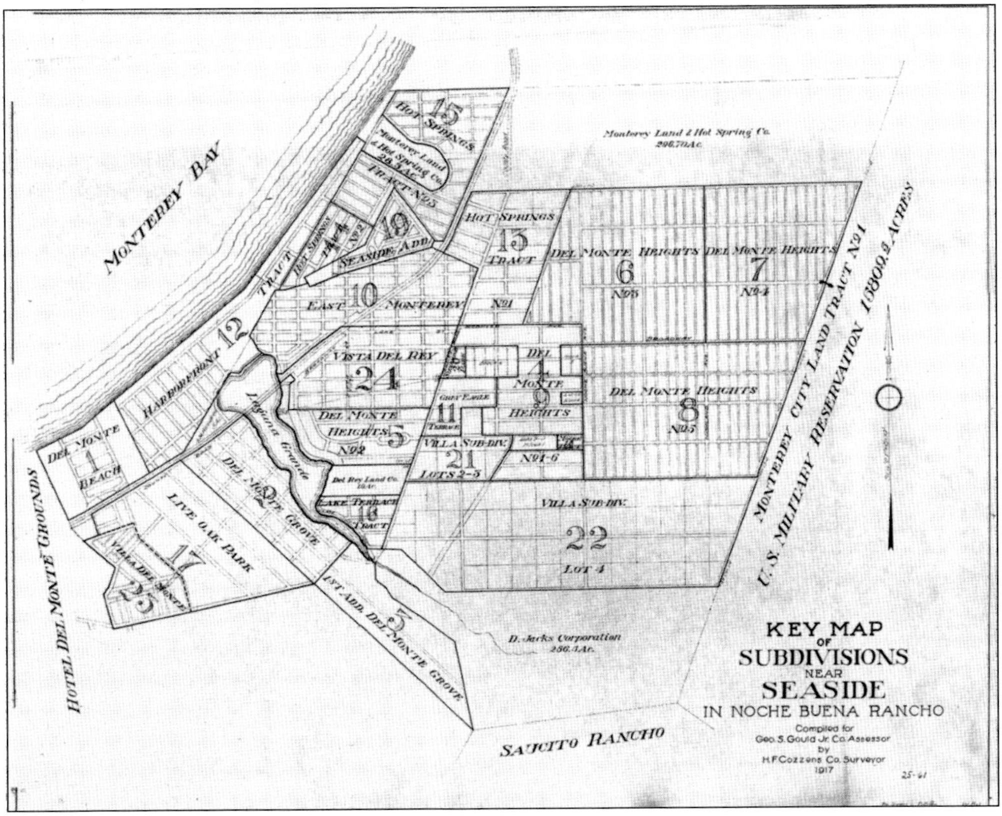

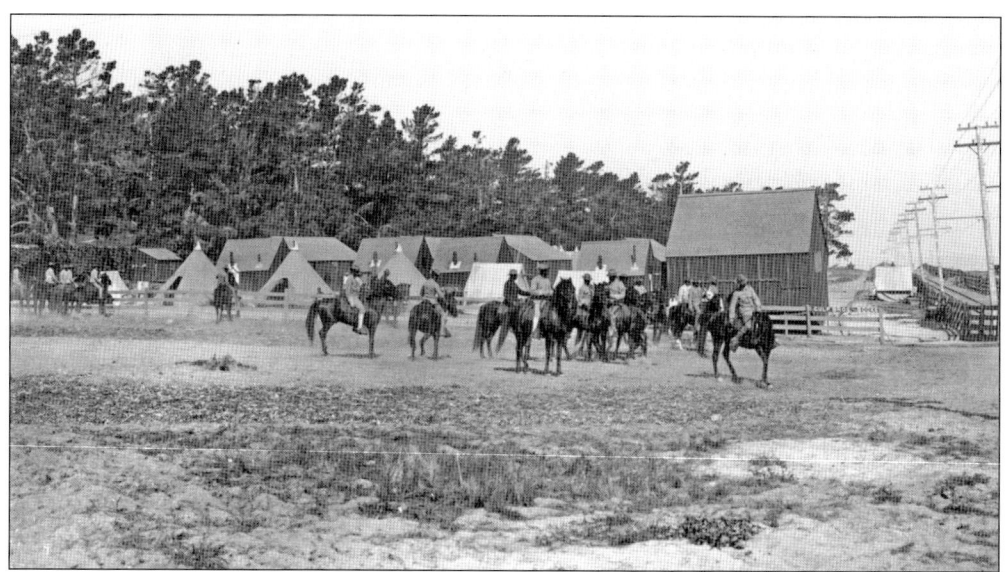

The black Buffalo Soldiers of the 1st Calvary (shown above) were actually trained at the Presidio in Monterey. The photograph below depicts officers at the Presidio. However, over the course of the next two decades, these and other soldiers at the Presidio would alter the face of Seaside from its Progressive Era suburban incarnation to a military town. (Both, courtesy of the Monterey Public Library, California History Room.)

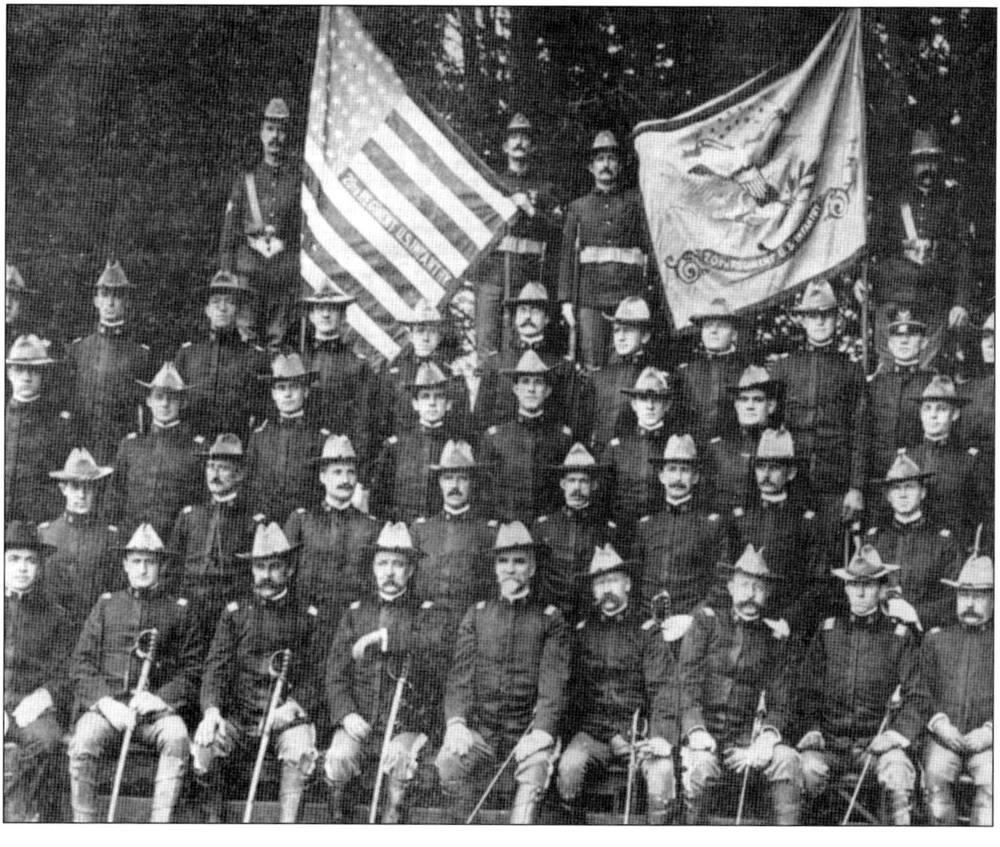

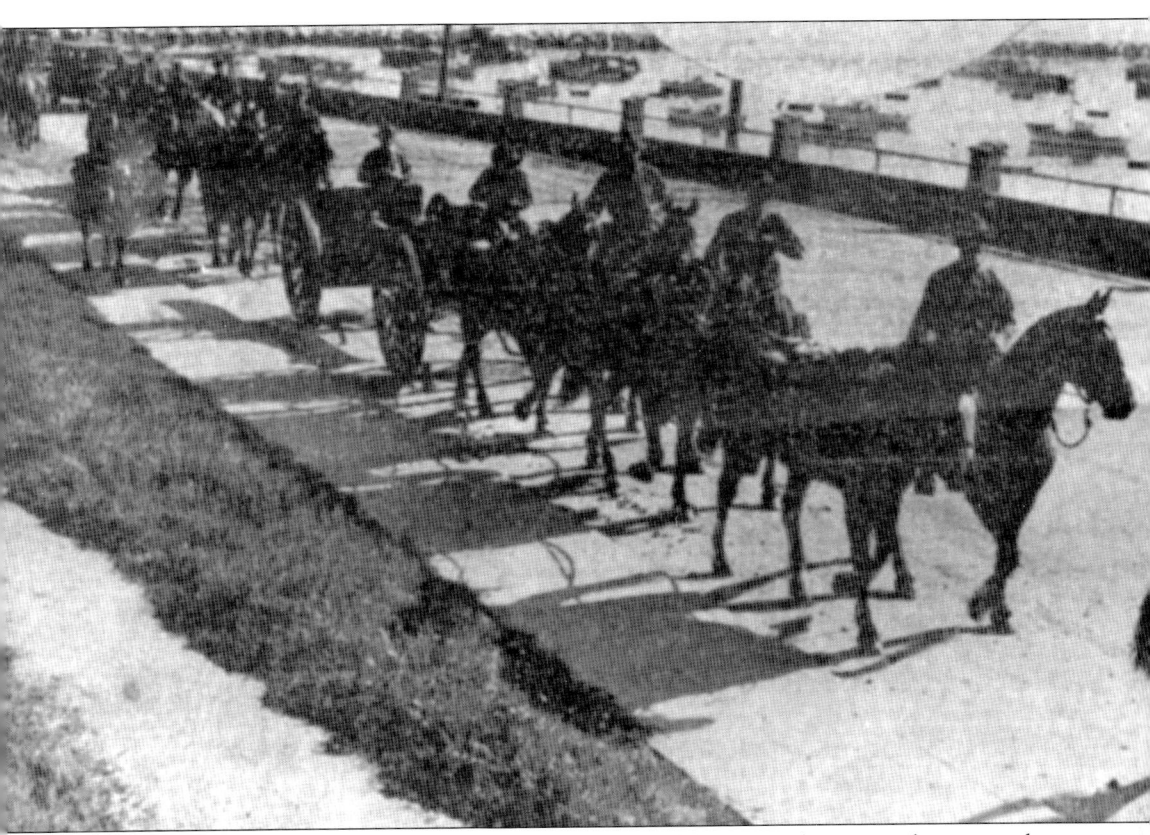

This photograph depicts Fort Ord in the years prior to World War II, when it was known as the Gigling Reservation and was used as a training base in conjunction with the Presidio of Monterey. Soldiers stationed at the Presidio were made up of veterans from the wars for territorial control of the American West. Many were Mexican American and Native American. These soldiers participated in actions in the Philippines and throughout the Pacific. During the 1930s and 1940s, soldiers and their extended families made homes in Seaside, creating a basis for Seaside as a segregated racial space within Monterey, as well as home to Fort Ord personnel and their families. (Courtesy of the Monterey Public Library, California History Room.)

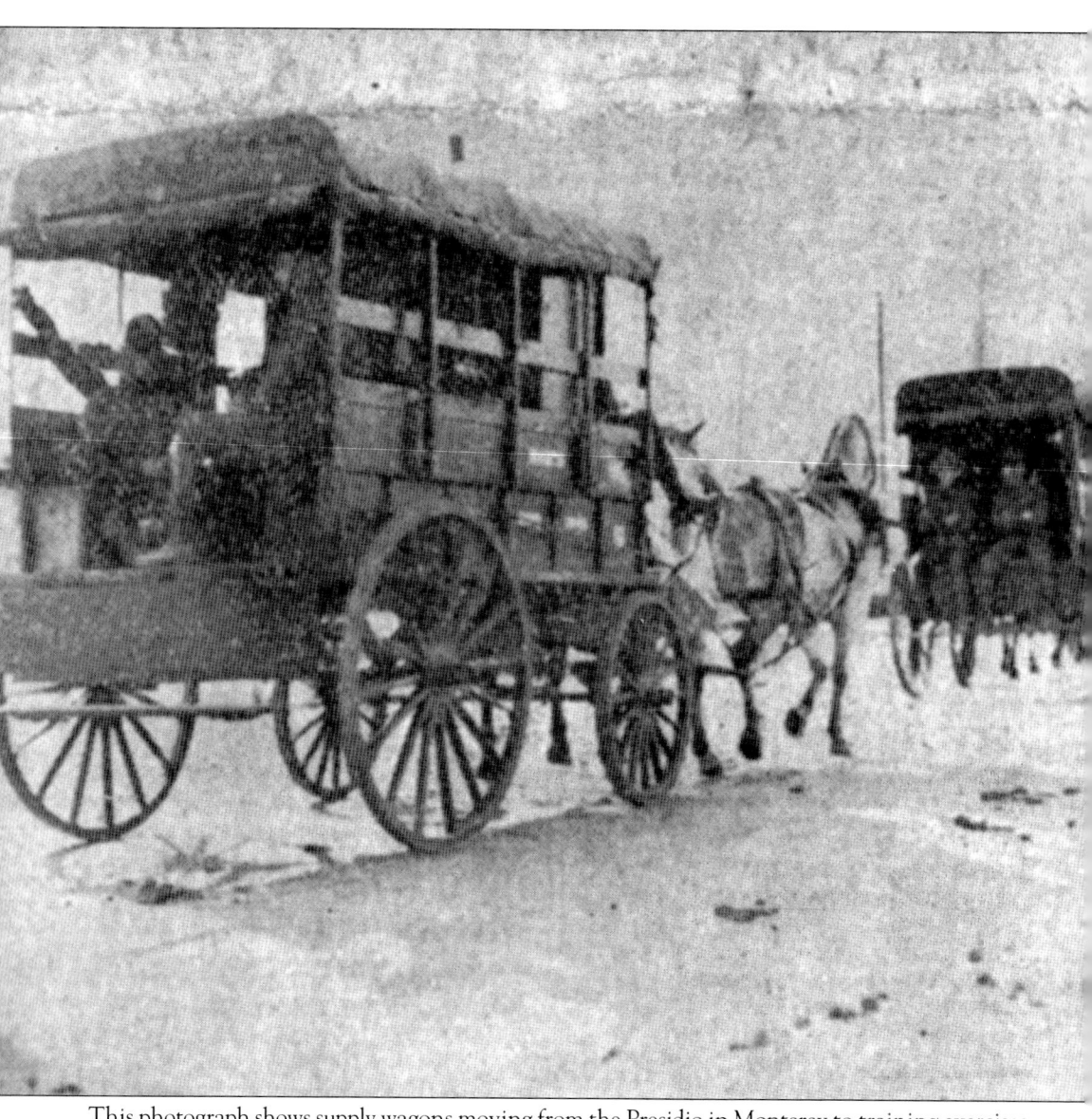
This photograph shows supply wagons moving from the Presidio in Monterey to training exercises in Seaside. (Courtesy of the Monterey Public Library, California History Room.)

Two

Depression, War, and the Creation of a Community

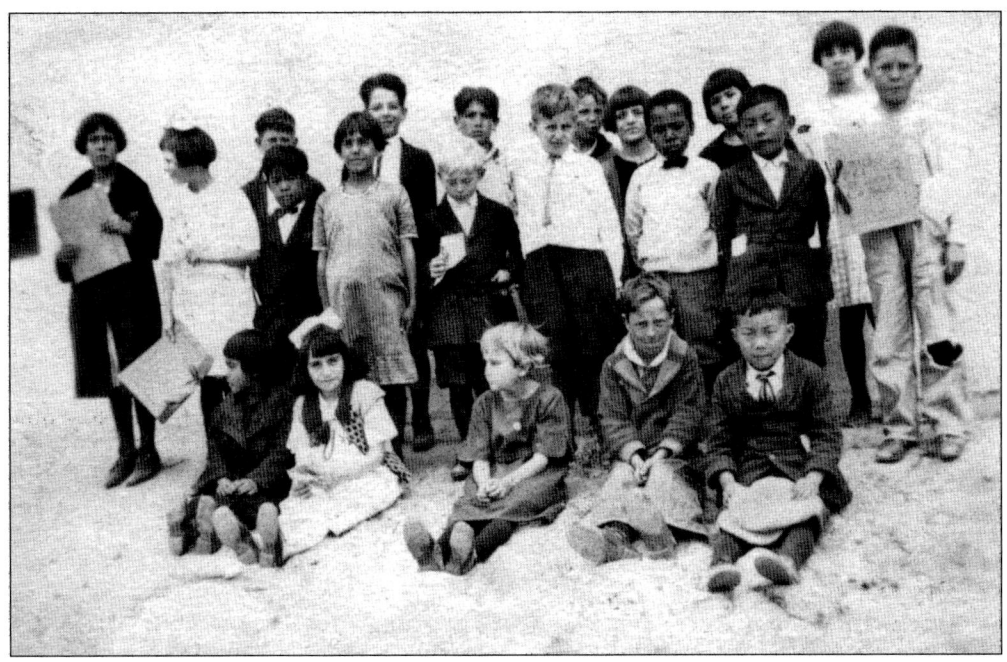

In contrast to the earliest period of settlement, the Depression brought new populations into Seaside from the Dust Bowl and from Southern Europe. The photographs of schoolchildren shown in the following pages illustrate a new population of working classes. The Seaside schoolchildren are shown here relaxing on the beach on June 28, 1925. (Courtesy of the Wasson Family Collection, City of Seaside Archive.)

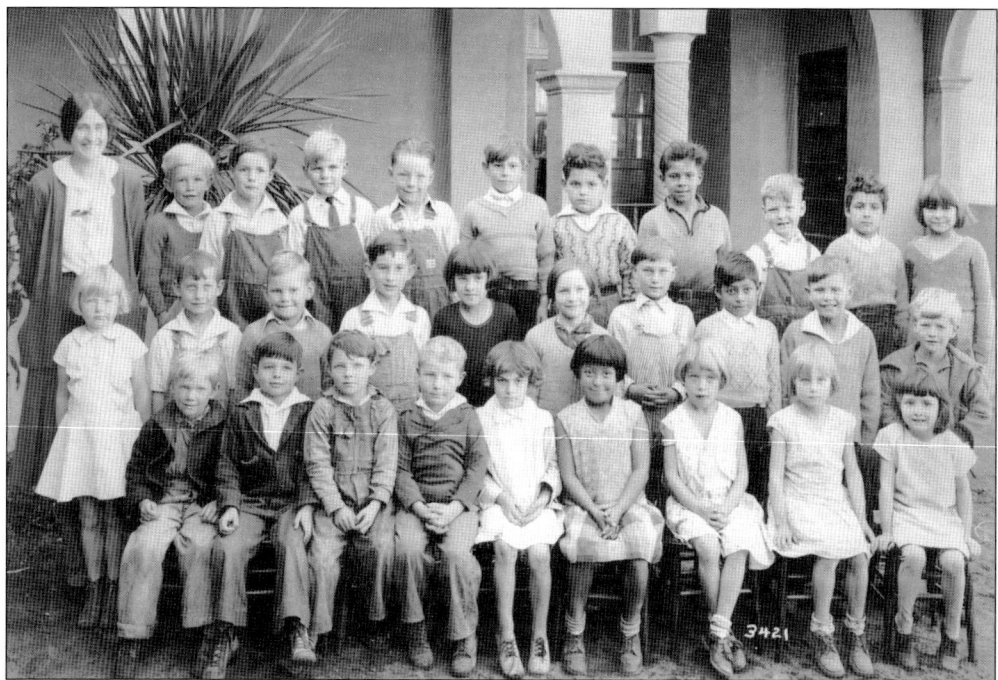

A diverse population of Mexicans, Italians, Japanese, and Portuguese, and a few African Americans began to settle in Seaside, which gave Seaside a reputation both as a poorer subdivision of Monterey and a multicultural enclave. In the photographs are unidentified schoolchildren in the 1930s. (Above, courtesy of the City of Seaside Archive; below, courtesy of the Lyle Quock Collection, City of Seaside Archive.)

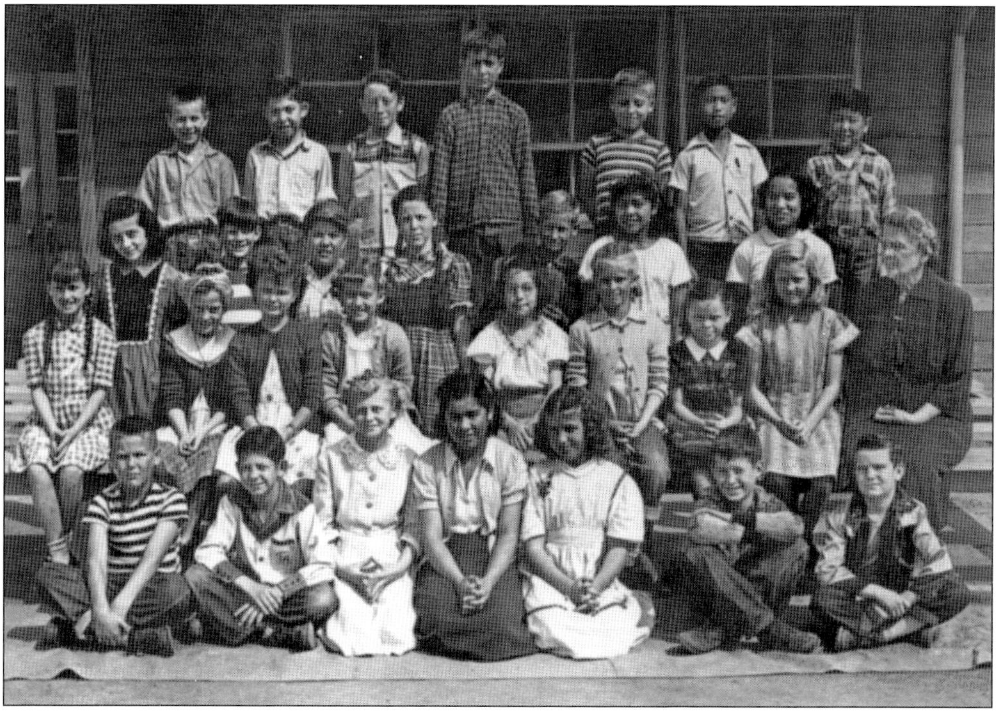

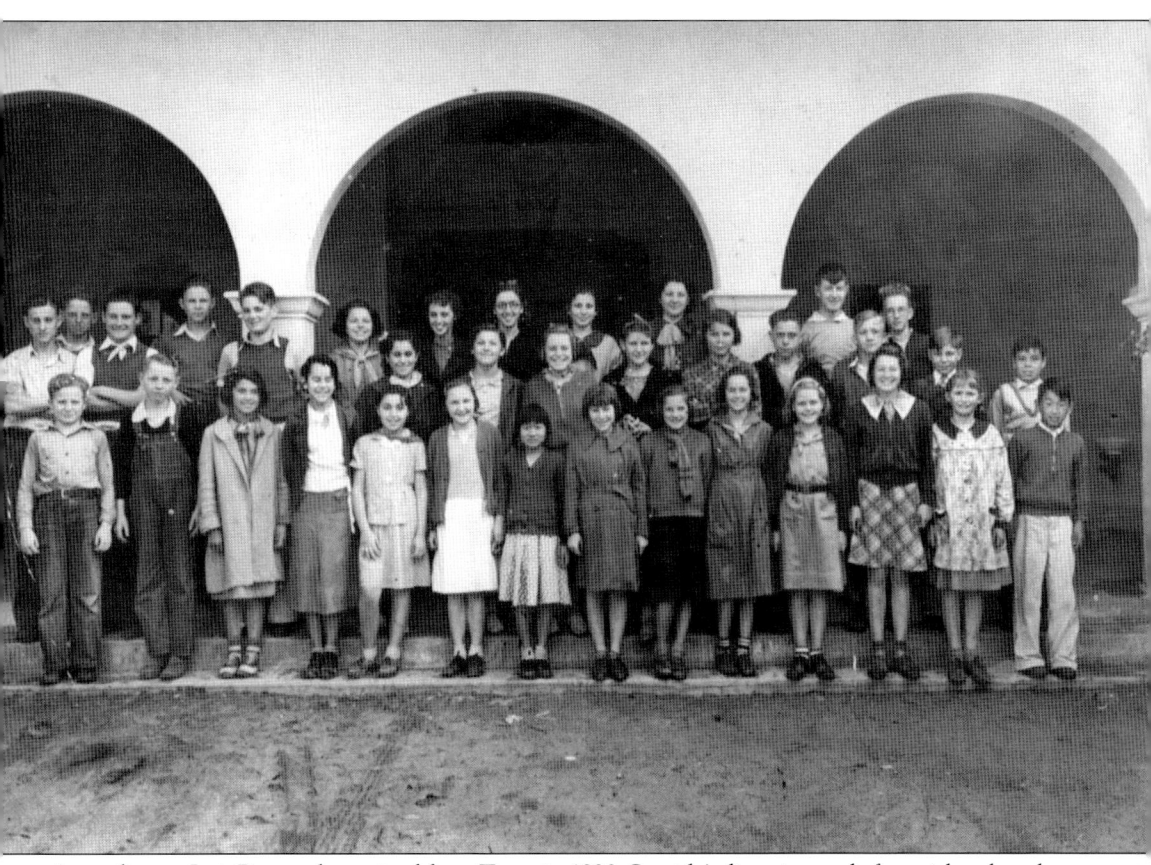

According to Luis Perez, who arrived from Texas in 1930, Seaside's diversity made for a rich cultural stew: "Right where we lived, which was up the hill [on Luxton Avenue], there were no streets, only little paths. There were about 20, 30 Mexican families. There was Fernando Mata and his wife—they were Mexican. Next to him was his compadre, Enrique Chacon. On the corner of Luxton and San Pablo—these were the Mexican people—we called him Pipirin—his real name was Melquiades Paredes. I remember there were those people [a Mexican family] who lived way down below. They had a restaurant. The name was Apodaka. There were the Molinas—they lived way on top of Del Monte. At the corner ,which is San Pablo, there was someone else—to me I think they were Gypsies or Arabs—they owned a little store. Mexicans, Portuguese and Italians were close. Let's face it; we were all going to work. We used to get together at our fiestas. . . . We were all together. At that time there were [few] blacks [in Seaside]. Blacks came maybe '48, '49. When Fort Ord got strong, there were more blacks." Pictured are unidentified 1930s schoolchildren. (Courtesy of the City of Seaside Archive, donated by Lucy Souza Giamona.)

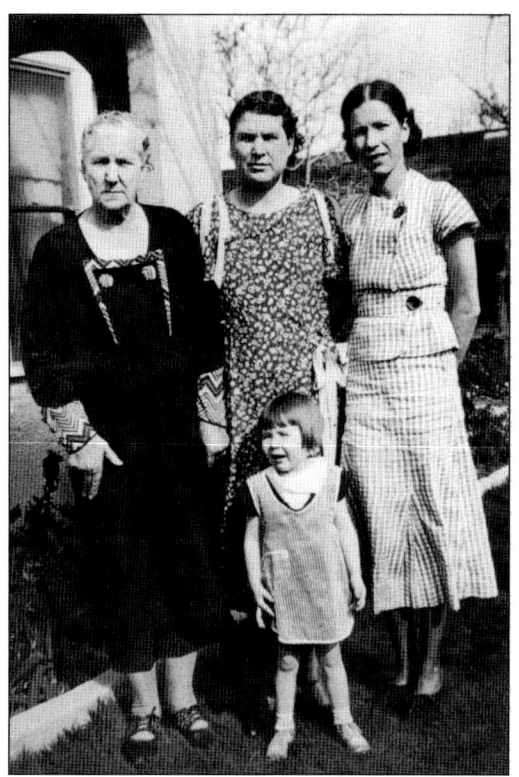

The working-class ethnic groups shown here are examples of just how far this community had moved away from the white middle-class subdivision it was in the late 19th century. It was still mostly white but not middle class. In the image at left are, from left to right, Lulu Pinkston, Bessie Morris, Opal Morris Hastie, and Donnie Hastie in 1936. Below is Arthur Morris in his home on Clementine Avenue in Seaside. (Left, courtesy of the Wasson Family Collection, City of Seaside Archive; below, courtesy of the Wasson Family Collection, City of Seaside Archive.)

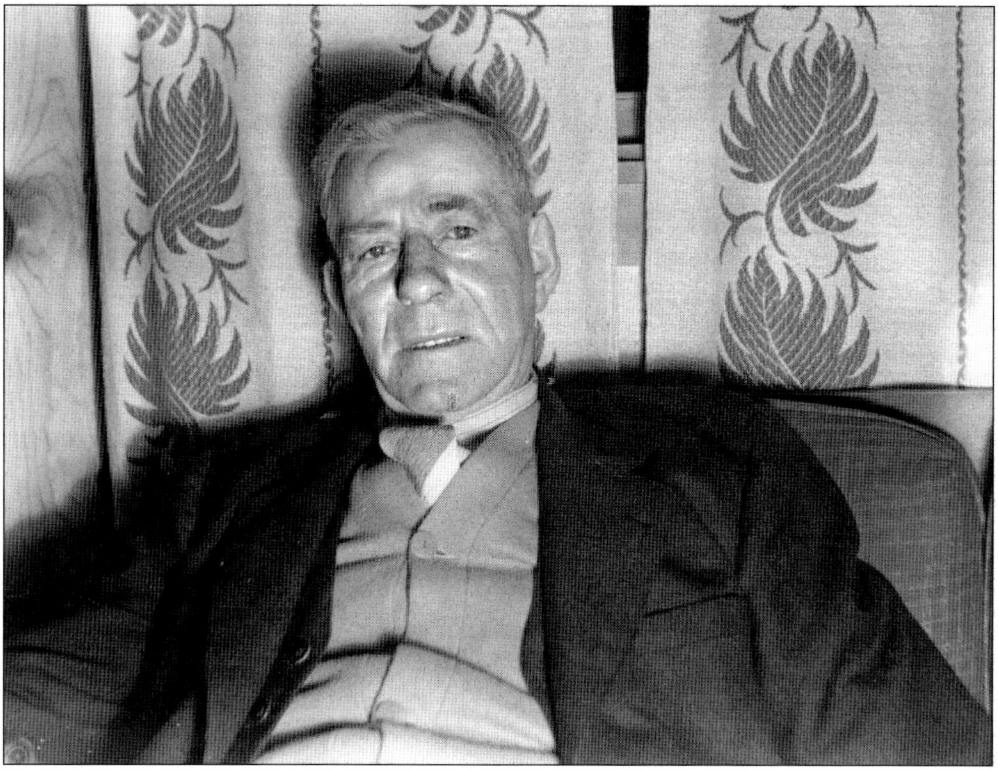

The ease, camaraderie, and working-class culture characterized the population of the subdivision in the 1930s. Seaside had truly become the part of Monterey that housed the cannery workers who were too poor even to live near the wharf on Cannery Row. In the image at right, the Chioino family is pictured—from left to right, Frances, Gloria, Arlene, Patrick, and Richard "Dickie" Chioino—at 415 Francis Street. In the picture below are Almondo Chioino (the father), Eddie, Johnny, Dickie, and Arlene Chioino. (Right, courtesy of the Gloria Scott Collection, City of Seaside Archive; below, courtesy of the Gloria Scott Collection, City of Seaside Archive.)

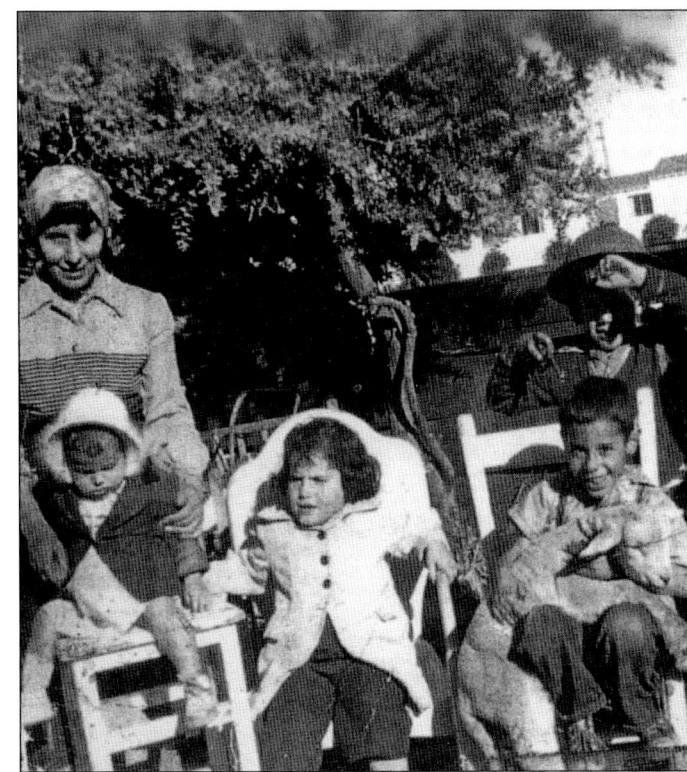

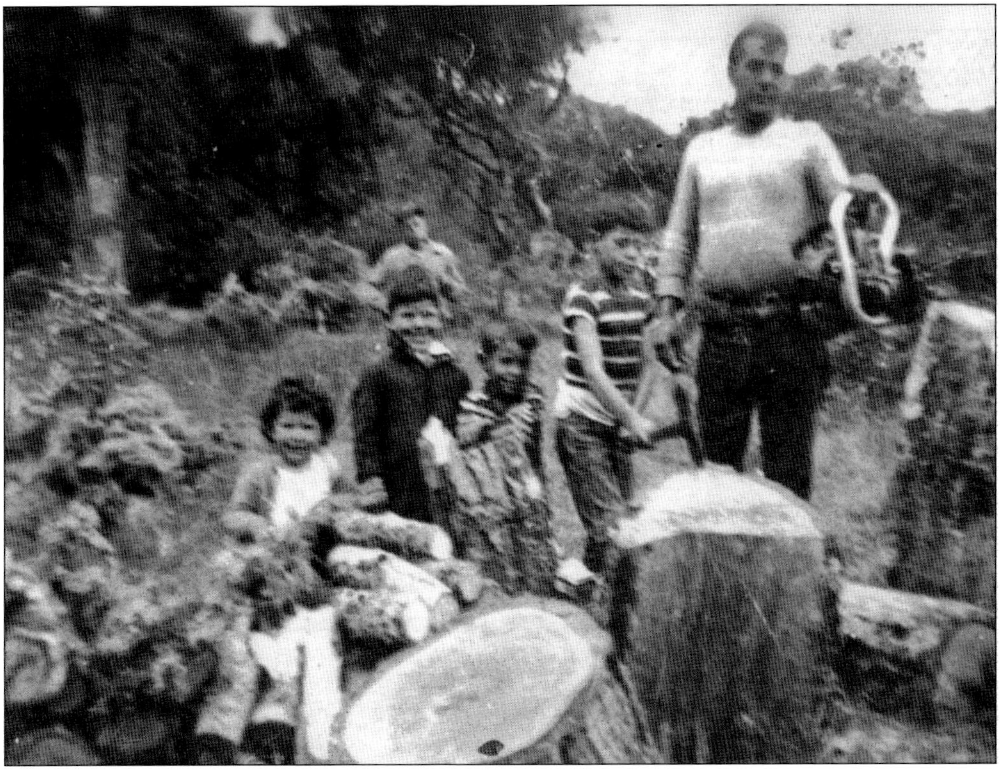

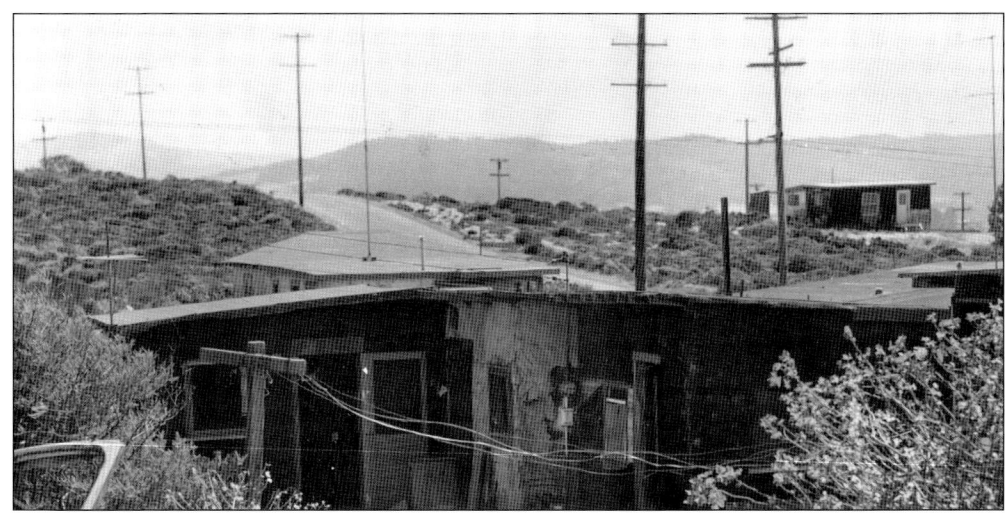

According to reports by residents of the time, Seaside in the 1930s had "no industry, streets were unpaved [and without] storm drainage, [and had] substandard shacks. [There were] septic tanks [rather than a sewer system], twenty-five foot lots bisected by thirty-foot streets, and with helter-skelter fashion of undeveloped land." Pictured above is a home located in the Del Monte Heights Redevelopment Area, and below is a home located at 1782 Yosemite Avenue. (Both, courtesy of the City of Seaside Archive.)

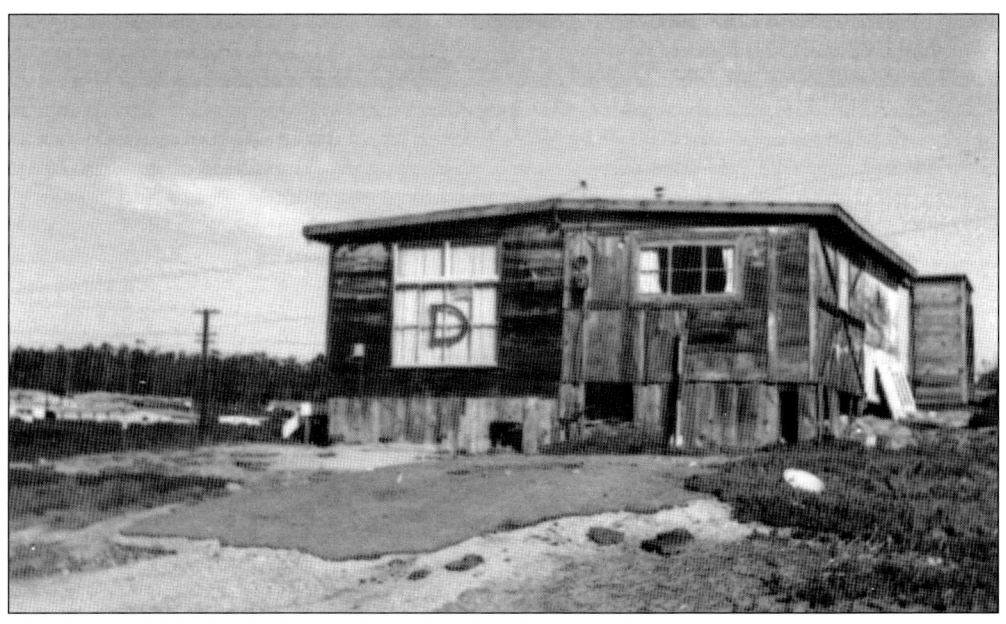

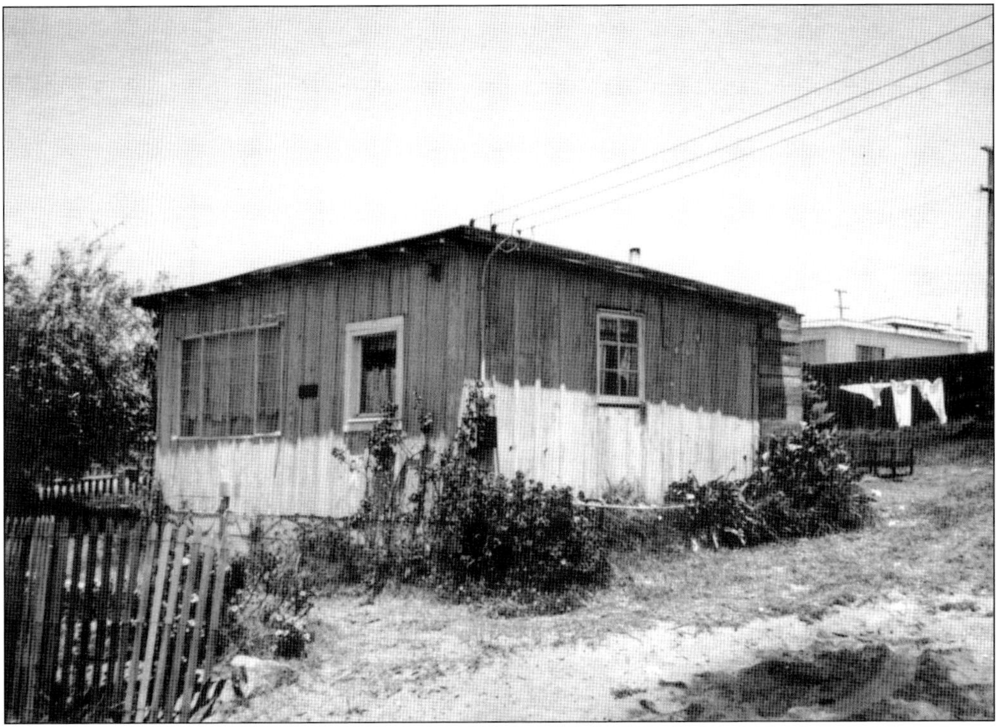

These photographs are graphic depictions of the type of housing that characterized Seaside in the 1930s and 1940s. One house was reputed to have been made entirely out of doors. These homes are at 1764 Helena Street (above) and 1787 Belle Street (below). (Both, courtesy of the City of Seaside Archive.)

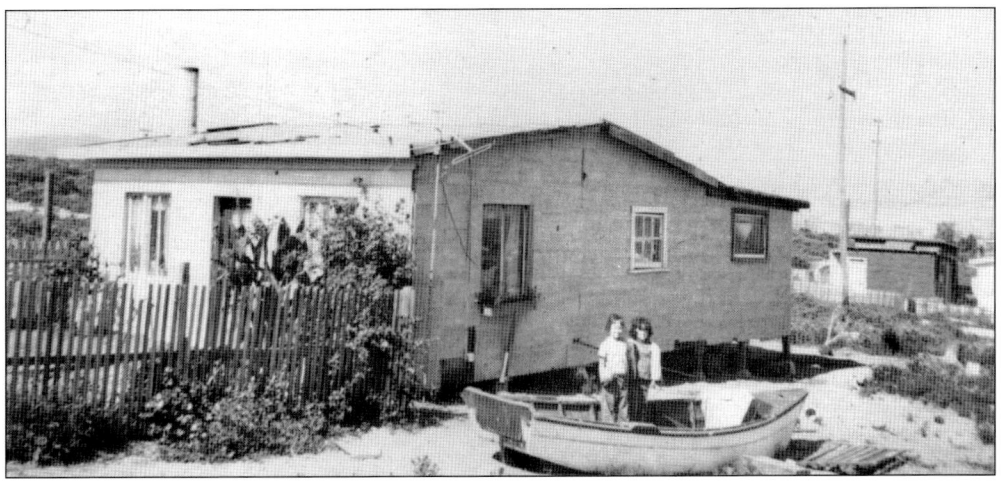

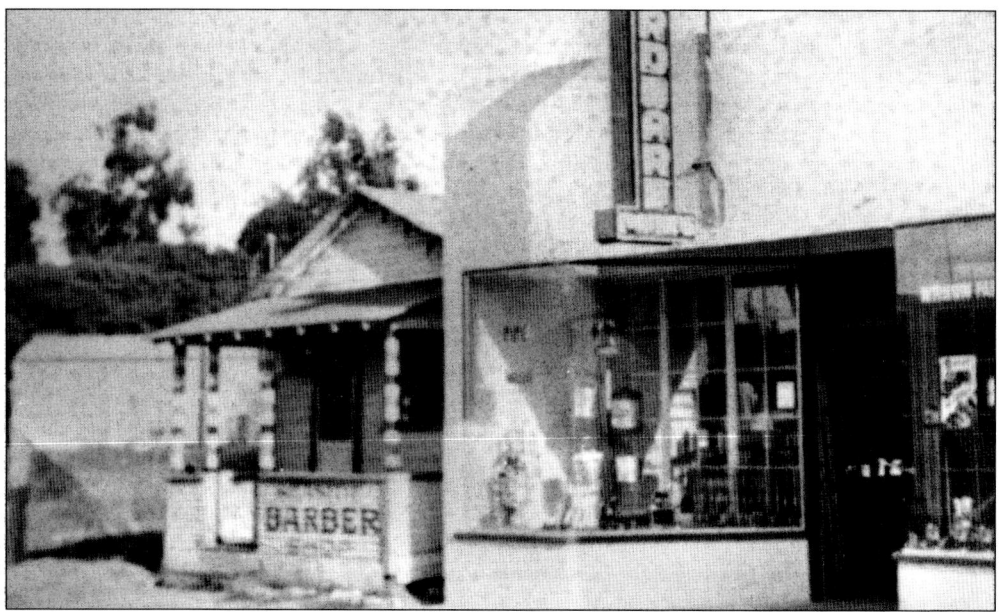

Along with the randomly built homes that proliferated during the Depression era in Seaside, some small businesses were established to serve the new population. These photographs depict one of Seaside's earliest barbershops (above) and Nelson's Emporium (below), which served as an important grocery and meat market, and as a meeting place for residents in the 1930s and 1940s. (Both, courtesy of City of Seaside Archive.)

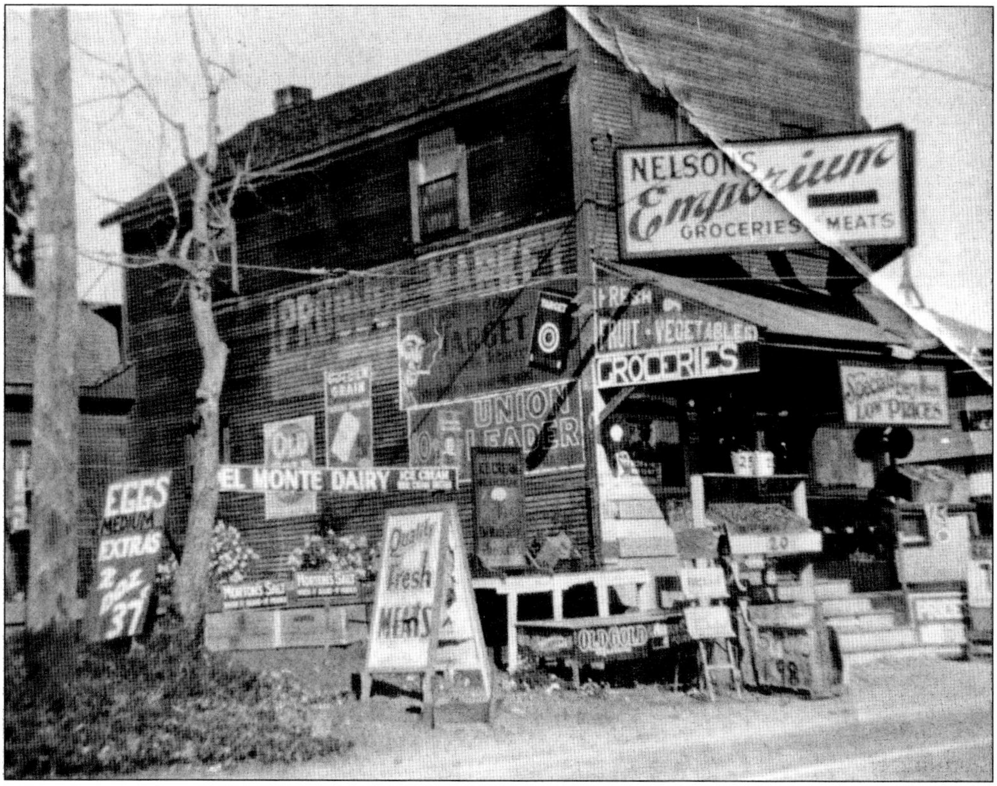

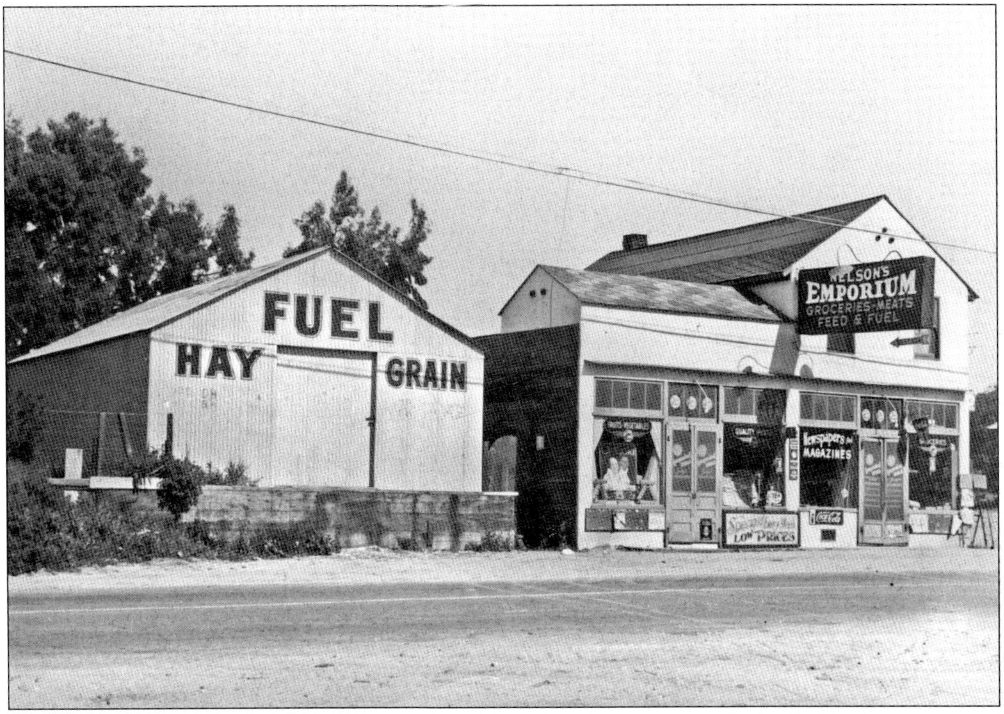

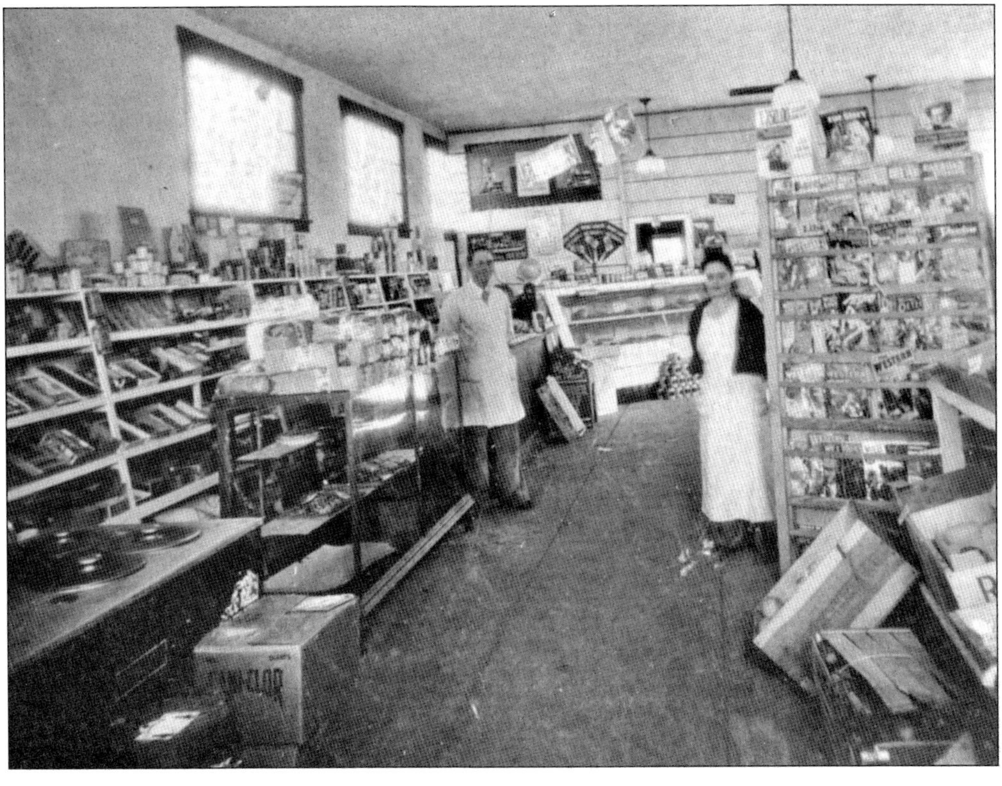

Shown here is Nelson's Emporium's exterior (above) and its interior (below). (Both, courtesy of Lyle Quock Collection, City of Seaside Archive.)

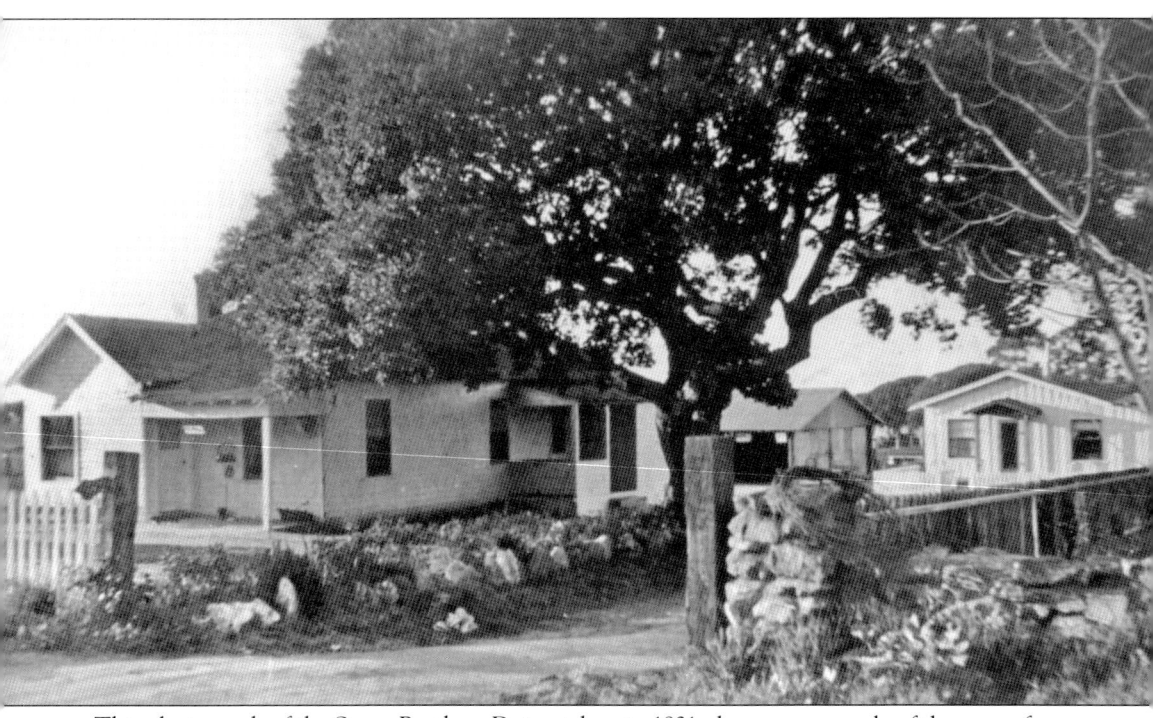

This photograph of the Sousa Brothers Dairy, taken in 1931, shows an example of the many farms, including large poultry and pig farms, that were typical in Seaside from the 1930s to the 1950s. Even with the new populations, the subdivision of Seaside remained a rural community on the outskirts of the more concentrated populations of Monterey proper. (Courtesy of the Monterey Public Library, California History Room.)

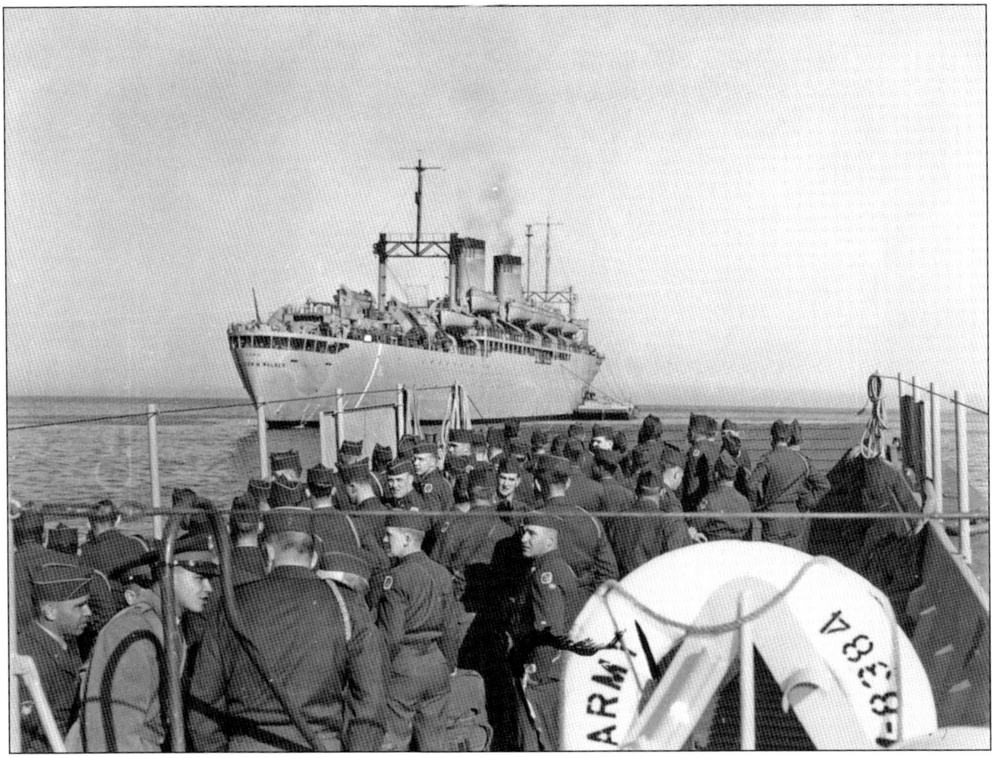

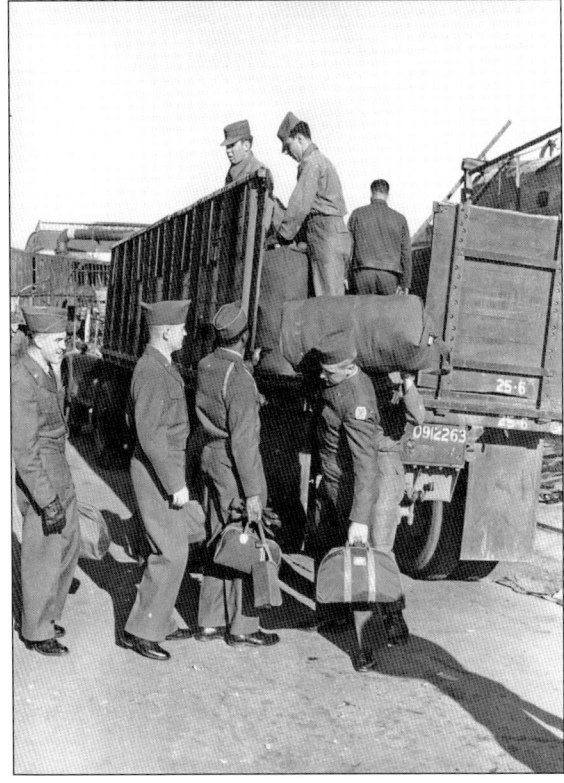

Fort Ord changed everything about Seaside. Fort Ord became the regional reception and training center for an enormous influx of soldiers in the 1940s as the United States mobilized for World War II. Built in 1940 on 28,514 acres, with an additional government purchase of 100,000 acres, at that time to be used for large-scale maneuvers and training, Fort Ord was located immediately to the north and northwest of Seaside. Many of these soldiers were not white, in contrast to the predominantly Caucasian makeup of all the armed services in the 1910s and 1920s. After 1940, the 3rd, 27th, 35th, and 43rd Infantry Divisions trained at Fort Ord, and a prisoner of war camp for Italian and German soldiers was located there during World War II. According to one observer, "At one time, there were more than 50,000 troops [stationed at Fort Ord], although the average was about 35,000." (Both, courtesy of the Monterey Public Library, California History Room.)

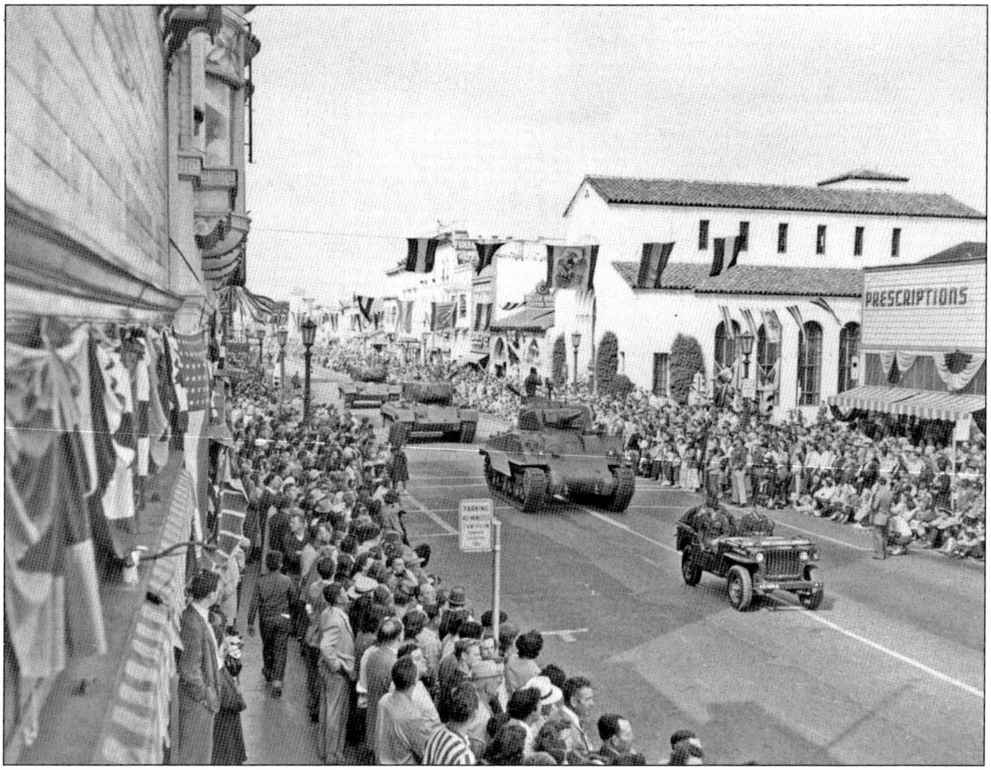

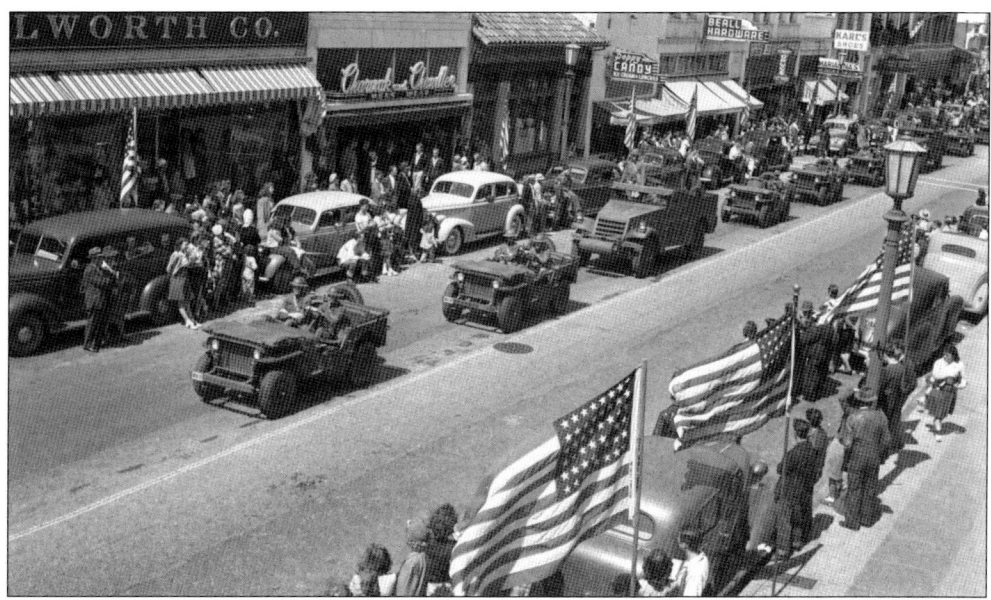

In April 1940, some 10,000 soldiers marched in review in Monterey, demonstrating with live ammunition—the 4th Infantry, the 30th Infantry, the 7th Infantry, the 50th Infantry, the 9th and 10th Field Artillery, the 11th Calvary, and the horse-drawn 76th Field Artillery. It was an impressive show of force. (Both, courtesy of the Monterey Public Library, California History Room.)

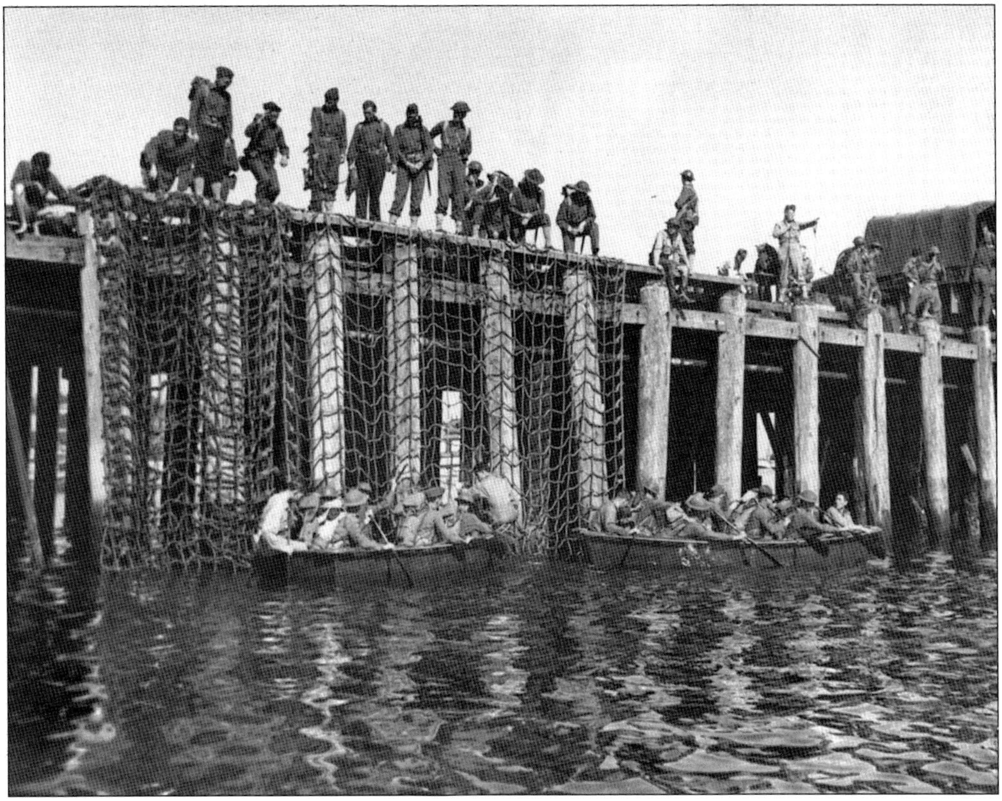

The 53rd Infantry, training at Monterey Municipal Wharf, is shown above in 1941. Pictured below is bazooka fire training at Fort Ord during World War II. (Both, courtesy of the Chamberlin Library Collection.)

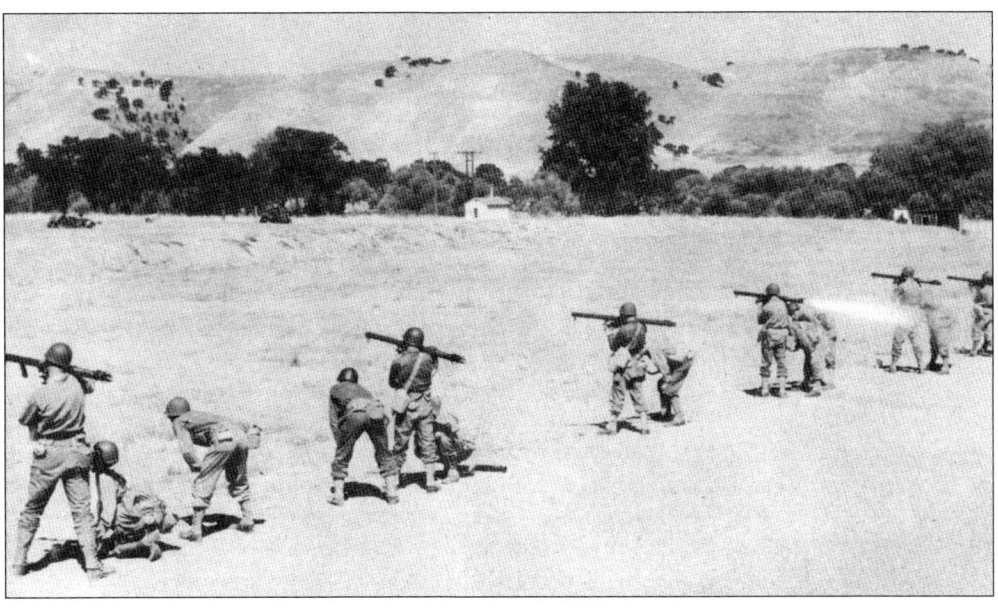

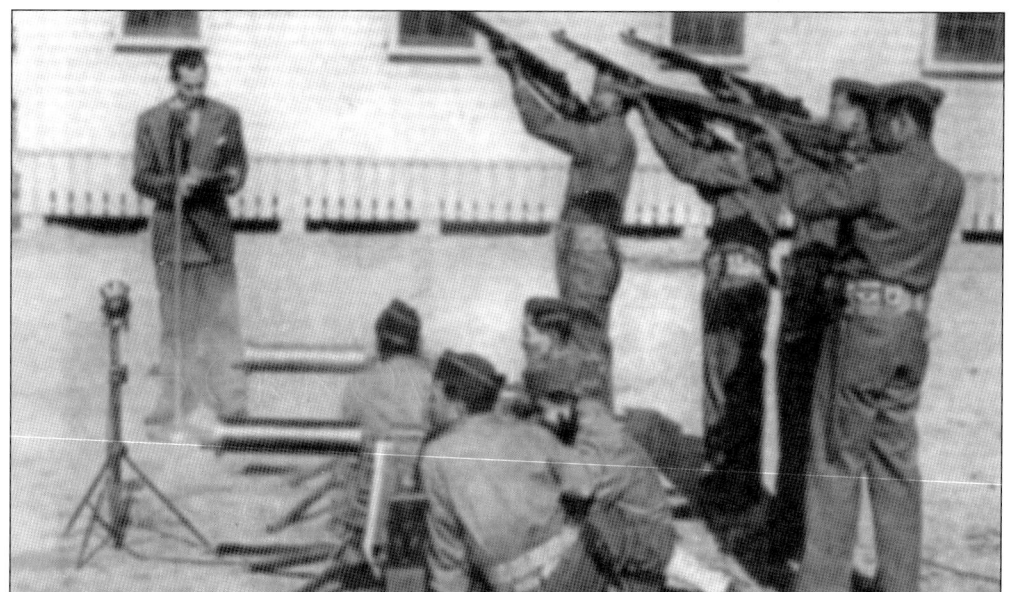

Although Filipinos had long faced serious discrimination in housing and employment, and could not become citizens or marry Americans, they responded with patriotic fervor to the advent of World War II. At the outbreak of World War II—actually, in the immediate aftermath of Pearl Harbor—Filipinos demanded the right to participate in the military, even though they were exempt from military service as noncitizens. On January 2, 1942, Pres. Franklin D. Roosevelt amended the Selective Service Act to allow Filipinos to join the armed services. By the end of May 1942, the 1st Filipino Infantry Regiment was formed in Salinas. Also in May 1942, the Philippine Naturalization Bill was passed, and Filipinos were sworn in en masse as U.S. citizens. Above is an image from November 20, 1942, of Fort Ord; below are Amy and Mike Cosio in the 1940s. (Both, courtesy of the Filipino American Clubs of the Monterey Peninsula.)

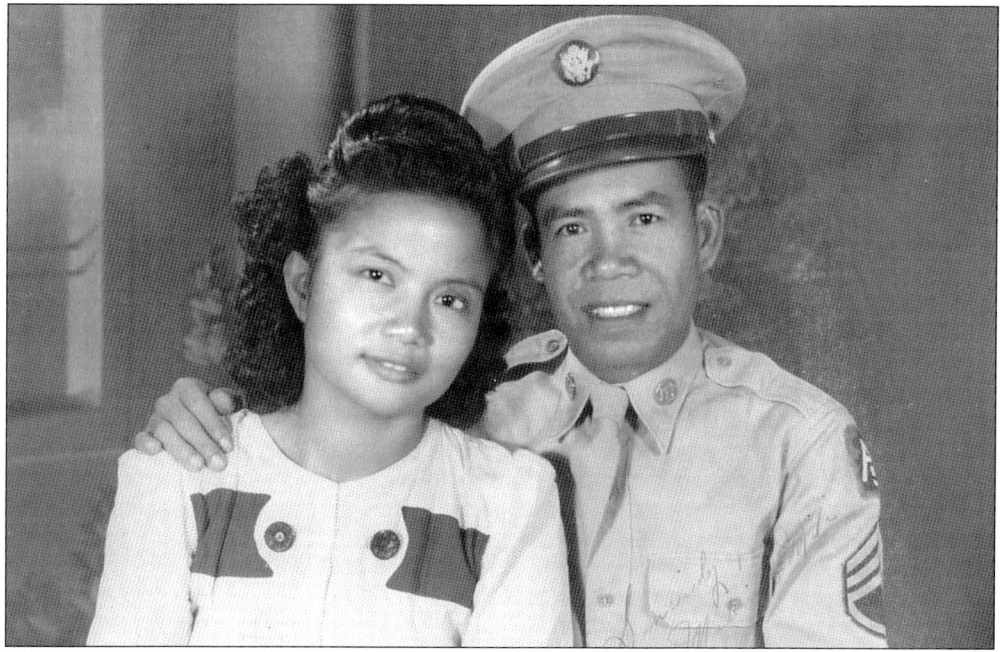

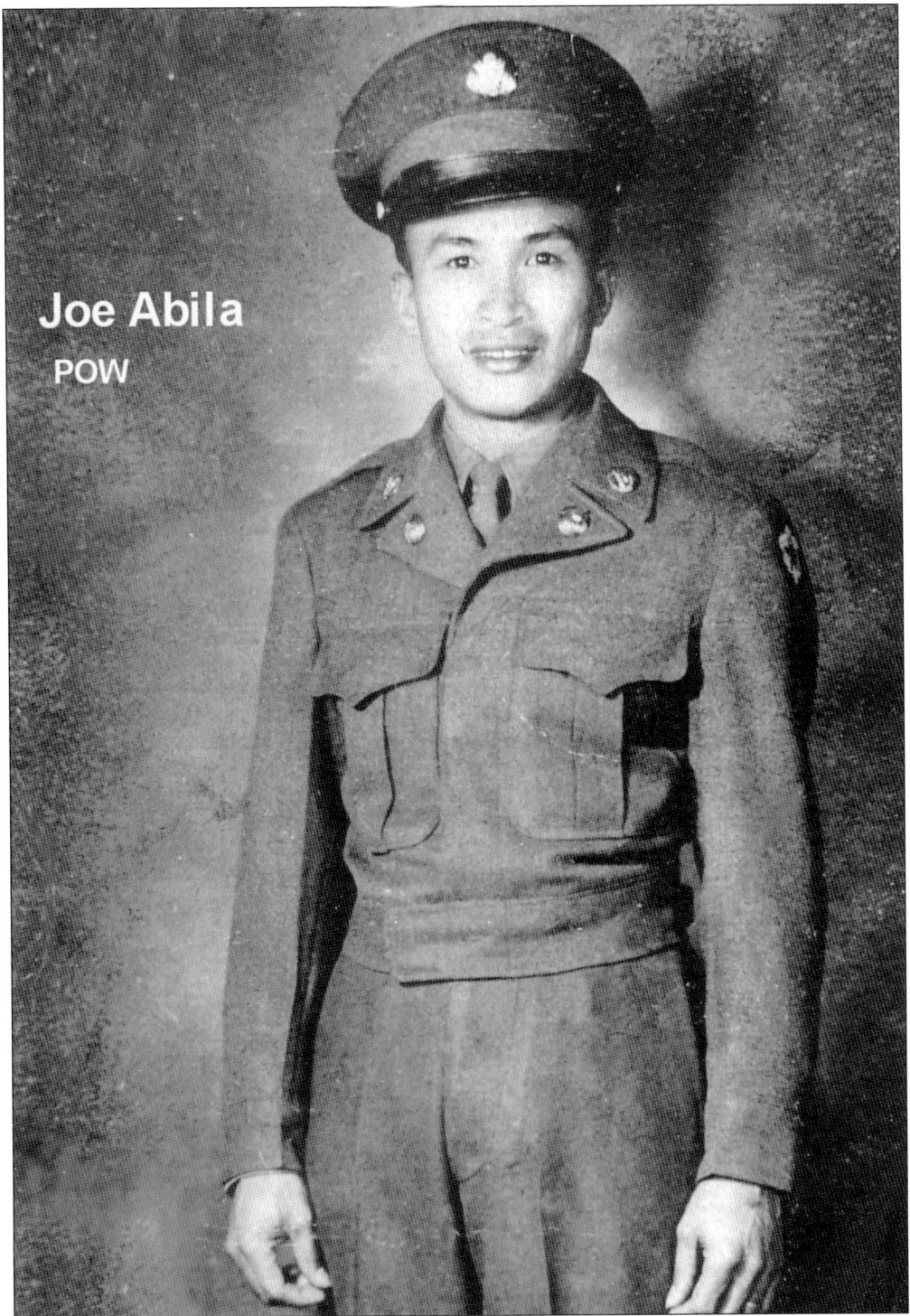

The 1st and 2nd Filipino Regiments trained at Fort Ord, after which they distinguished themselves in the Battle of Leyte and on the Bataan Peninsula. Shown here is Joe Abila. (Courtesy of the Filipino American Club of the Monterey Peninsula.)

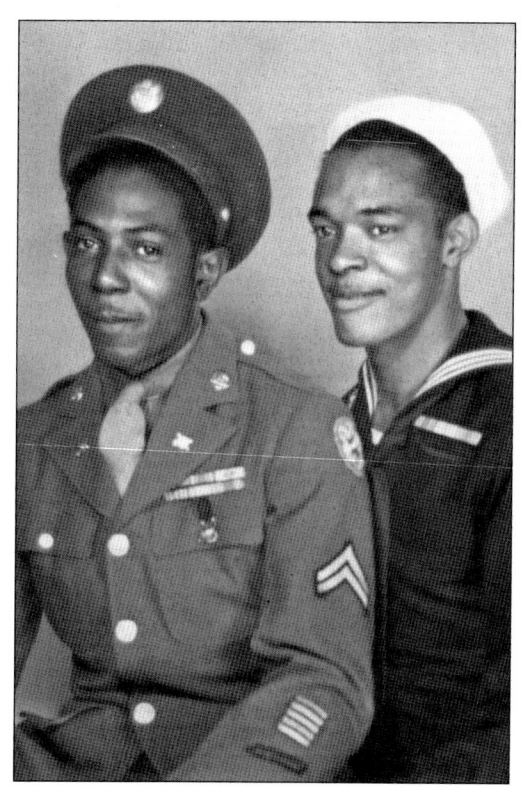

Adding to the diversity of the military personnel and of the city, African American soldiers were assigned to Fort Ord, especially after the army integrated in 1948 by order of Pres. Harry S. Truman. At left, Lonnie and Samuel Welch are pictured in 1946. In the image below on the far right is John Bean; the others are unidentified. (Left, courtesy of the Diedre Banks Collection, City of Seaside Archive; below, courtesy of the Lenora Bean Collection, City of Seaside Archive.)

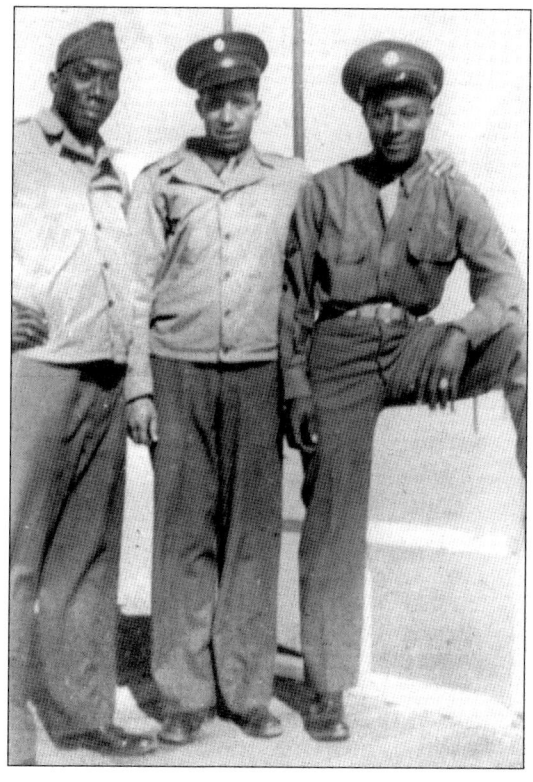

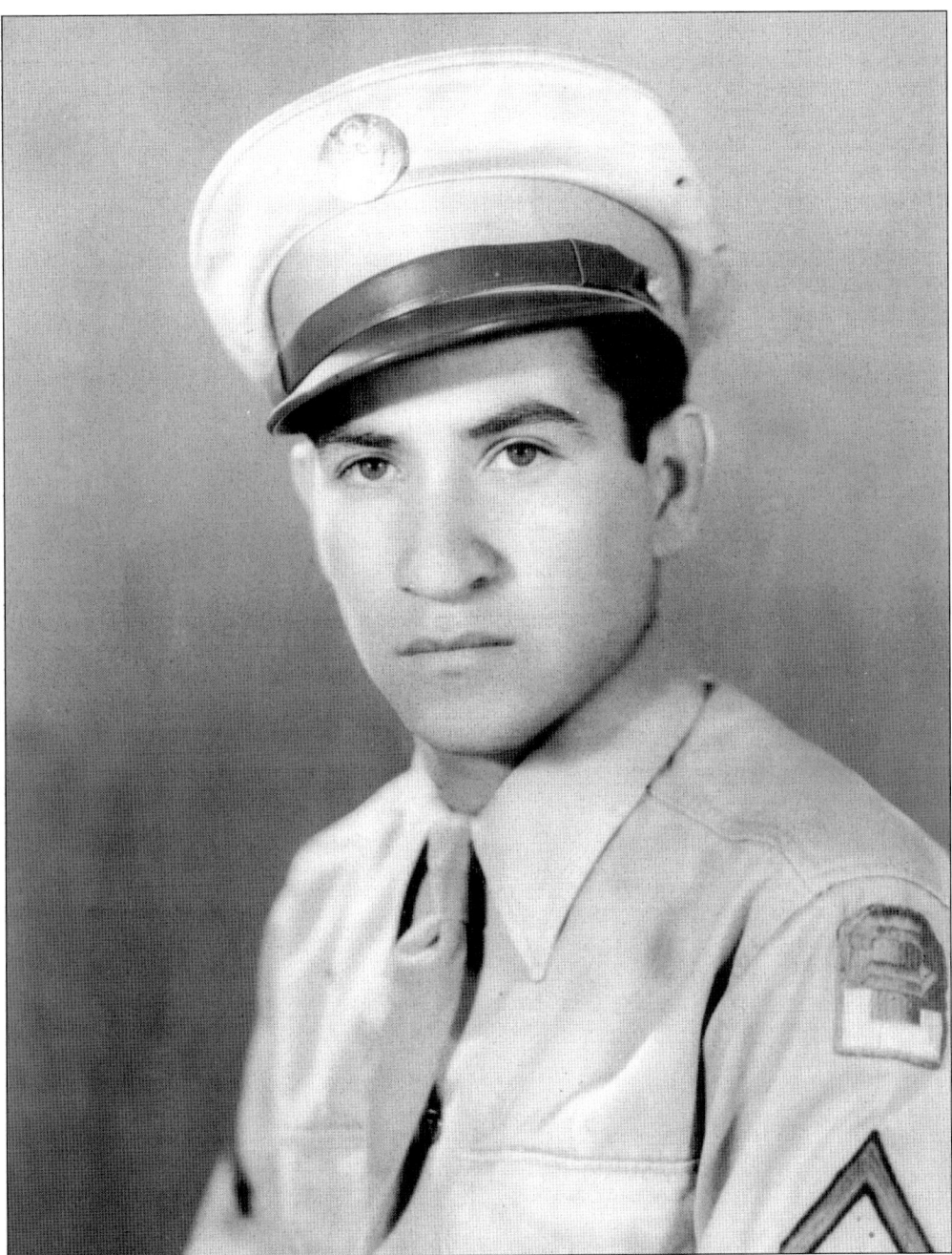

The 7th Infantry Division, which included a sizable number of African Americans and also had "an unusually large percentage of Mexicans and Indians," was the largest and perhaps most significant example of an expanded and diverse new army, according to Maj. Park Wollam in his unpublished paper entitled "Fort Ord in World War II," written in May 1998. This is a photograph of Orancio Perez in 1941. (Courtesy of the Evangelina Perez Collection, City of Seaside Archive.)

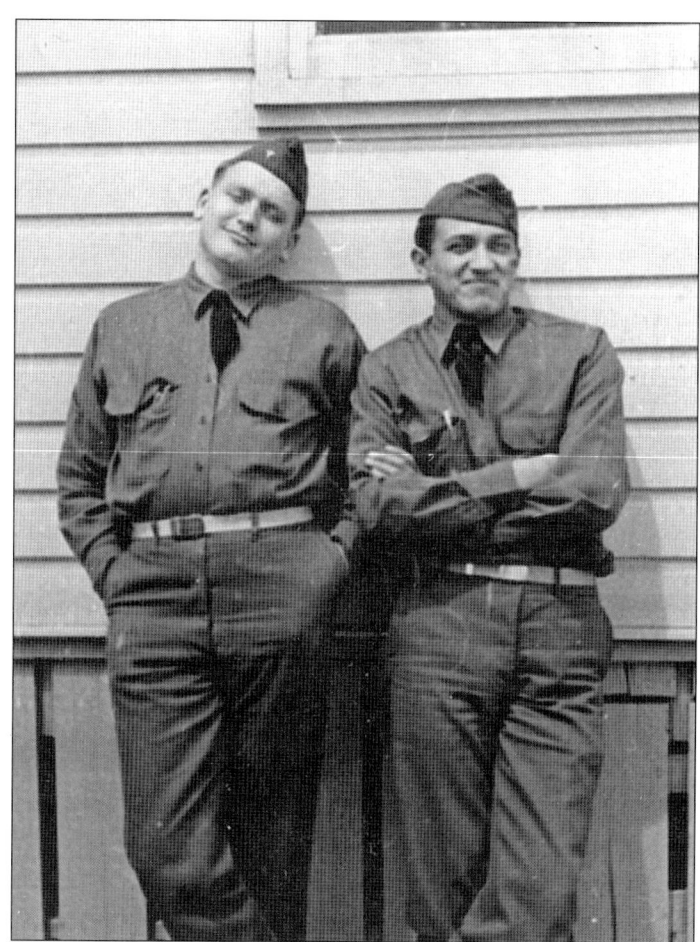

These snapshots of soldiers on and off base in Seaside show how integral they became to the city landscape during the war years and immediately thereafter. The men at left, pictured around 1940, are unidentified. Below are Ray Wasson (far right) and another unidentified sailor on leave. The other two men are also unidentified. (Left, courtesy of the Steven Levinson Collection, Fort Ord Museum and Archive; below, courtesy of the Wasson Family Collection, City of Seaside Archive.)

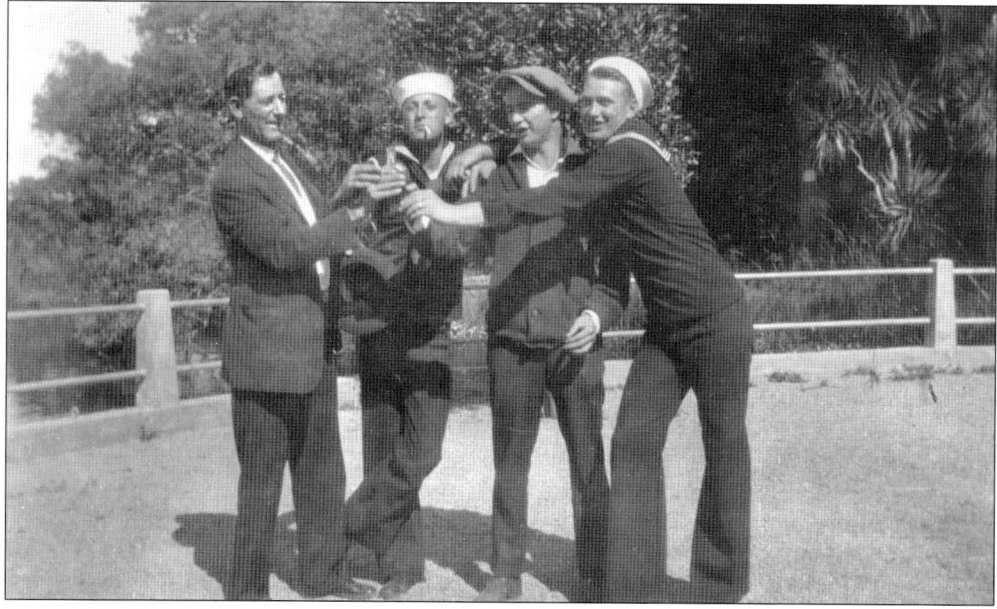

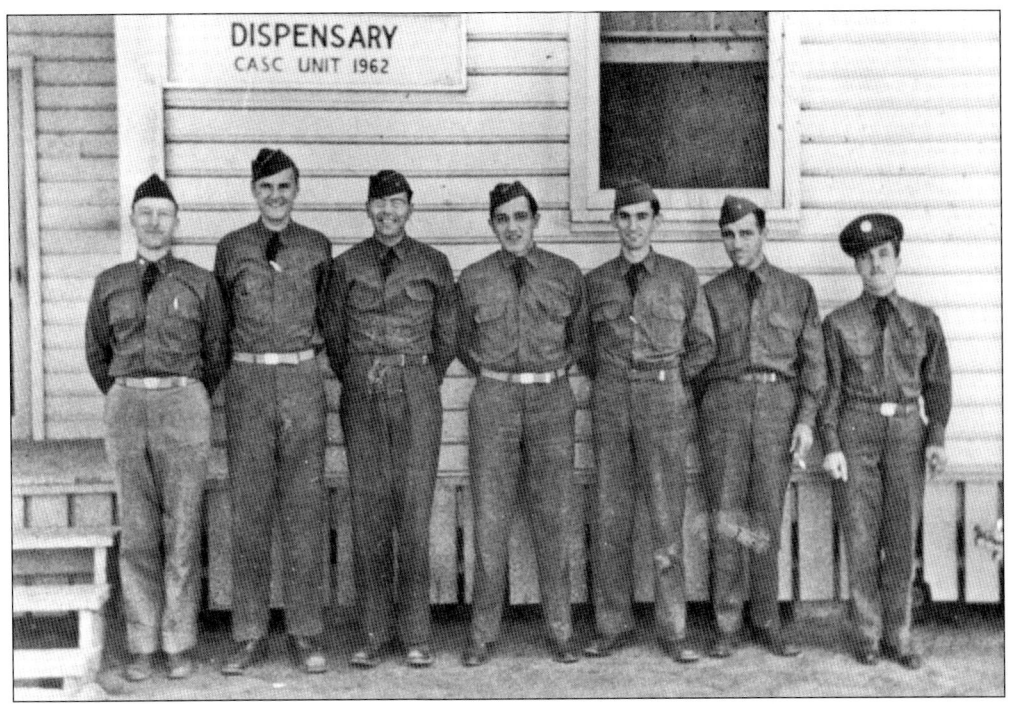

By the end of World War II, Seaside had truly become a military town. In the photograph above, from left to right, are Lt. ? Havenhill, Sgt. ? Lamb, D. Rios, Cpl. M. Clapham, and three unidentified. (Above, courtesy of the Steven Levinson Collection, Fort Ord Museum and Archive; below, courtesy of the City of Seaside Archive.)

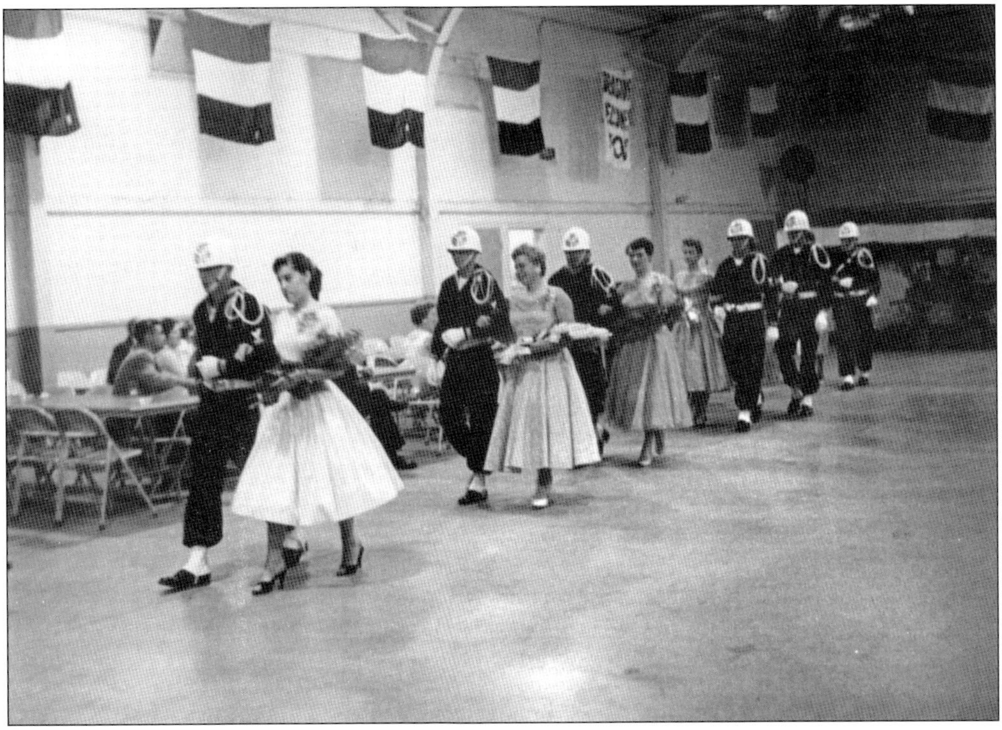

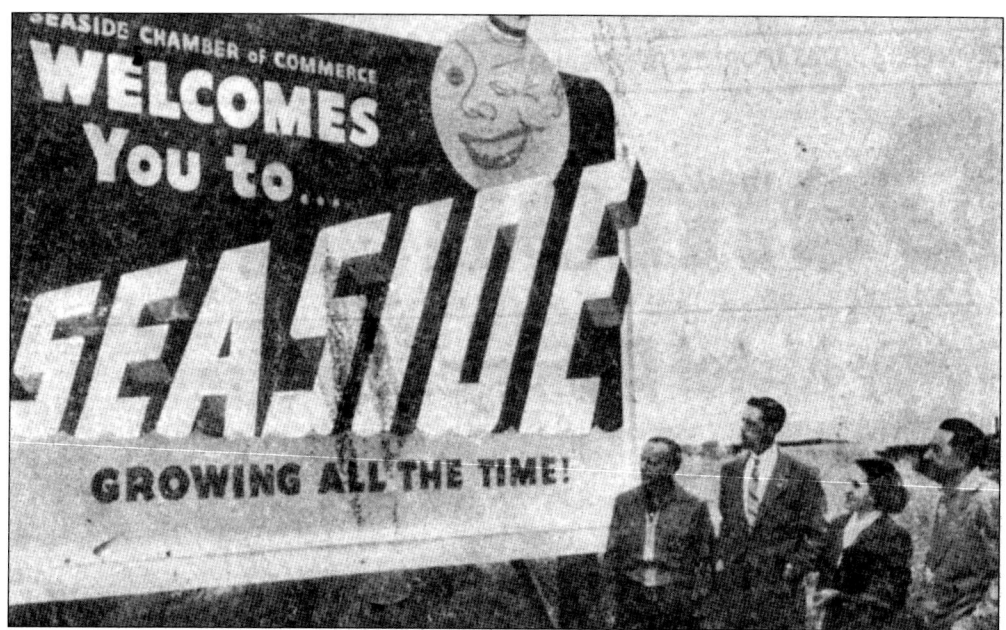

The Seaside Chamber of Commerce, established in 1941, became the first governing body for the subdivision as residents began to plan for a drive to incorporate and separate from the City of Monterey. The photograph above shows a mix of patriotism and pride in the emerging suburb of enterprising small business people and military families. The map (below) is evidence of the beginning of urban planning. (Above, courtesy of the Amy Stuart Scrapbook Collection, City of Seaside Archive; below, courtesy of the Monterey Public Library, California Room.)

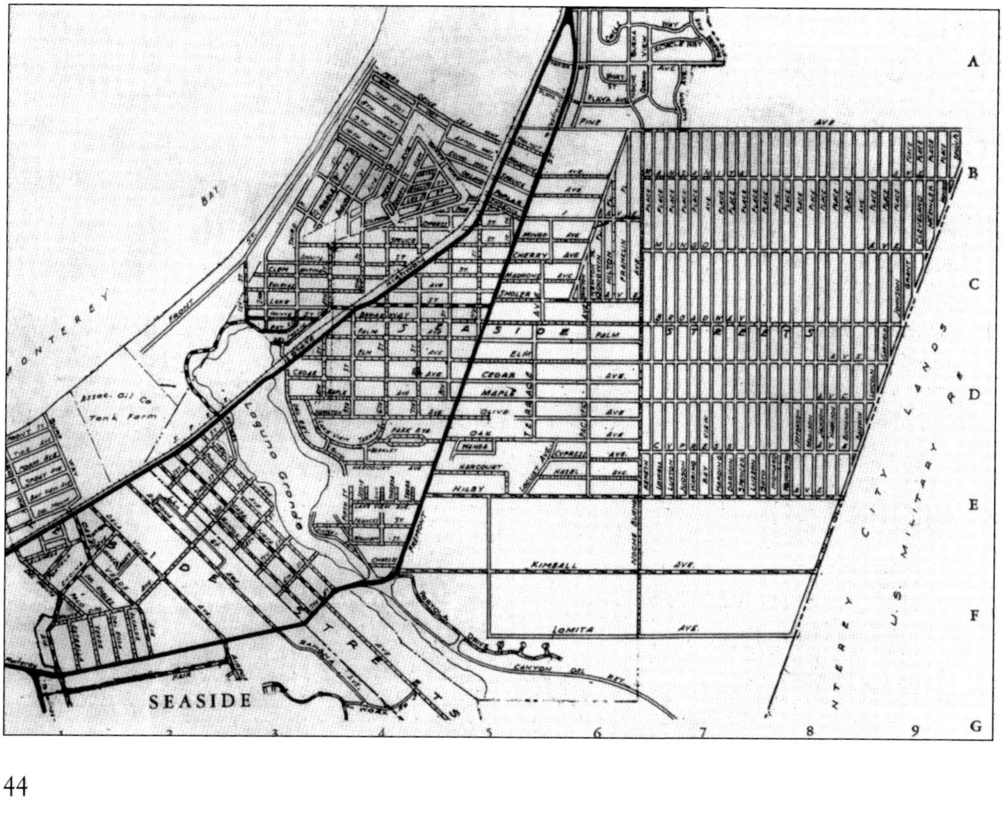

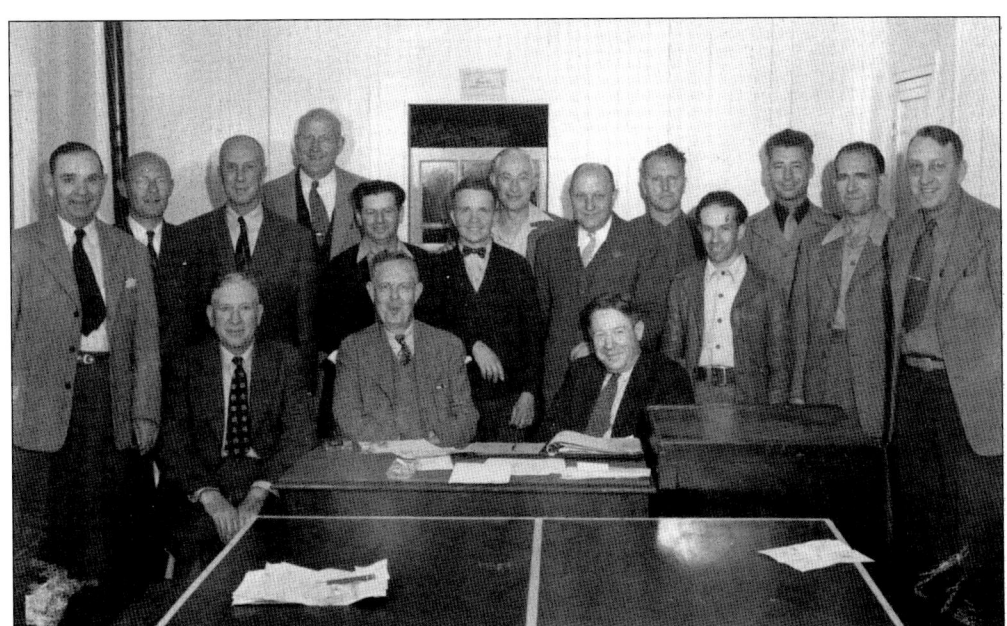

Despite the mixed-race population, the first chamber of commerce members were all white and all male. The first directors of the Seaside Chamber of Commerce are shown above in June 1944. From left to right are (seated) E. H. Galpin, Clark Sturgis, and W. C. Forsyth (the first president); (standing) Norman Stevens, "Doc" Cooper, Harry Reed, Al Grube, William Pacehetti, J. W. Benson, Lester Krumbholdtz, G. T. "Sarge" Cunningham, Charles Bently, Same DeMello, Tony Puglizevich, Ed Hawes, and Dan Greenwald. (Both, courtesy of the Amy Stuart Scrapbook Collection, City of Seaside Archive.)

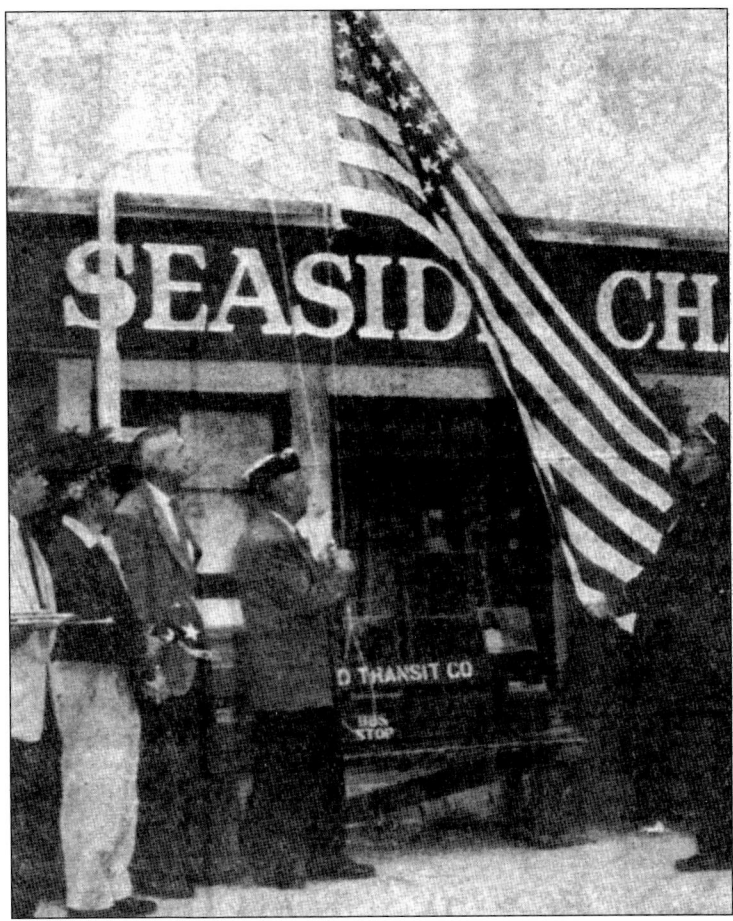

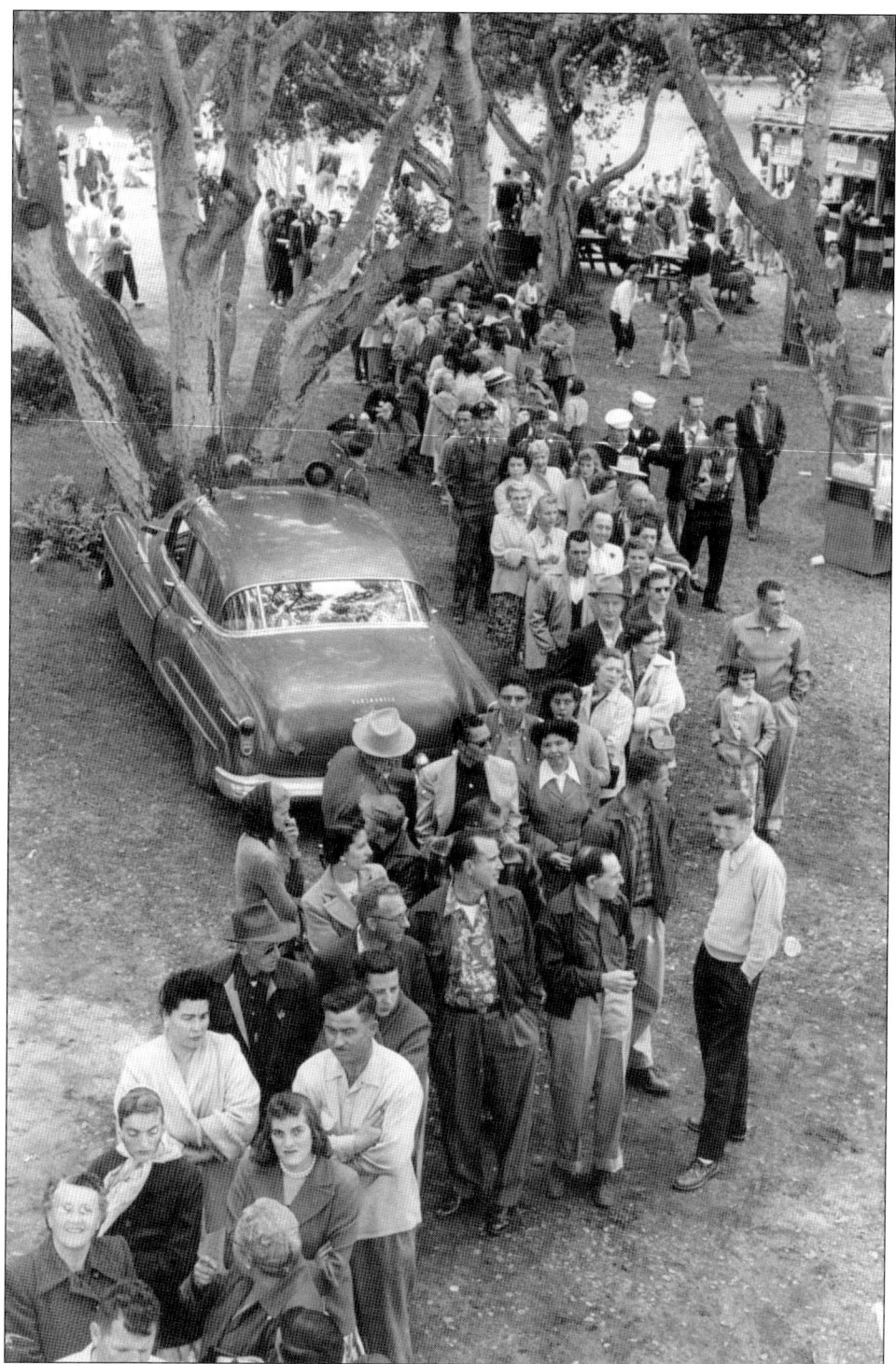
This photograph of residents gathering at the Monterey County fairgrounds, located on the border of Seaside and Monterey, depicts the increasing population of the area and a continued military presence. (Courtesy of the City of Seaside Archive.)

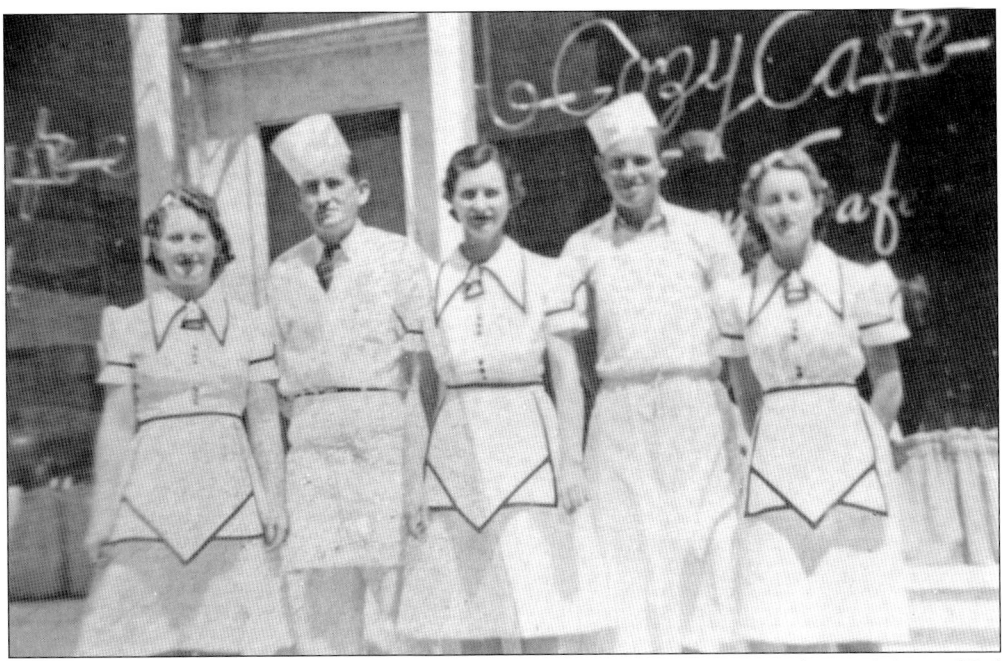

Seaside residents were proud of establishing small businesses along the main thoroughfares of Del Monte Avenue, Broadway, and Noche Buena Street in the 1940s and 1950s. These photographs are examples of the many small cafés and shops that defined the neighborhood before the urban renewal of the 1960s. (Above, courtesy of the City of Seaside Archive; below, courtesy of the Cecil Bindel Collection, City of Seaside Archive.)

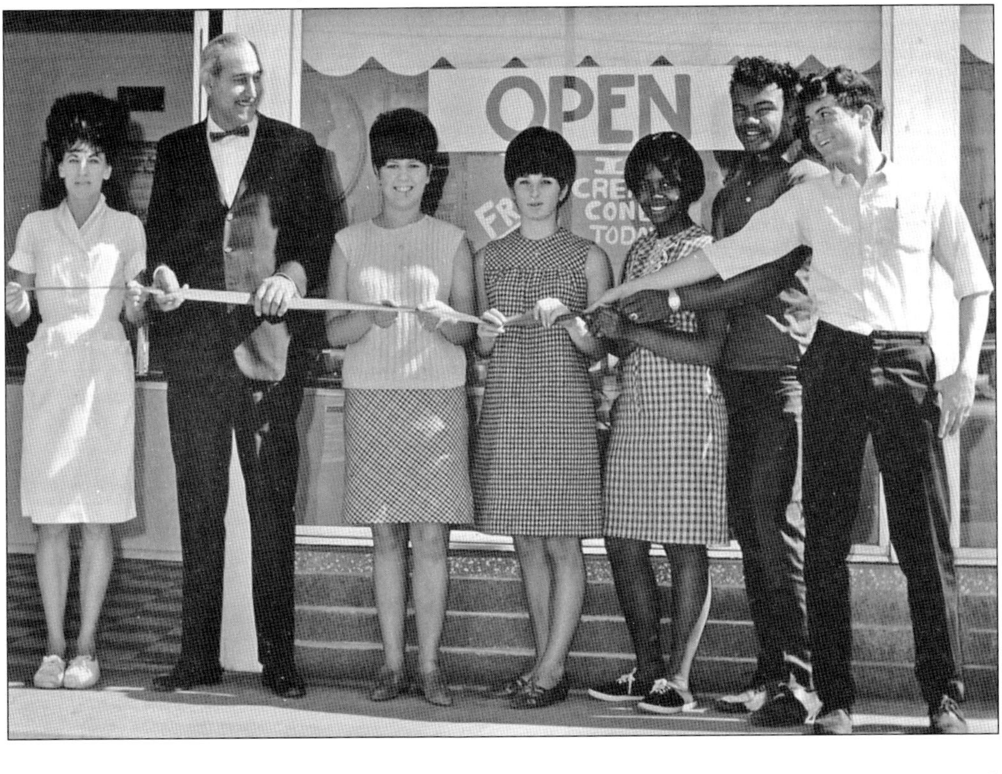

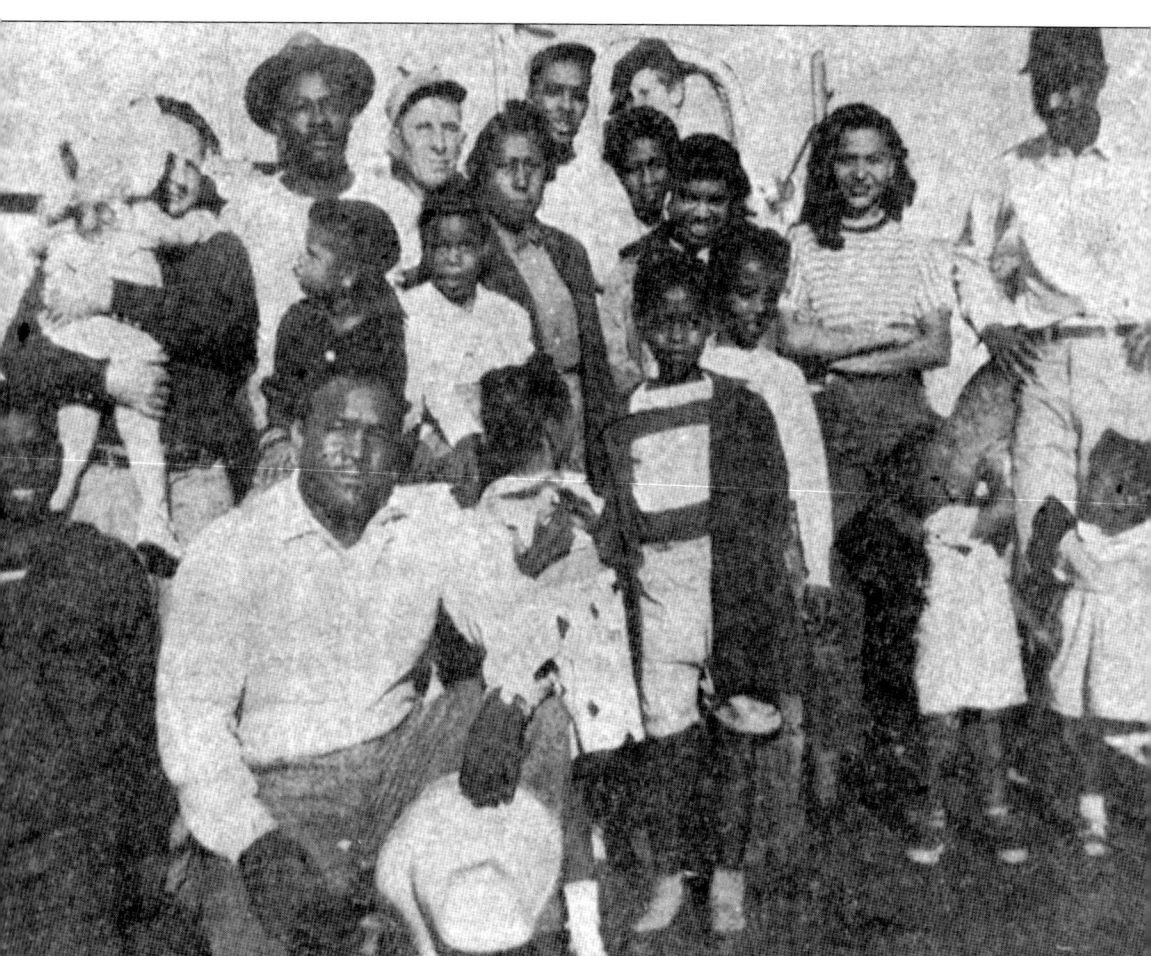

The Civic Voters League, organized and led by African Americans Richard Joyce (standing, far right), John Bean (standing, far left), and Jack Simon (kneeling, first row), was part of an effort to register voters and promote incorporation. Although the organization and the drive to incorporate was mixed race, the leadership and participation of African Americans in Seaside made incorporation a success in 1954. (Courtesy of the Amy Stuart Scrapbook Collection, City of Seaside Archive.)

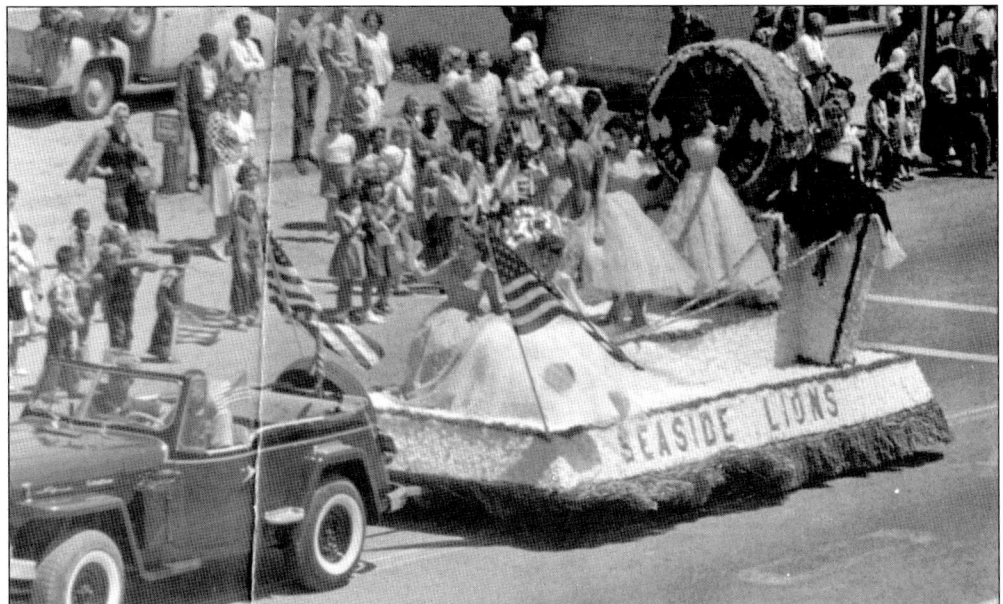

In addition to small businesses, Seaside residents organized chapters of numerous clubs such as Kiwanis, Lions, and Boy Scout and Girl Scout troops. All were meant to give residents a sense of community apart from Monterey. The photographs here depict a Boy Scout troop (above) and the local Lions Club. (Above, courtesy of the City of Seaside Archive; below, courtesy of the Amy Stuart Scrapbook Collection, City of Seaside Archive.)

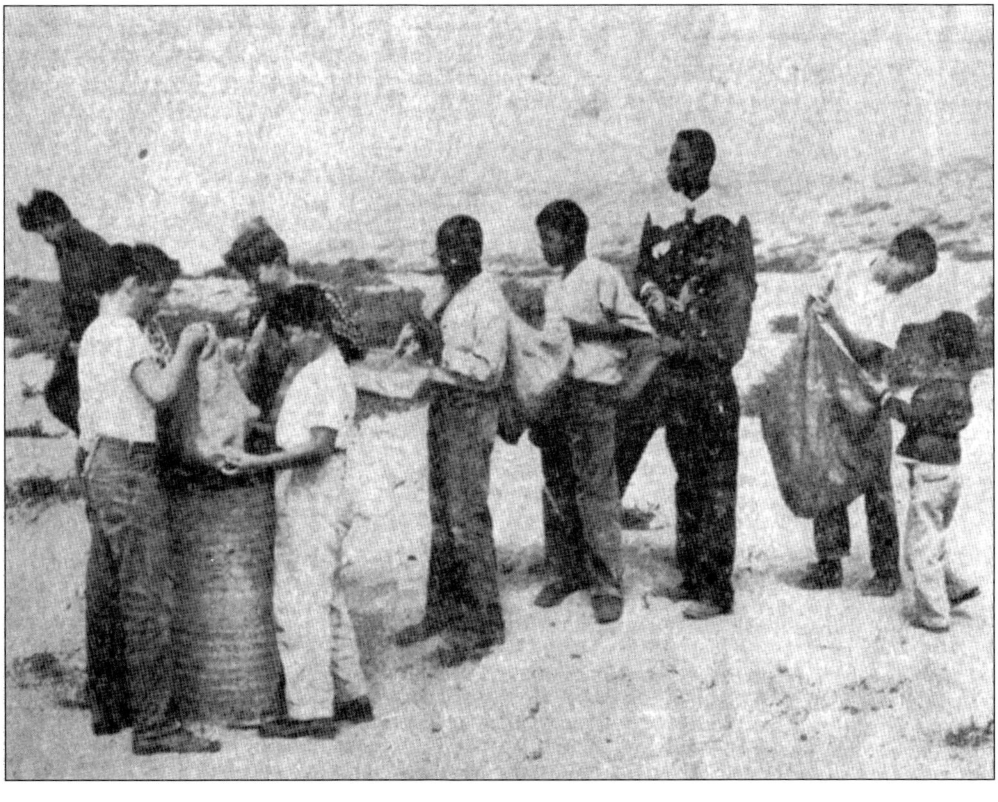

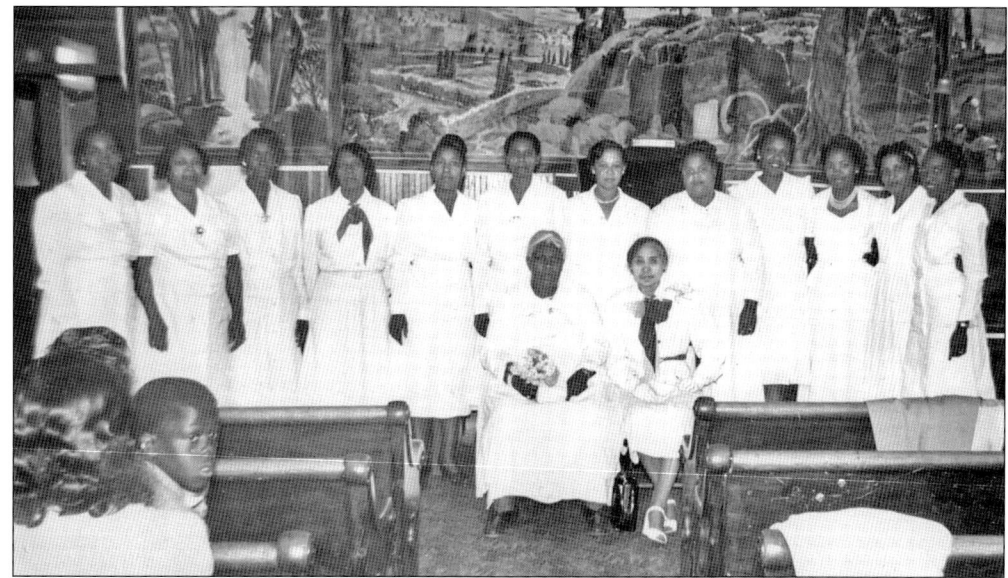

Missionaries Society First Baptist Church in Pacific Grove included, from left to right, (seated in pews) Steven Bailey, Mother Dora Isom, and (far right) the reverend's wife, Ella Bailey; (standing) unidentified, Lottie Rodgerg, Lucy Baily, Effie Greenwell, Elenora Rodgers, Rachel Welch, Bessie Lucas, unidentified, Belle Morris, Rosie Ross, Charlotte Jackson, and Johnnye Bush. Churches played an important role in Seaside civic life. Military families formed congregations based on race and on shared regional origins so that, by the 1950s, Seaside boasted 35 different churches, many of which were traditionally African American. This included Victory Temple, first established in 1943, numerous Baptist and Methodist churches, a Russian Orthodox church, and St. Francis Xavier Catholic Church, which was known for its multicultural, mixed-race membership. The picture below is of Rev. S. R. Martin and the Victory Temple Church of God and Christ in 1969. (Above, courtesy of the Diedre Banks Collection, City of Seaside Archive; below, courtesy of the City of Seaside Archive.)

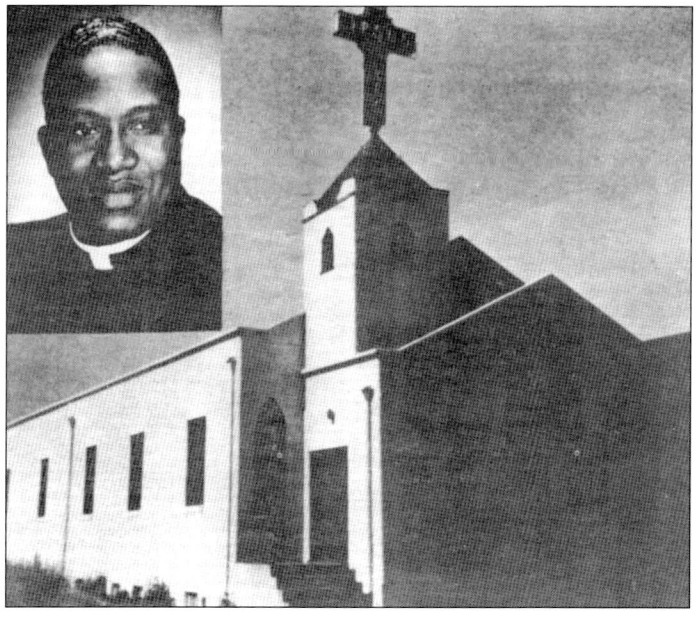

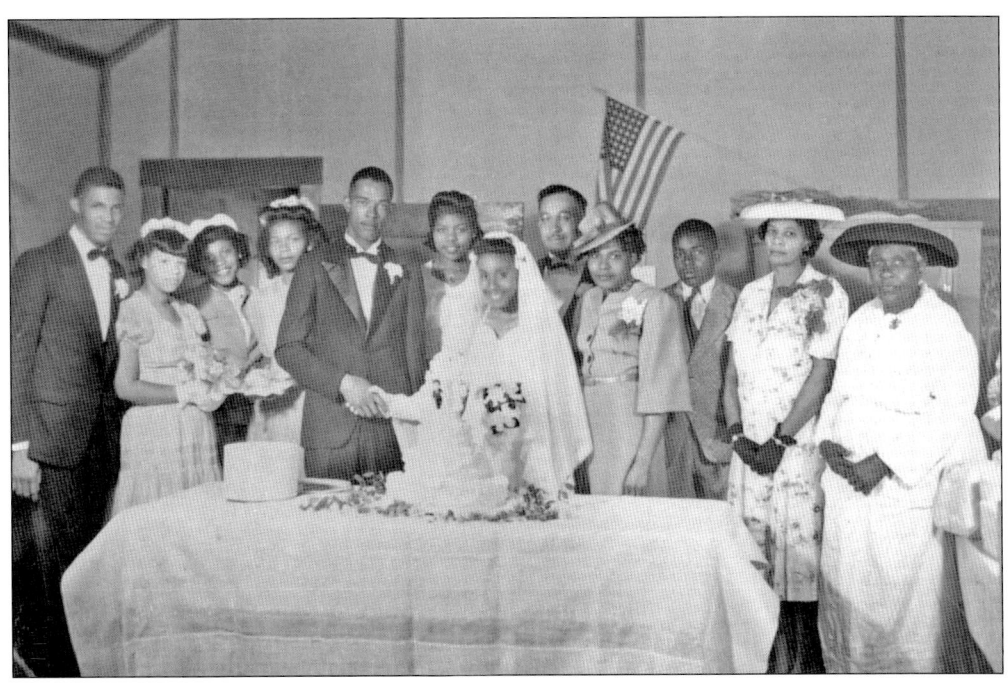

Pictured above is a wedding ceremony at a Baptist church in Pacific Grove for Sam Welch and Murietta Ratliff in 1949. Sarah Ratliff is the mother of Murietta. Walter Jones stands behind the bride and groom. The rest are unidentified. Among those pictured below are Rev. E. B. Stewart, Bob Johnson, Dale Ward, Mayor L. K. Smith, Gene Trenner, Rev. S. R. Martin, Mrs. J. F. Dukes, and Mrs. L. Fascon. (Both, courtesy of the Diedre Banks Collection, City of Seaside Archive.)

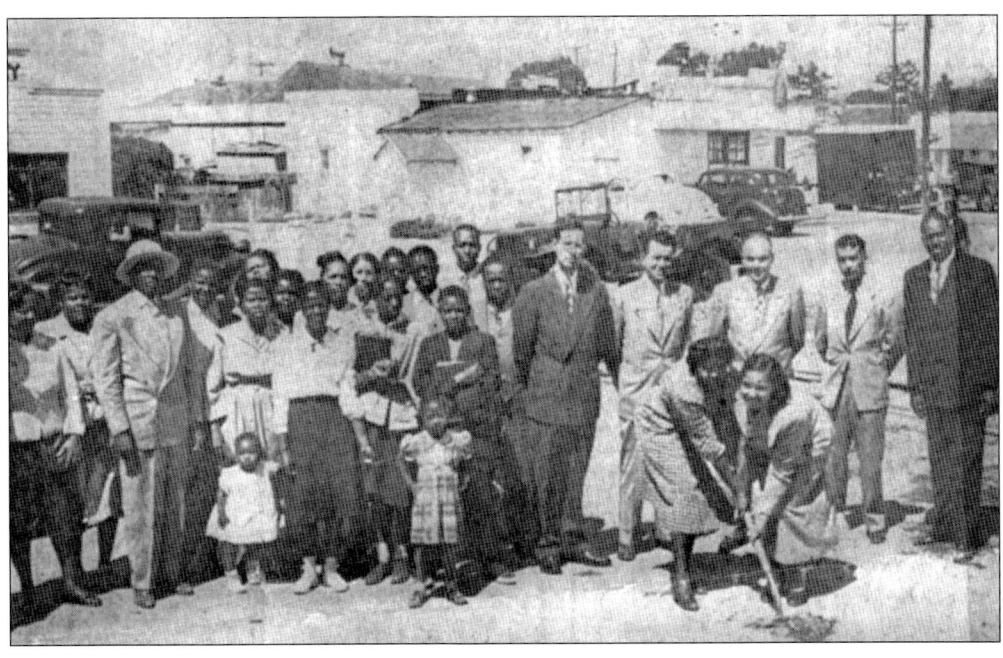

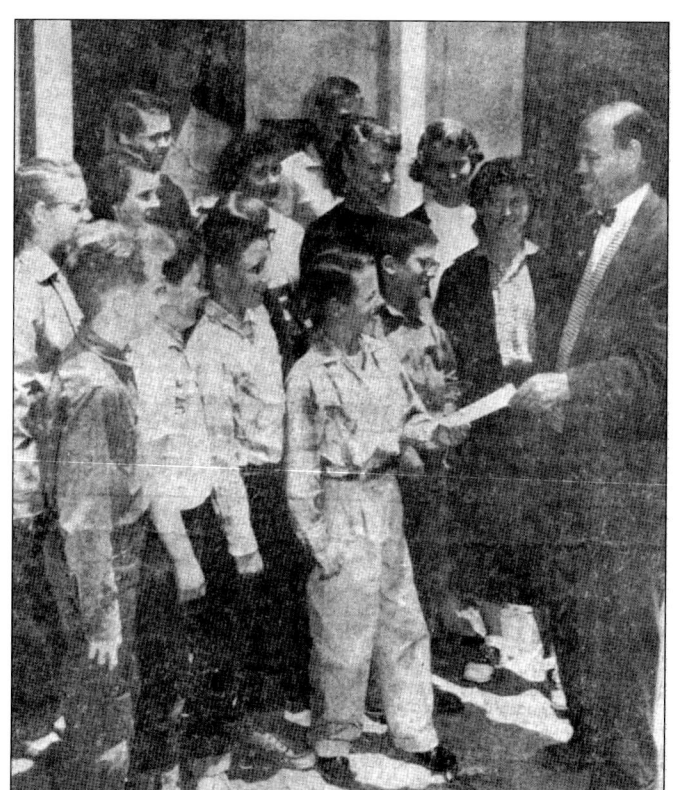

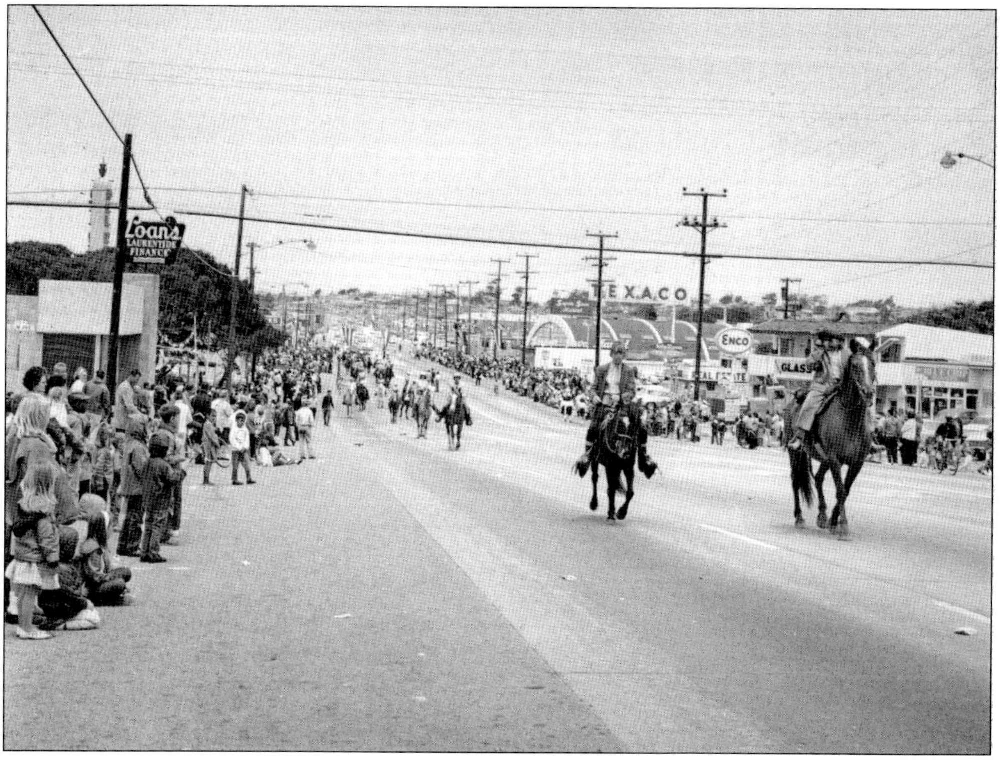

As Seaside emerged as a suburb in its own right, residents proudly participated in all sorts of public events to show off their community spirit. (Both, courtesy of the City of Seaside Archive.)

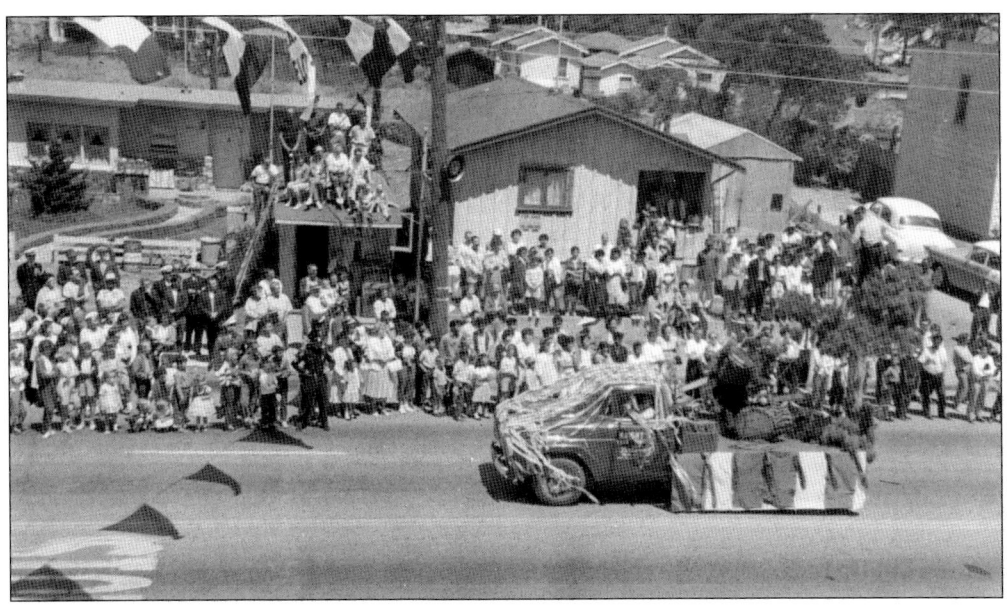

Parades were particularly important, and Seasiders spent weeks collectively building floats for the Monterey festivals and their own. (Both, courtesy of the Amy Stuart Scrapbook Collection, City of Seaside Archive.)

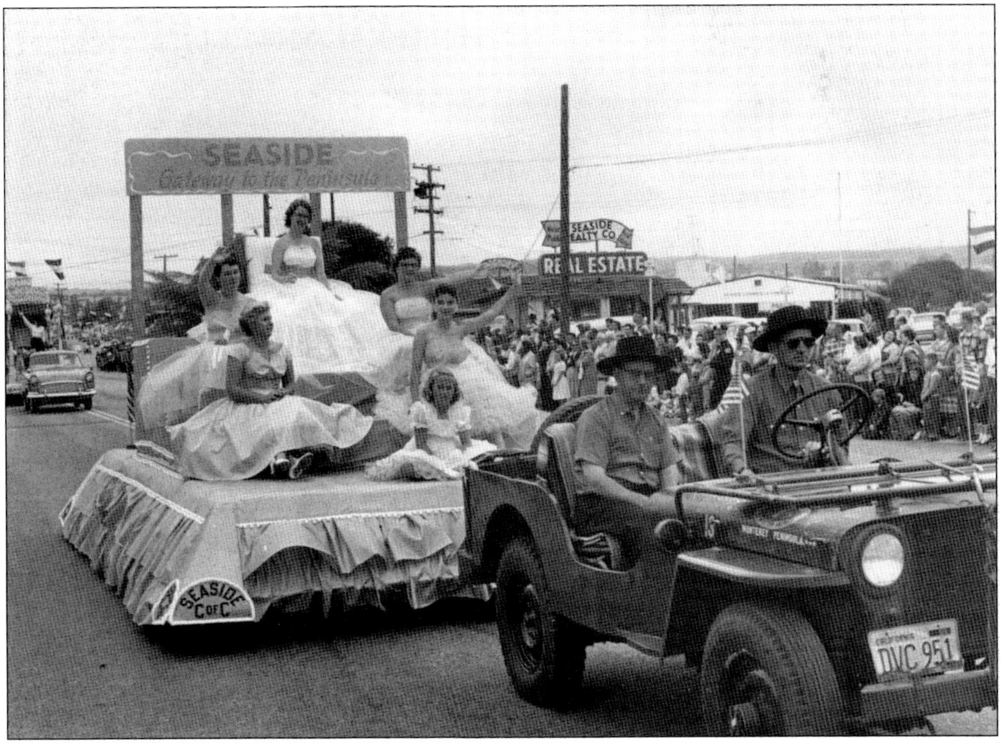

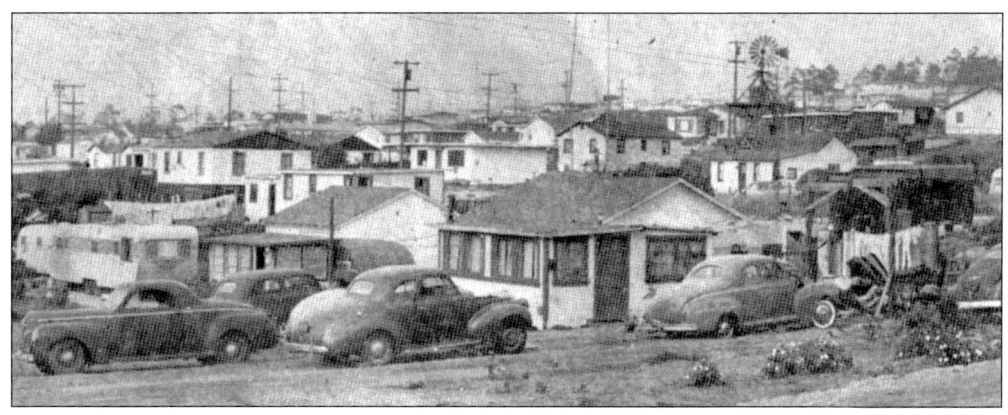

These photographs depict Seaside as it looked in the 1950s postwar period. It was an increasingly crowded military suburb of Fort Ord and a community of small homes with little or no landscaping. The hastily built shacks of the 1930s and 1940s gave way to neighborhoods with streets. The population of a few hundred prior to World War II soared to 10,226 by 1950 and 21,750 by 1956. By 1968, Seaside was the largest city on the Monterey Peninsula, with a population well over 32,000. Minorities were well represented throughout these years. By 1980, thirty percent of Seaside's population was African American, and the city had become a minority-majority suburb. (Both, courtesy of the Amy Stuart Scrapbook Collection, City of Seaside Archive.)

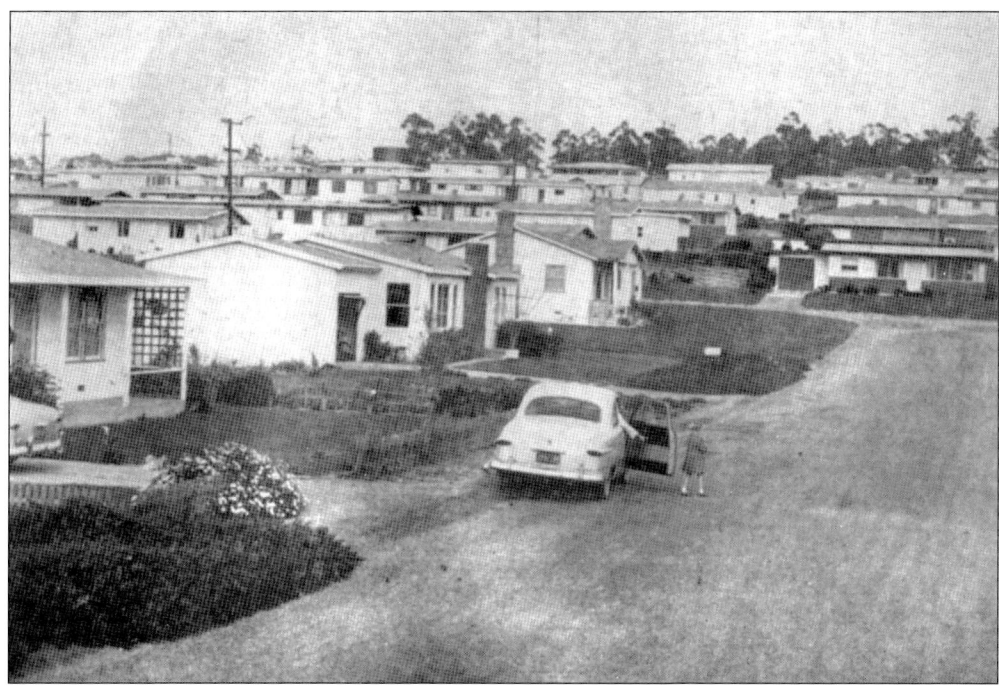

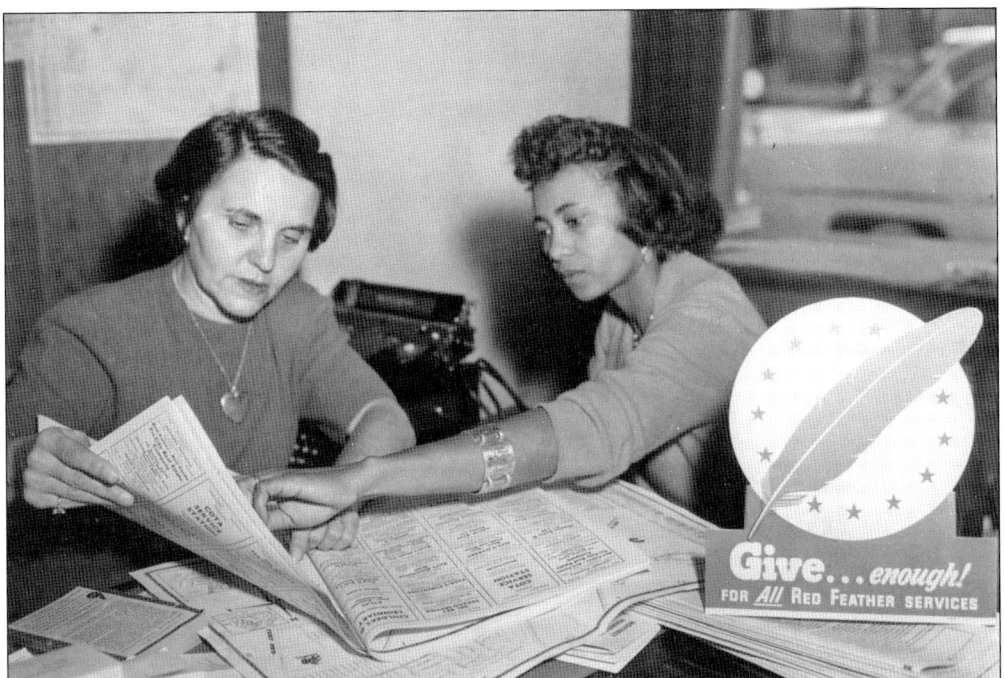

Seaside residents worked together to organize politically. Lenora Bean (right), a prominent African American resident, is shown above organizing charitable giving with a colleague. In the picture below are, from left to right, (standing) Joe Cota, John Bean, Sam DeMello, John Pattulo, and Al Underwood. Seated is redevelopment director Francis Geary. (Both, courtesy of the Lenora Bean Collection, City of Seaside Archive.)

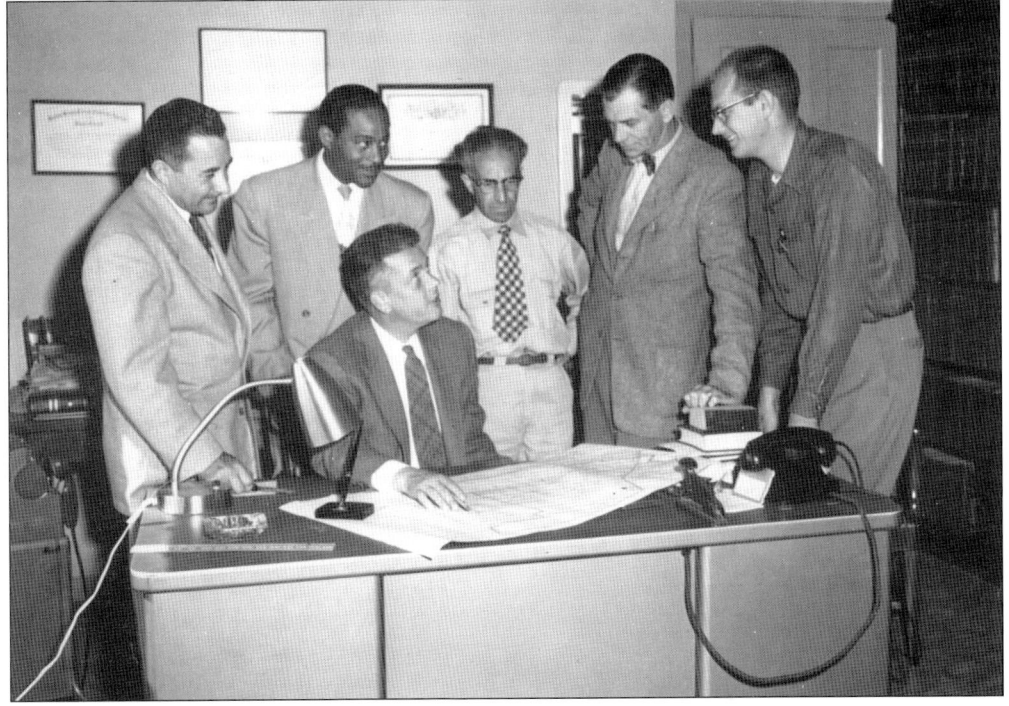

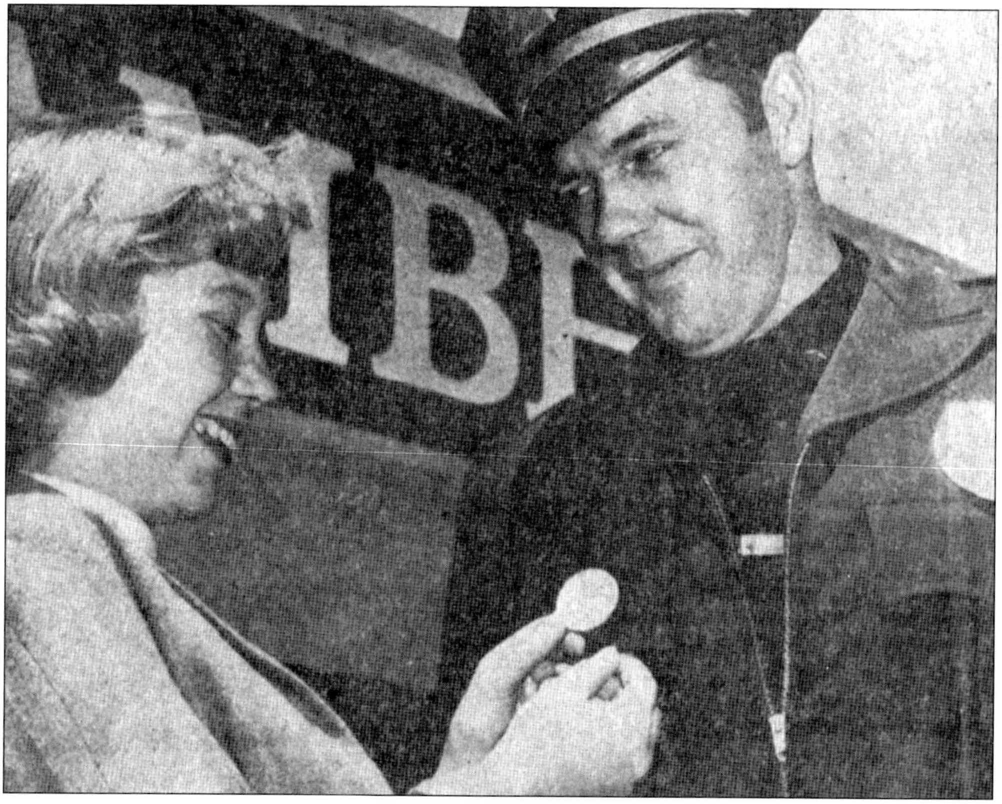

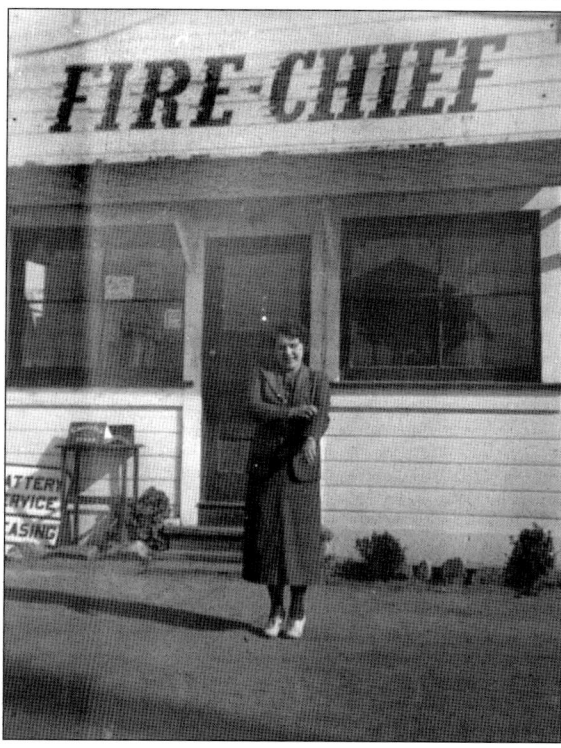

Seaside residents were eager to ensure that, although they were known as a military town, they also supported a strong police force and fire department to keep order. Photographs such as these were commonplace efforts at public relations in the local press. Pictured above are Anita Irwin (left)—Miss Liberty—and an unidentified police officer. (Above, courtesy of the Amy Stuart Scrapbook Collection, City of Seaside Archive; left, courtesy of the Monterey Public Library, California History Room.)

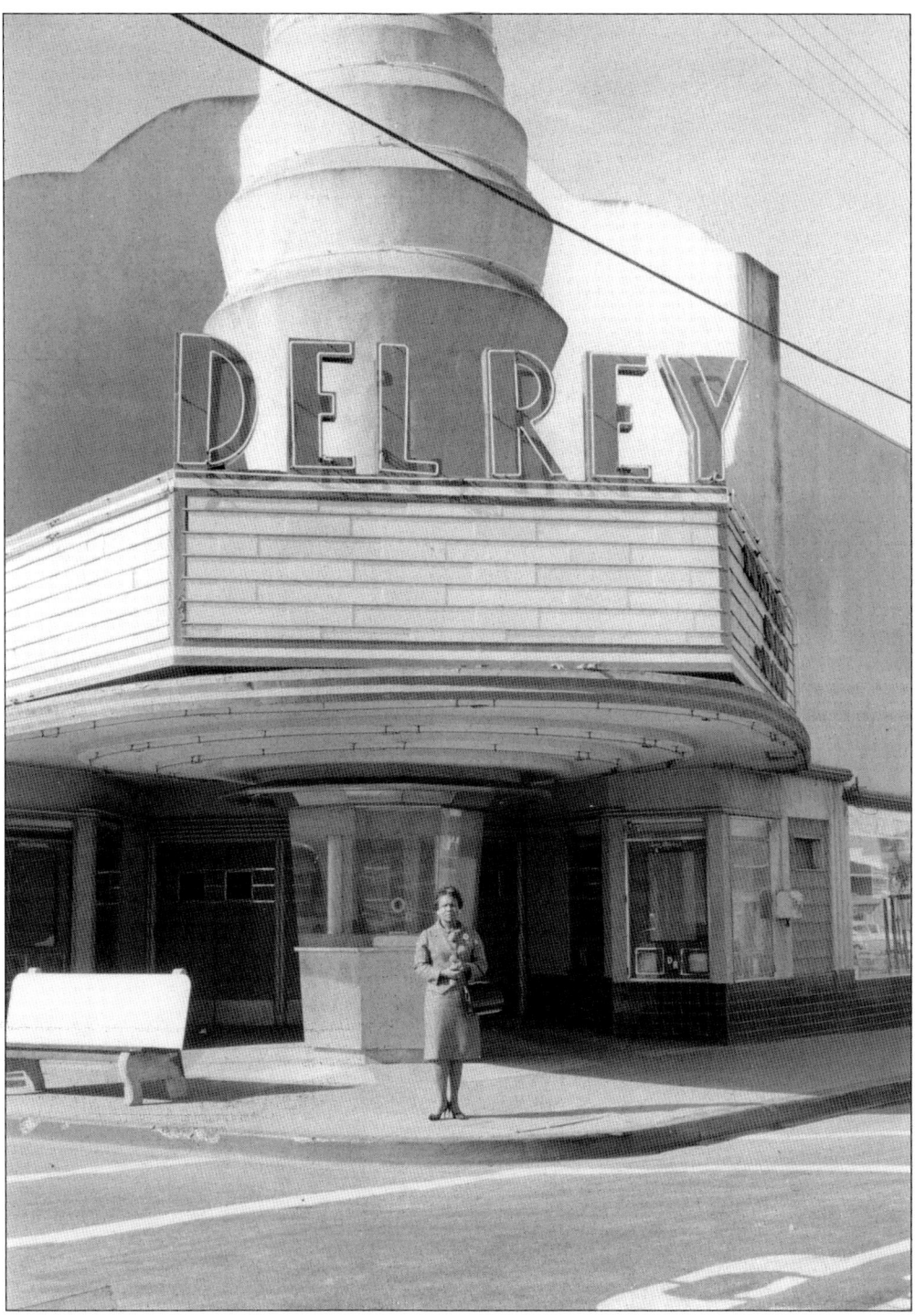

The Del Rey Theater was one of Seaside's most important landmarks. It was unfortunately destroyed by fire in the mid-1970s. This photograph shows Pearl Carey, one of Seaside's most important leaders in the civil rights movement, standing in front of the Del Rey Theater in the 1950s. (Courtesy of the Pearl Carey Collection, City of Seaside Archive.)

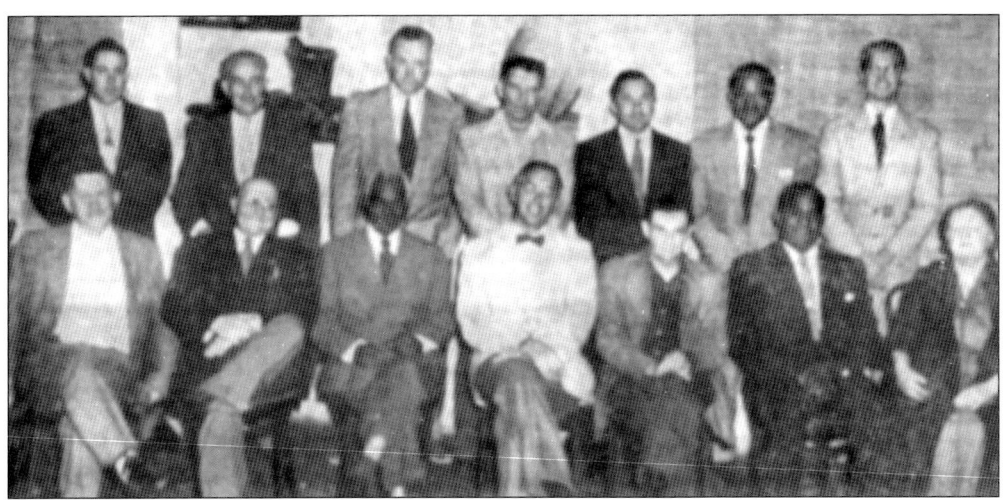

The race for city council began in 1954 as Seasiders prepared to fight for incorporation. The candidates pictured above show the participation and leadership of African Americans, in contrast to the chamber of commerce photograph 10 years earlier. Politics in Seaside was dynamic and contentious. The photograph below represents some of the lively discussion among businessmen in Seaside over the issue of incorporation. *The People Speak*, which aired over KXXL each Thursday at 7:30 p.m. by the Monterey Peninsula Jaycees, presented the first in a series of panel discussions on current political issues in Seaside. Panel members were (clockwise, beginning at far left) Herman Olsen, president of Ord Terrace Property; George Polluck; Dr. John Craige; city councilmen Pat Patterson; official of the Seaside Democratic Club; Walt Eggers; and moderator S. J. Neckele, the program chairman. (Both, courtesy of the City of Seaside Archive.)

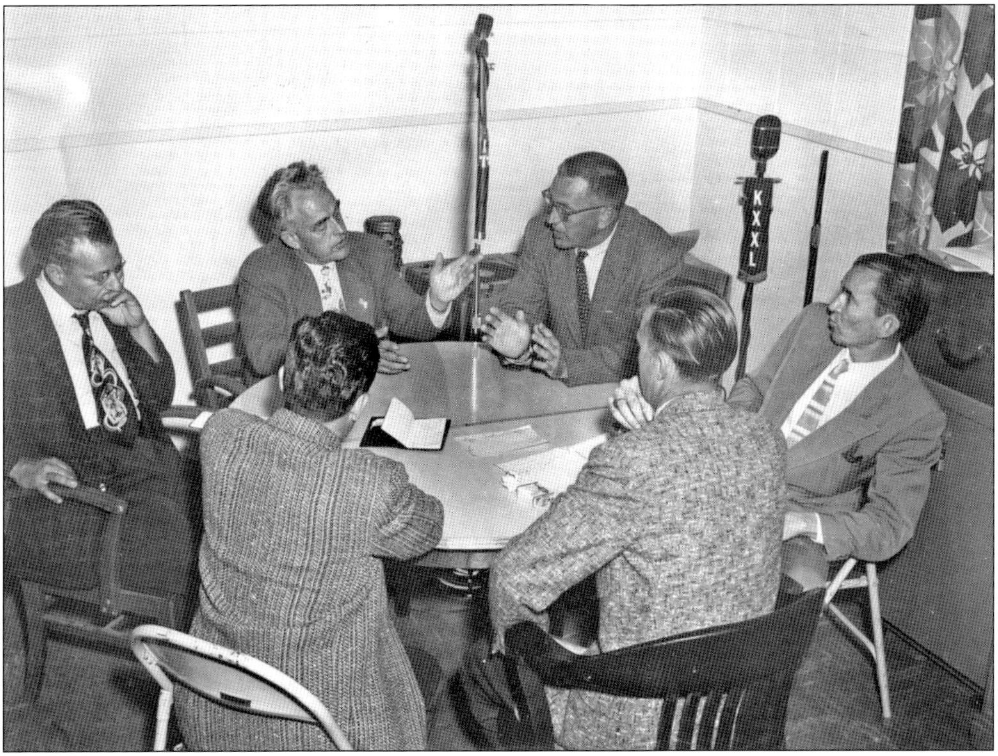

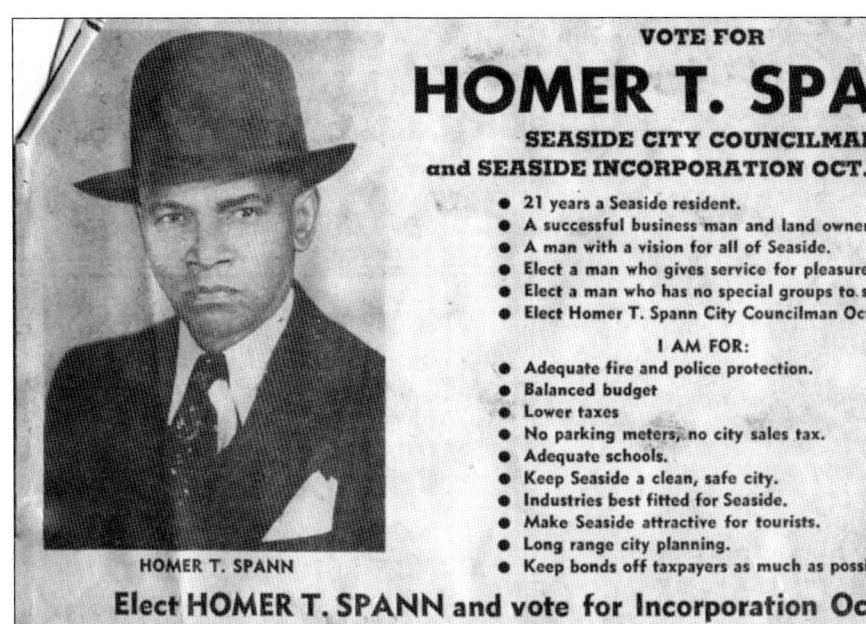

The first millionaire in Seaside, Homer Spann had moved with his family from his native Florida to Los Angeles in 1909 when he was nine years old. He lived in Carmel for six years before moving to Seaside in 1933 and began buying property and developing the city. A strong advocate of incorporation, he ran for city council in 1954. In his campaign literature, he was quoted as saying, "Seaside is not only the gateway to the Monterey Peninsula, but the power of the Peninsula." (Courtesy of the Amy Stuart Scrapbook Collection, City of Seaside Archive.)

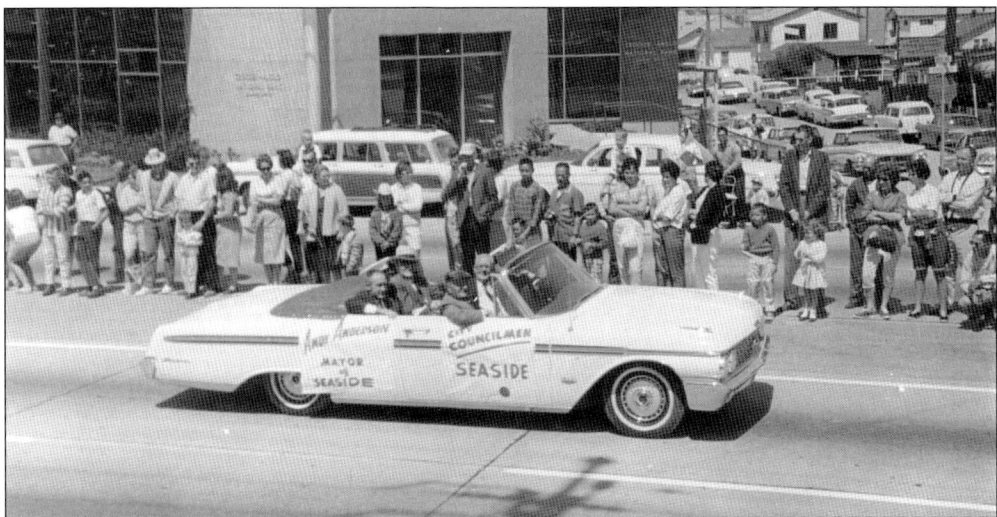

Here is Seaside's mayor from 1960 to 1964, Beauford T. "Andy" Anderson, campaigning in a Seaside parade. Anderson grew up on a Wisconsin farm and became a war hero during World War II, earning a Medal of Honor. He reenlisted and was stationed at Fort Ord, where he remained after leaving the service in 1952. He started a floor covering and linoleum business in Seaside. Anderson, like almost all of Seaside's political leaders in the postwar decades, was a small businessman with direct connections to the military and Fort Ord. (Courtesy of the City of Seaside Archive.)

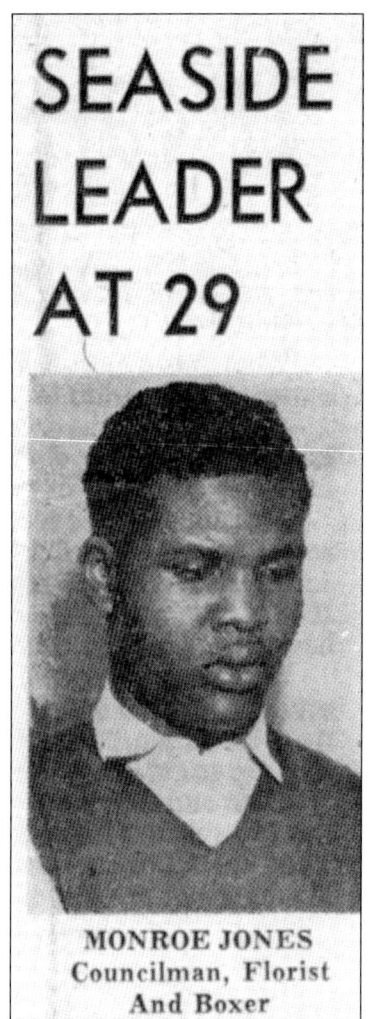

MONROE JONES
Councilman, Florist
And Boxer

Monroe Jones arrived in Seaside in 1943 with his uncle, the Reverend S. R. Martin, who was the founder of one of Seaside's most important black churches, the Greater Victory Temple Church of God in Christ. Monroe Jones, a 29-year-old former boxer and head custodian for Del Rey School, ran and won a city council seat in 1956. He shared a background as an army veteran with the rest of the candidates for city council and was described as a "soft-voiced man with a talent for political oratory." Jones not only won reelection to the city council for two years, but he also won with the highest number of votes and, according to the *Seaside News Sentinel*'s front-page headline, "Swept the Field" with a multiracial political coalition supporting him. He was one of only three black city councilmen in the state of California. (Courtesy of the Amy Stuart Scrapbook Collection, City of Seaside Archive.)

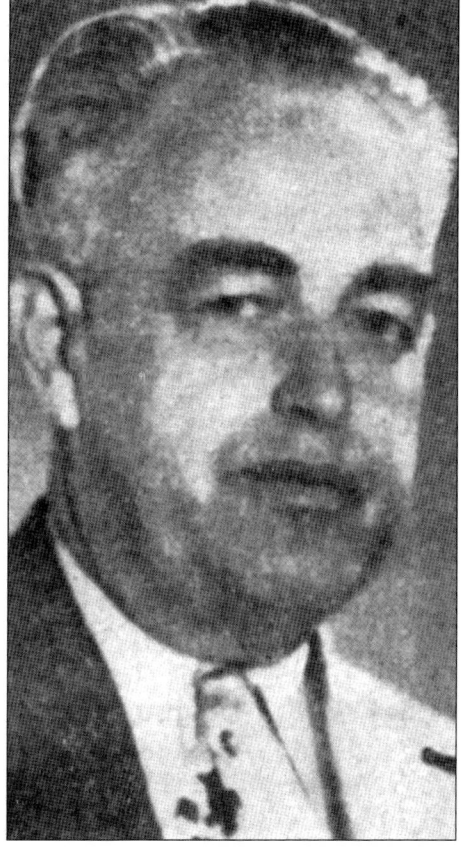

Not everyone supported incorporation. George Pollack is depicted here in a campaign photograph. Pollack, a labor-rights attorney, owner of the water company in Seaside, and former president of the chamber of commerce, stood to lose his water company if the city incorporated and water systems were publicly owned. Pollack led the fight against incorporation, but when petitions were passed to put incorporation to a vote, he ran and won a seat on the first Seaside City Council. (Courtesy of the Amy Stuart Scrapbook Collection, City of Seaside Archive.)

John Bean came to Seaside as part of the 7th Infantry in 1943; in retirement, he became the first African American realtor in Seaside and an active participant in Seaside politics. Bean was also a strong advocate for incorporation and made it a centerpiece of his campaign for city council in 1954. Although he lost the election, he remained a prominent member of Seaside's elite business community and an activist in Seaside's civil rights movement. (Courtesy of the Lenora Bean Collection, City of Seaside Archive.)

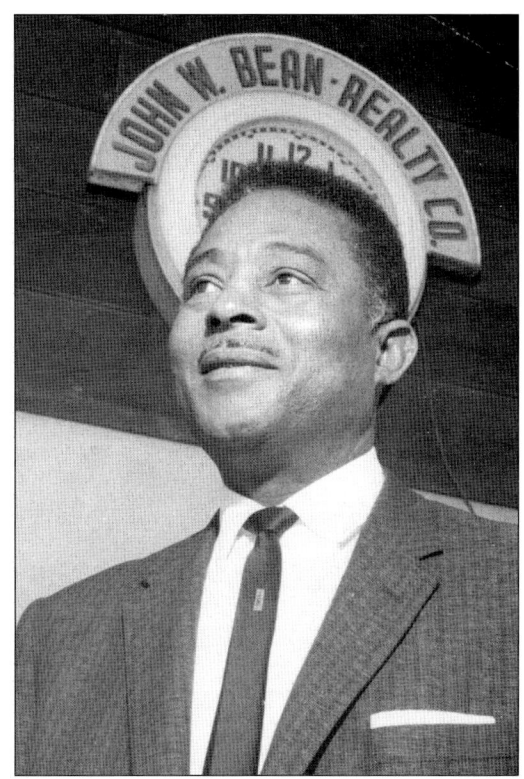

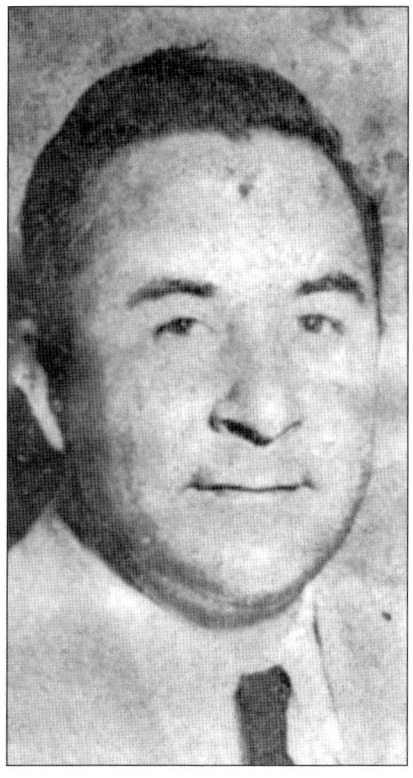

This photograph depicts Joe Cota, who came from Salinas to Seaside in 1948 and who owned a moving and storage company. He had been actively involved in everything from the local Lions Club to the Seaside Chamber of Commerce. He was elected mayor of Seaside in 1958 and served one term, although he remained a crucial member of Seaside's business community and governing elite through the 1960s. (Courtesy of the City of Seaside Archive.)

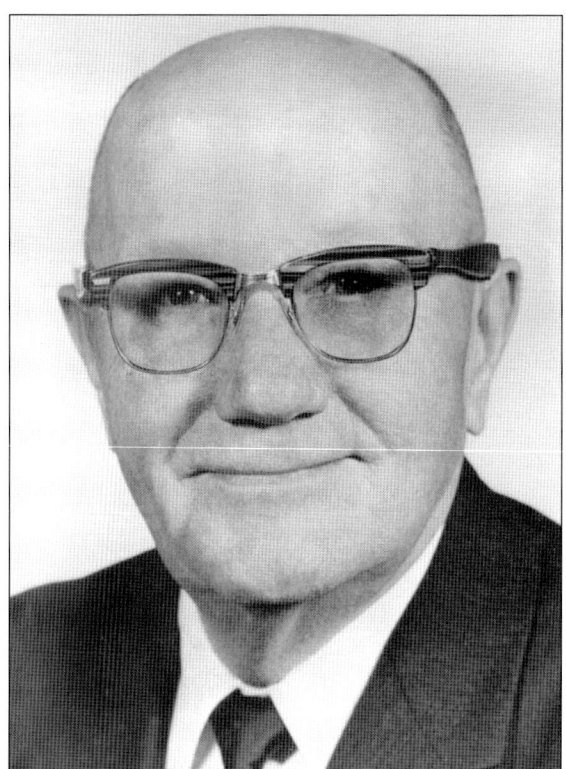

G. T. "Sarge" Cunningham managed the Del Rey Theater and was an army veteran who had lived in Seaside for 14 years before being elected to the city council in 1954. Cunningham served as mayor from 1956 to 1958. (Courtesy of the City of Seaside Archive.)

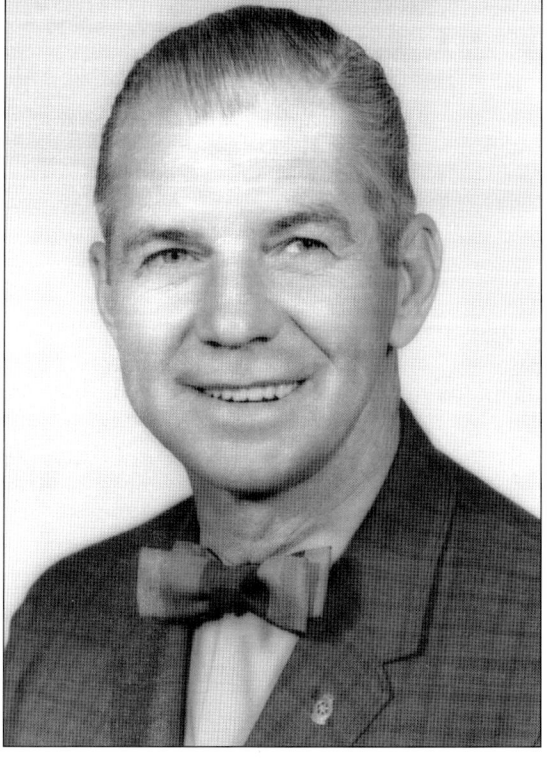

John Pattulo was an insurance and real estate agent and a former civil engineer who arrived in Seaside in 1948 from Nebraska. He was elected to the city council and appointed mayor in 1964. The municipal pool in Seaside was later named after him. (Courtesy of the City of Seaside Archive.)

Jack Oldemeyer, elected Seaside's first mayor, was an automobile mechanic who came to Seaside in 1928 and became actively involved with establishing a fire district in Seaside, an issue that generated great support among residents who felt neglected by the county. He described himself as "100 percent American." However, he became embroiled in racial politics with the Seaside Police Department shortly after assuming office and narrowly survived a recall election. The controversy resulted in strong responses from the African American community, and by the next election, the first black city councilman, Monroe Jones, was elected with overwhelming support. Oldemeyer continued to be involved in community organizations but left politics. The most important community center in Seaside, the Oldemeyer Center, was named after Jack Oldemeyer. (Courtesy of the City of Seaside Archive.)

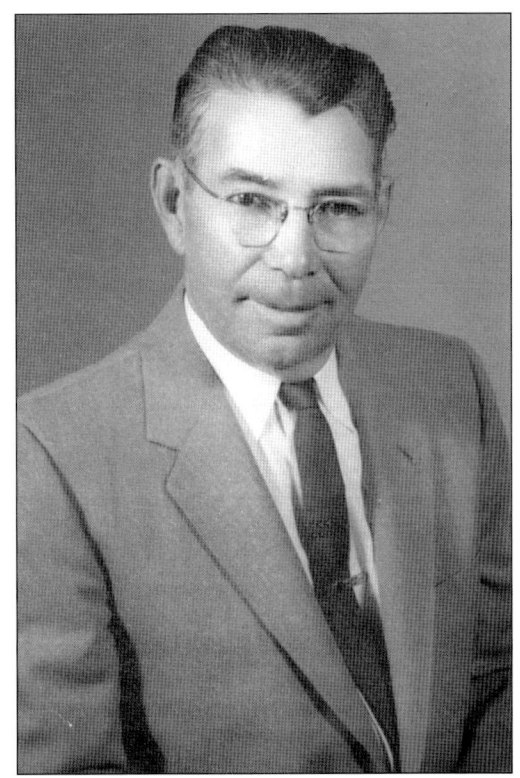

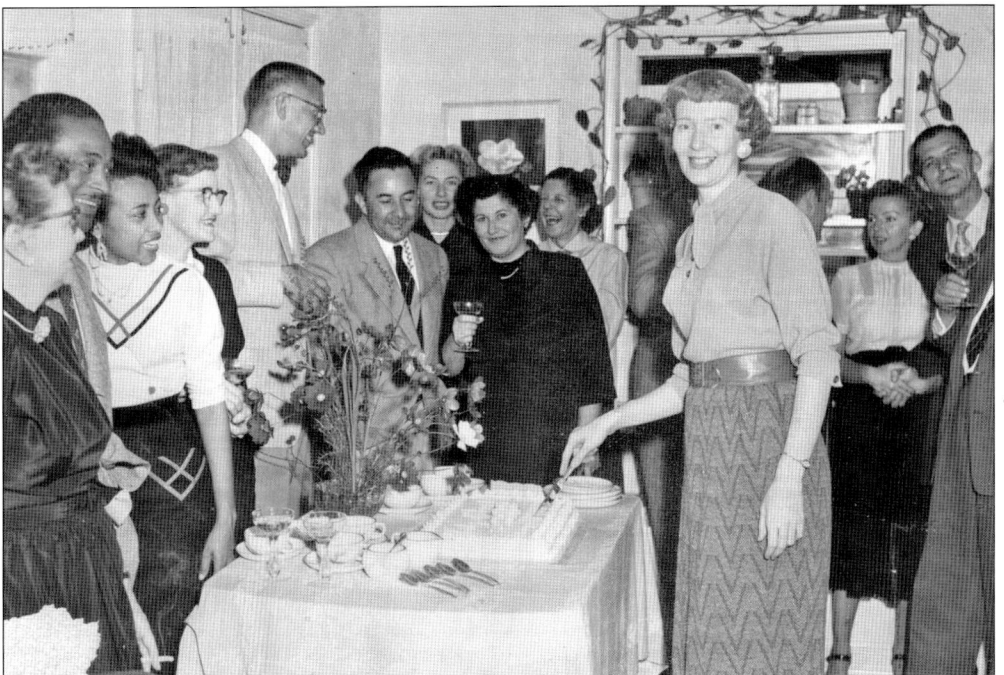

This 1954 photograph depicts the celebration party in the aftermath of the successful vote for incorporation in Seaside. The celebrants were all active proponents of the move to incorporate. (Courtesy of the Lenora Bean Collection, City of Seaside Archive.)

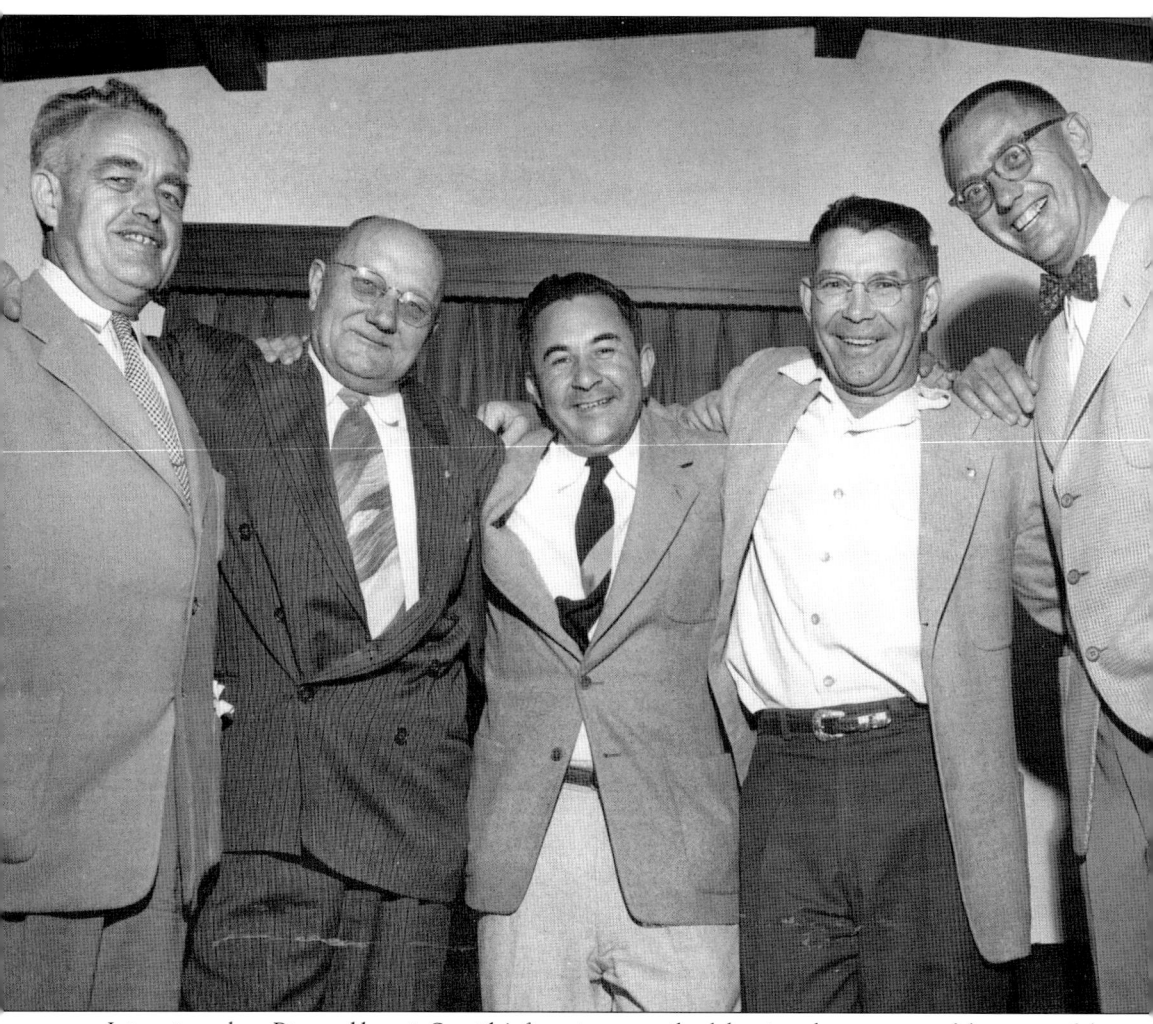

It is a city at last. Pictured here is Seaside's first city council celebrating the outcome of the successful drive to incorporate. From left to right are George Pollack, "Sarge" Cunningham, Joe Cota, Jack Oldemeyer, and veterinarian John Craige. (Courtesy of the City of Seaside Archive.)

Three

REVITALIZING THE POPULATION IN THE POSTWAR ERA

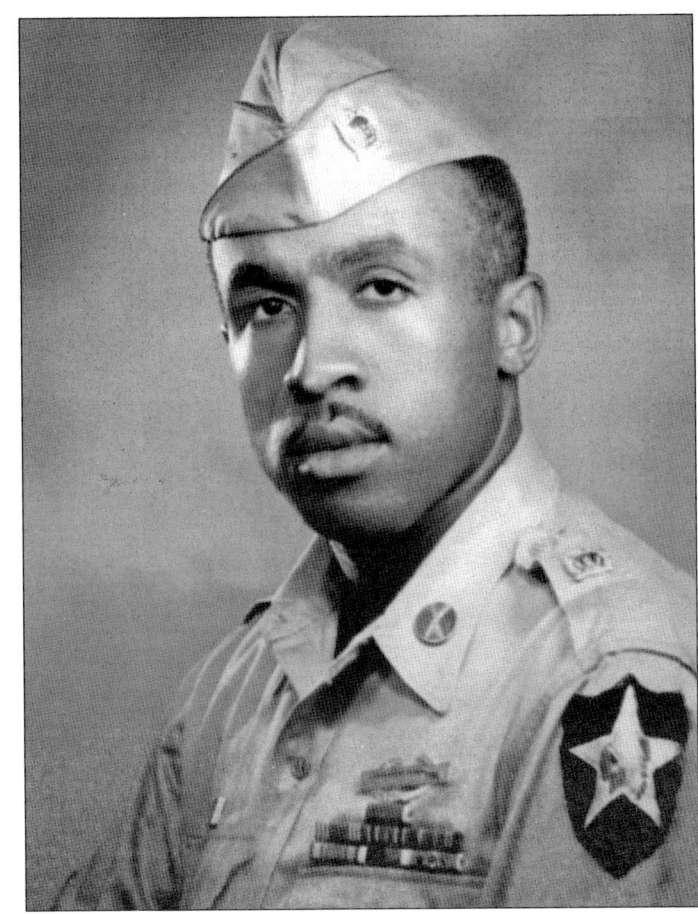

The following photographs of black soldiers stationed at Fort Ord show the effects of Pres. Harry S. Truman's Executive Order 9381 in 1948, which desegregated the military "with equality for all people." Here is Bernard Miller in 1951. (Courtesy of the Veterans of Foreign Wars Collection, City of Seaside Archive.)

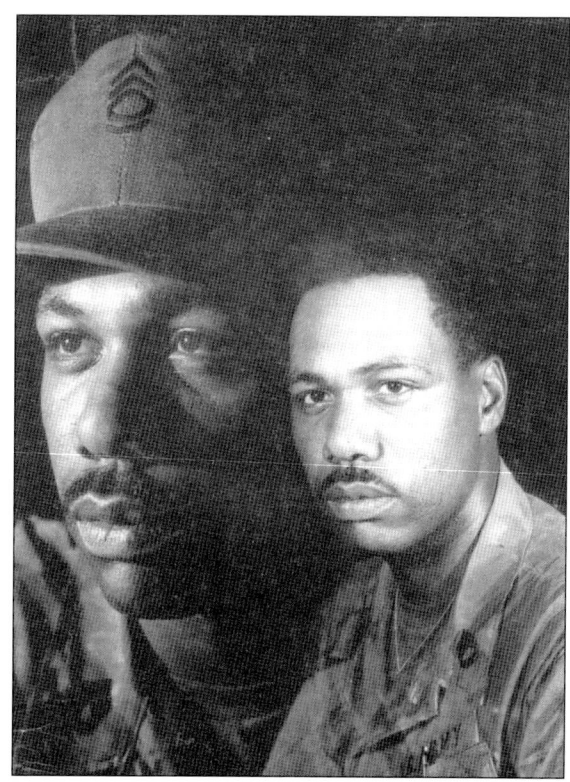

Fort Ord became an integrated training base practically overnight. The population of Seaside exploded into a brilliant multiracial mix, with a predominance of African American soldiers and their families, who were forced to settle in mostly segregated areas of Seaside because they encountered racial restrictions on housing on the rest of the peninsula. Pictured at left is Tony Martin in 1970; below is Tom Dorsey, just out of basic training in 1944. (Both, courtesy of the Veterans of Foreign Wars Collection, City of Seaside Archive.)

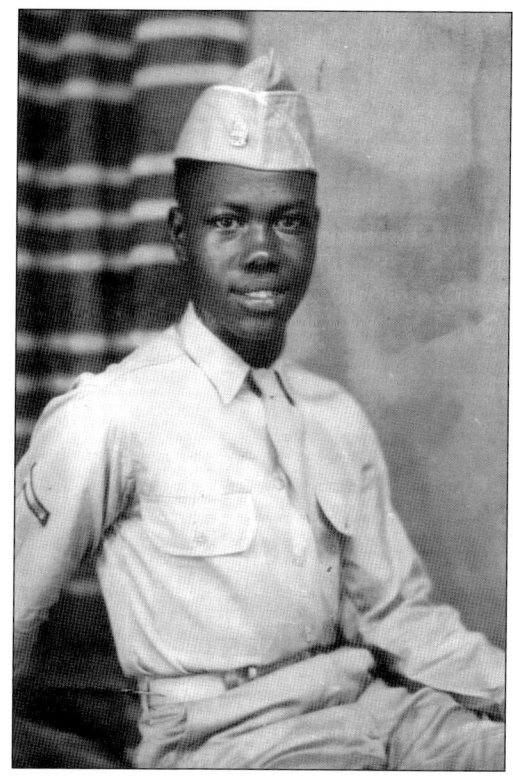

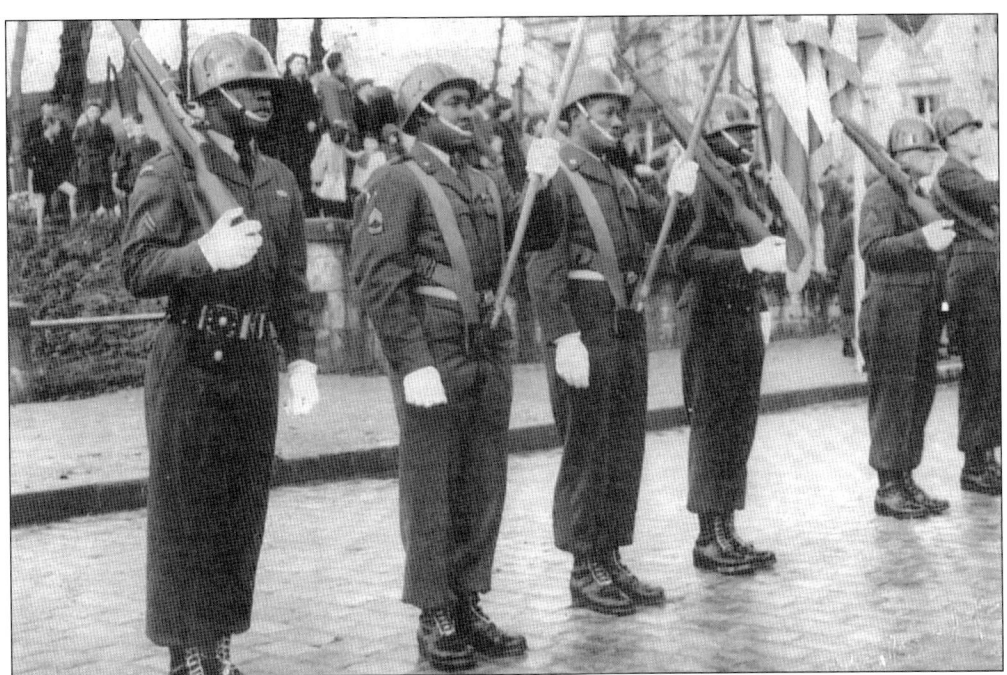

By 1980, fully one-third of Seaside's population of 33,000 was black. Pictured above are unidentified soldiers in Germany, and at right is Thomas Joyce in the 1940s. (Above, courtesy of the Veterans of Foreign Wars Collection, City of Seaside Archive; right, courtesy of the Richard Joyce Collection, City of Seaside Archive.)

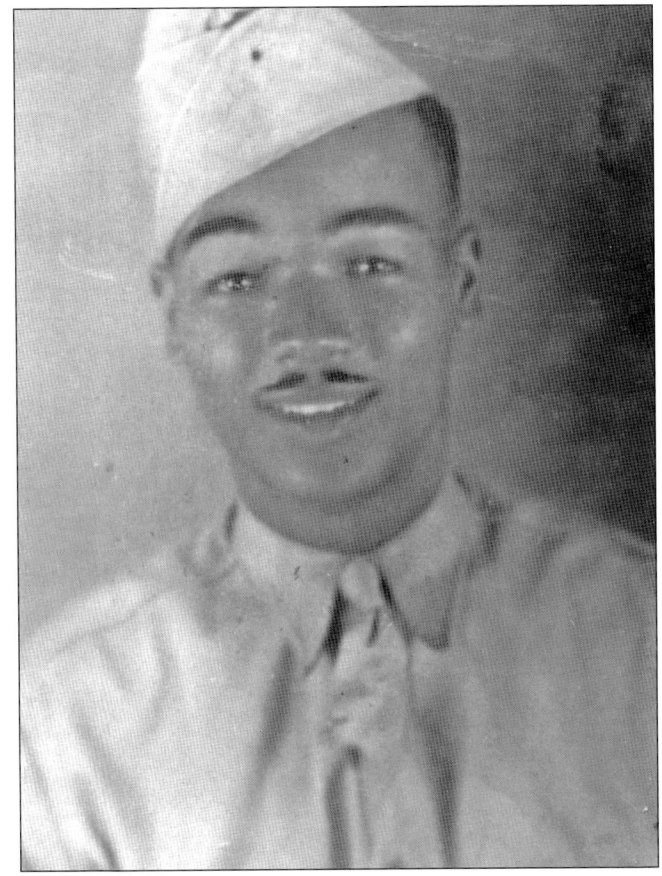

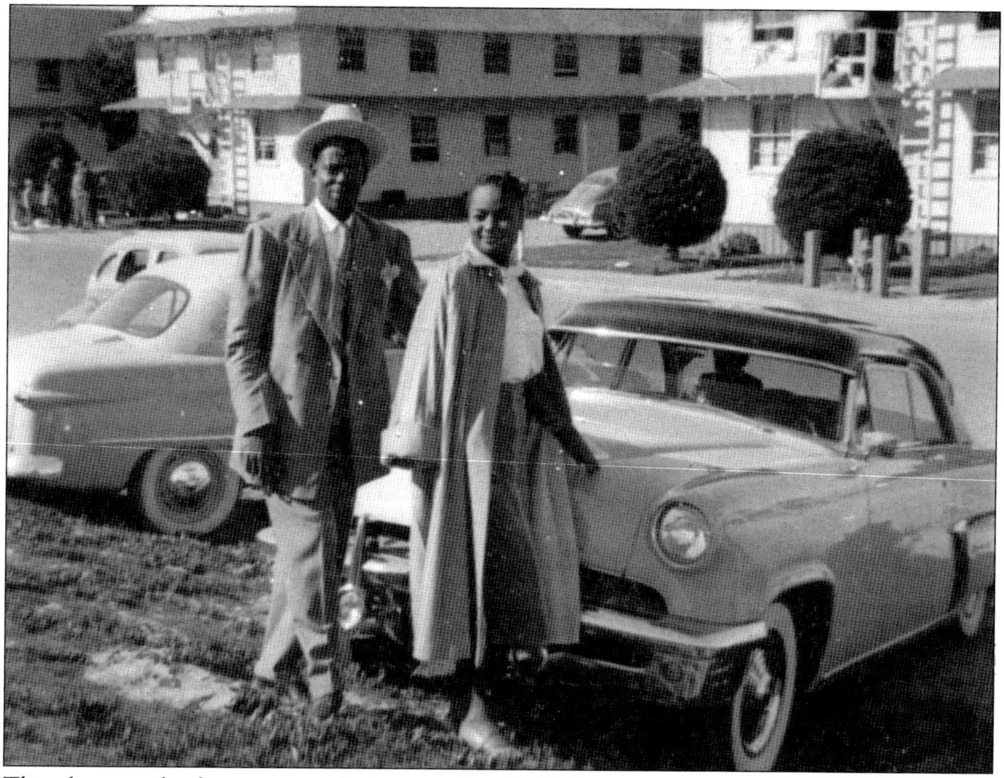

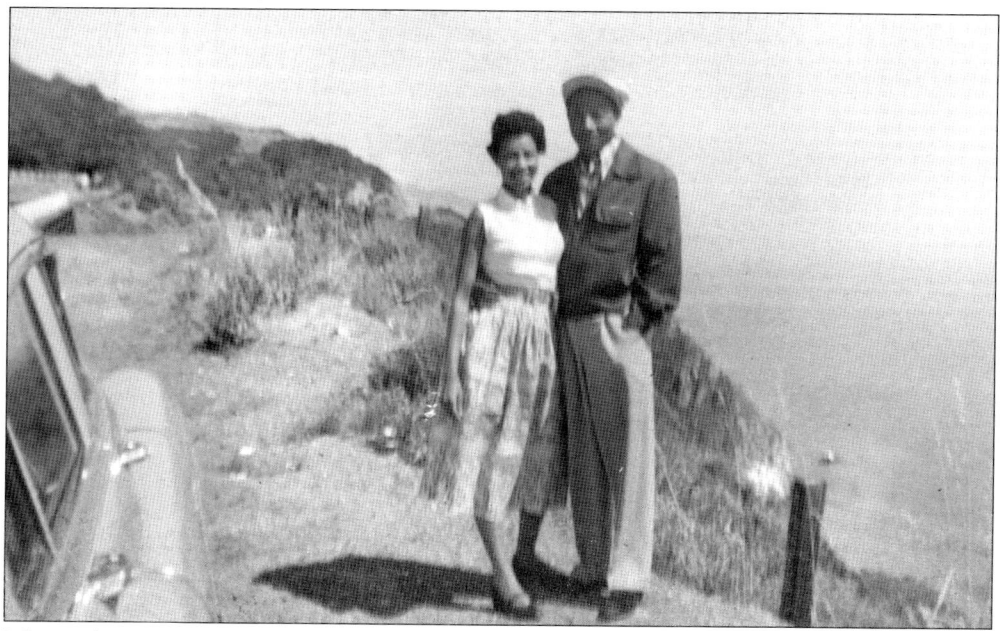

This photograph of a young couple, Joyce and Leslie McKinney, just arriving in postwar Fort Ord was taken in front of military housing there in 1954. (Courtesy of the Richard Joyce Collection, City of Seaside Archive.)

John and Lenora Bean are pictured after they first arrived in Seaside in 1956. (Courtesy of the Lenora Bean Collection, City of Seaside Archive.)

Most African Americans who arrived in Seaside came by way of the American South, just like the white families that preceded them in the 1930s. At right is a photograph of Ruthie Watts, who arrived in Seaside from North Carolina, along with her daughter. The image below is of Lenora Bean, 11th from left, at a Writers Club in the 1950s. (Right, courtesy of the Ruthie Watts Collection, City of Seaside Archive; below, courtesy of the Lenora Bean Collection, City of Seaside Archive.)

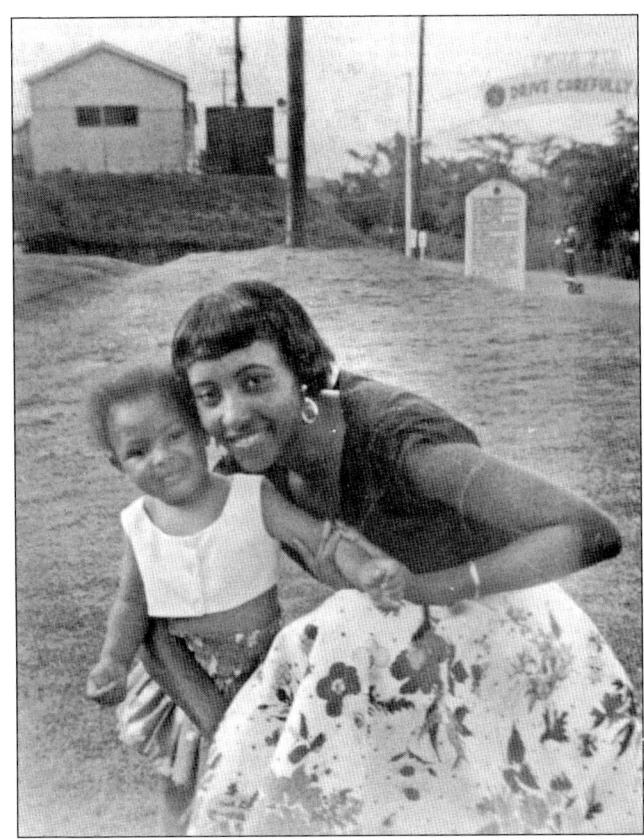

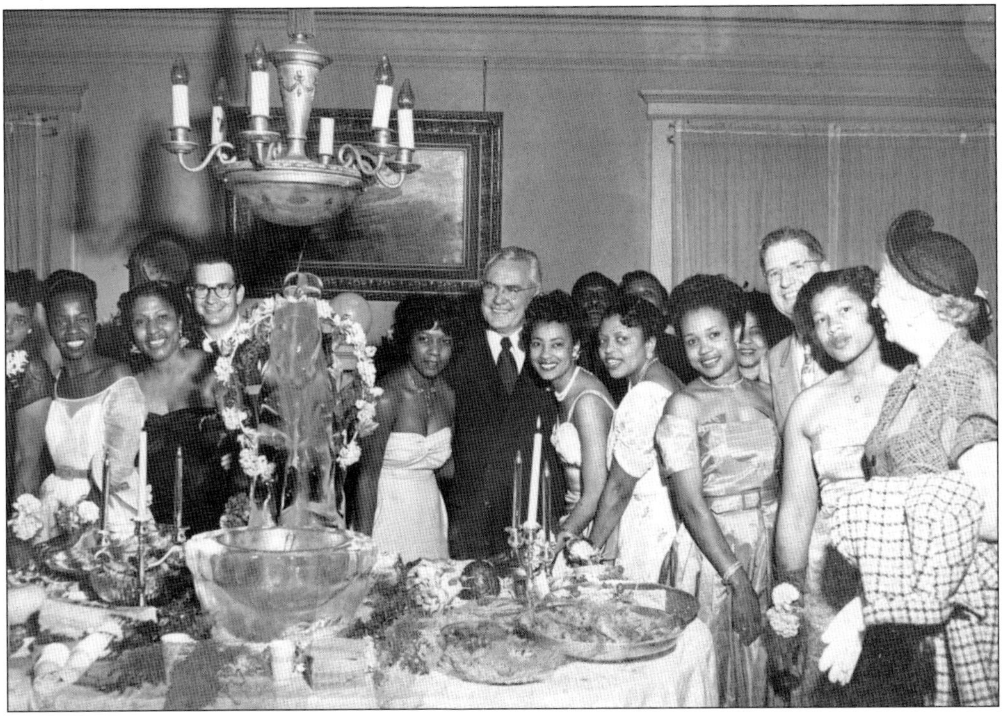

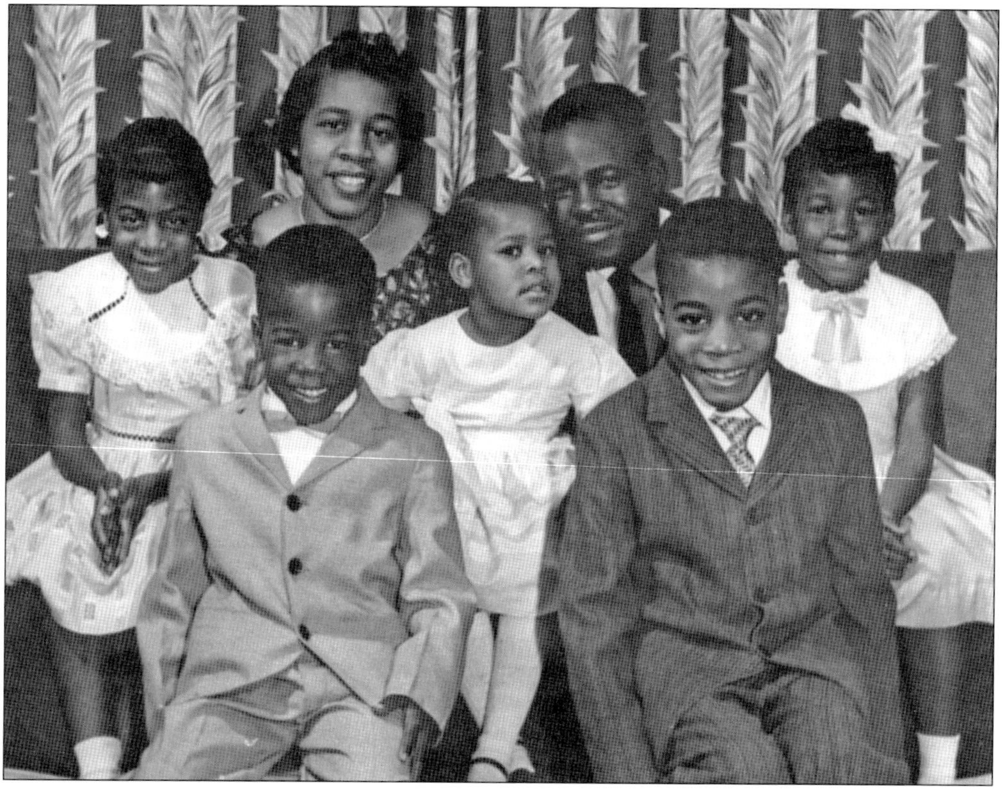

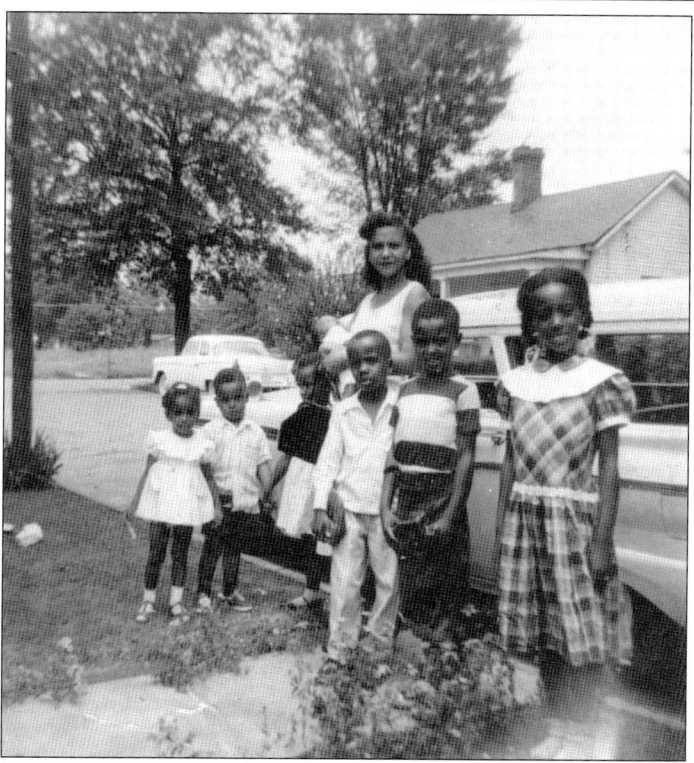

The African American families shown here in Seaside in the 1950s represented many elite families of officers and higher ranking enlisted men, creating a strong middle-class black community that would redefine the city throughout the 1950s and 1960s. The image above is a Danridge family portrait with, from left to right, Bula, Rossilyn, Leland, Mary, Ray Jr., Donna, and Raymond Danridge in 1963. At left is the Joyce family on Harding Street in 1957. (Above, courtesy of the Raymond Danridge Collection, City of Seaside Archive; left, courtesy of the Richard Joyce Collection, City of Seaside Archive.)

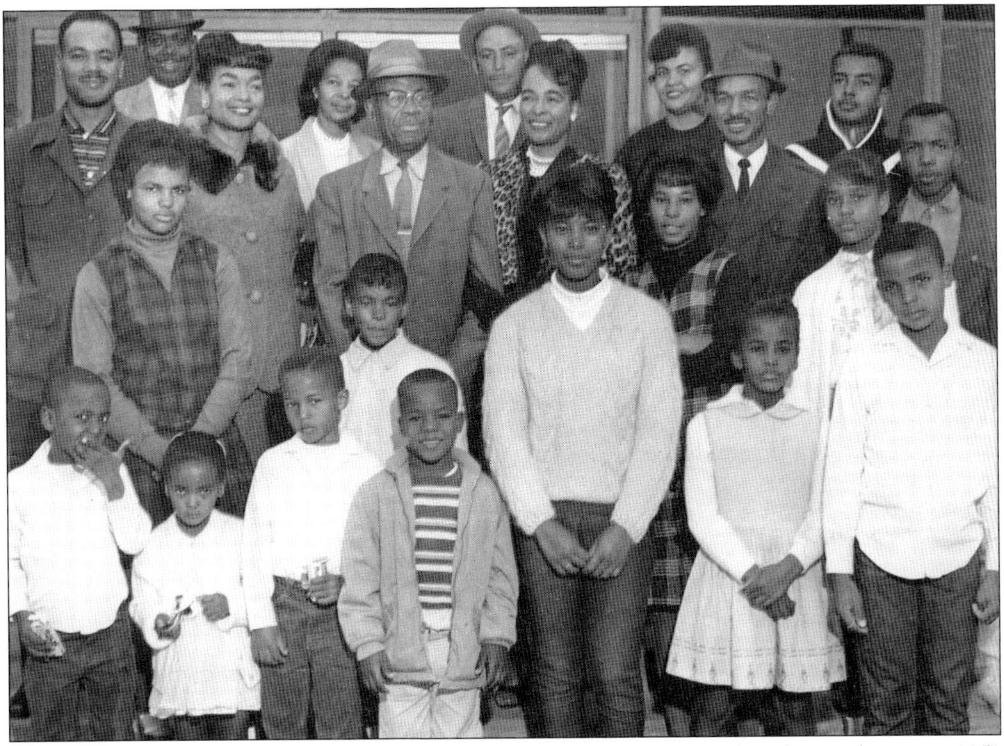

The Joyce family is pictured above in 1963. The image below is of church members at a 1951 picnic. (Above, courtesy of the Richard Joyce Collection, City of Seaside Archive; below, courtesy of Rev. Welton McGee, City of Seaside Archive.)

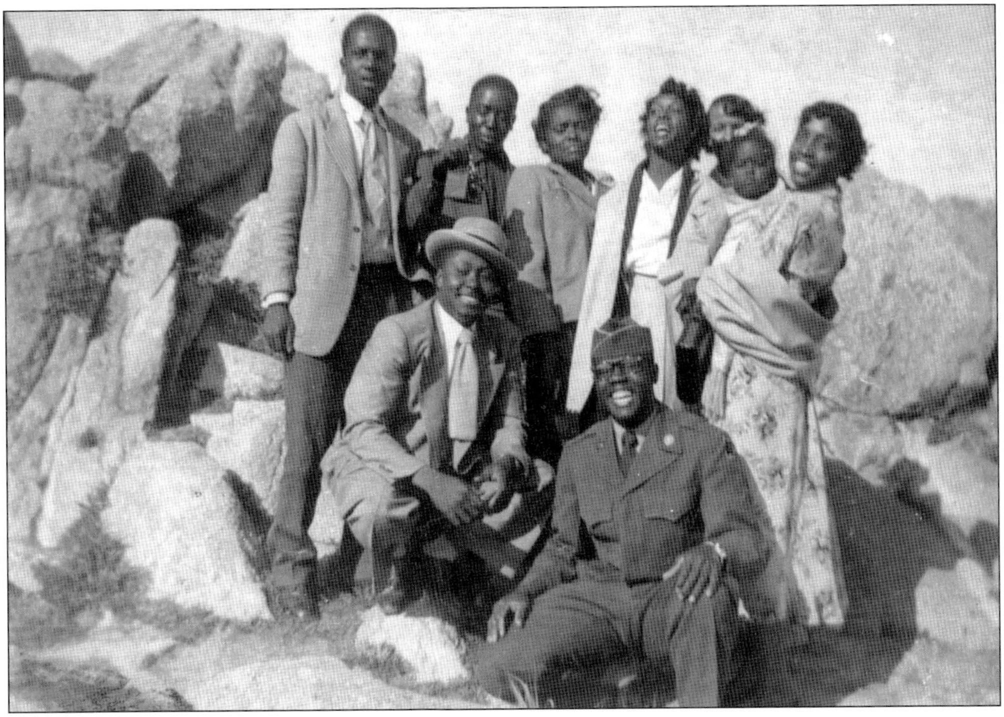

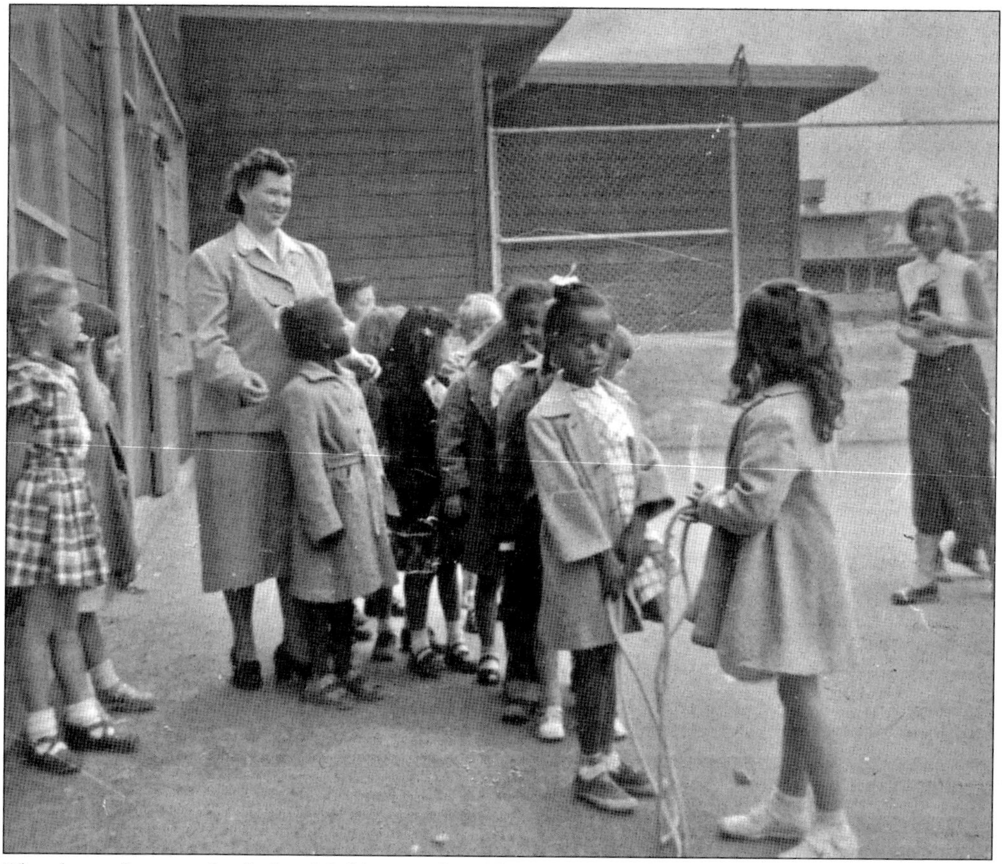

The above photograph of schoolchildren in the 1950s is an example of the changing and increasingly diverse population. It shows the Noche Buena School kindergarten class in 1953. Below, these Seaside Little Leaguers also shows diversity and integration in sports, even though housing remained segregated in this era. (Both, courtesy of the City of Seaside Archive.)

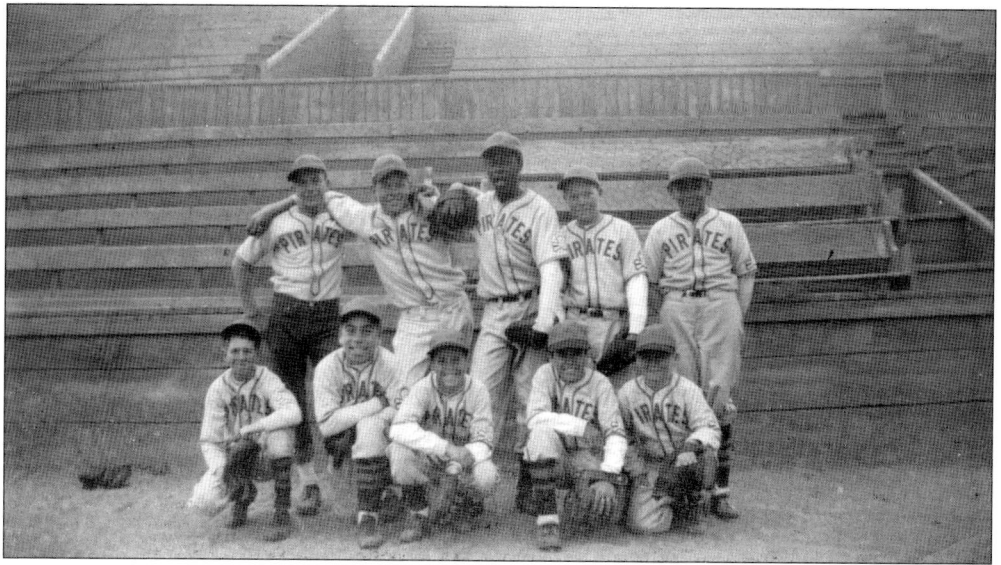

The Japanese immigrants and Japanese Americans (the Nisei generation) who were survivors of the internment camps had to start over after World War II ended, and without question, the most affordable, promising place to do so was in Seaside. At left is the Matsuyama family in the 1950s at 48 Harcourt Avenue; below is a Matsuyama family portrait taken at their Harcourt home. (Both, courtesy of the Matsuyama Collection, City of Seaside Archive.)

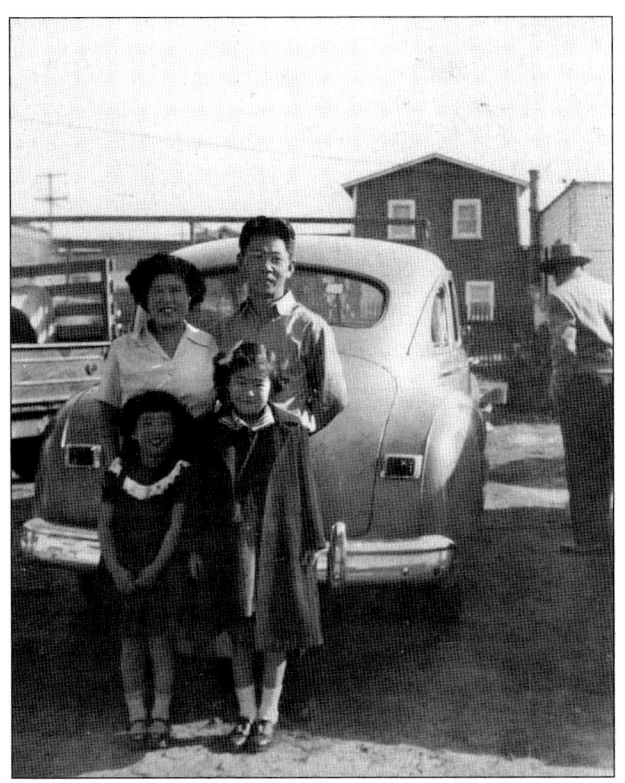

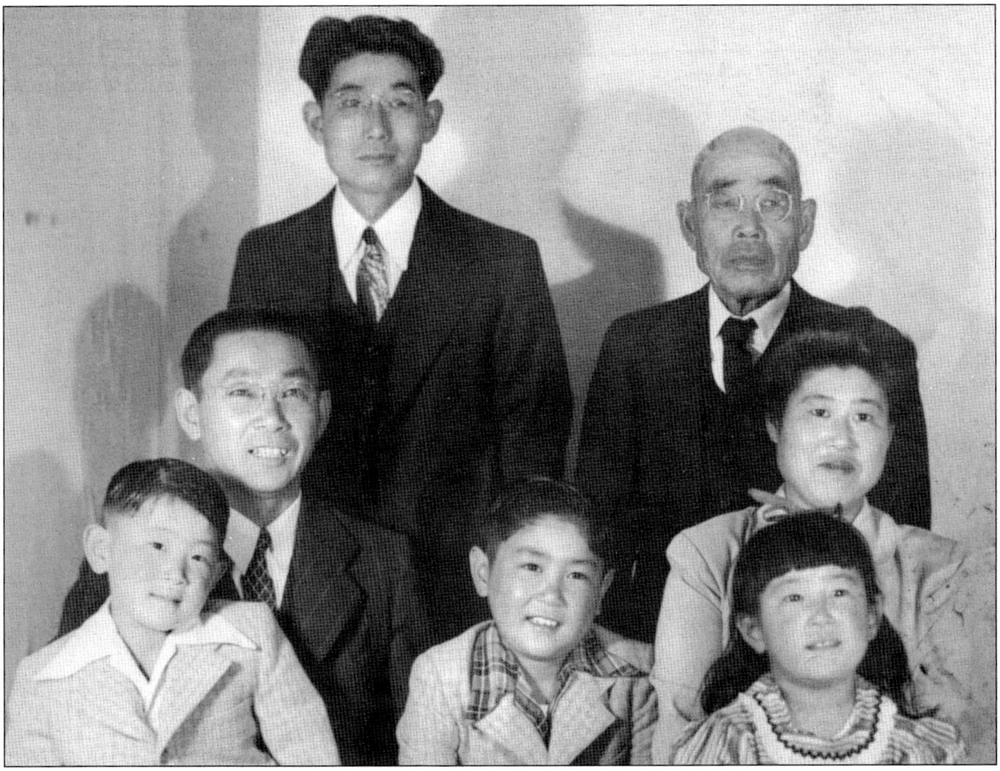

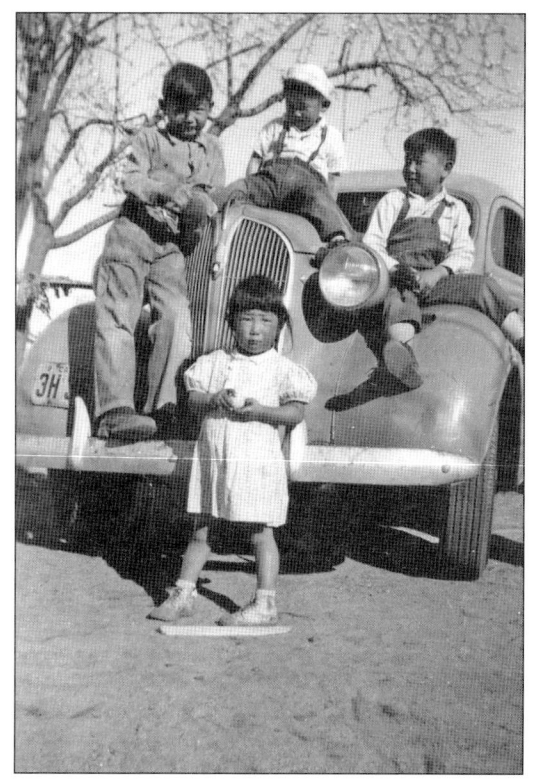

The new Japanese community established in Seaside after 1945 included residents formerly from Monterey and Salinas. The picture at left shows Kazuko Matsuyama (in front) and Robert Suki, Sam Matsuyama, and Jimmy Matsuyama on the family car in 1948; the image below shows the Matsuyama family Christmas in 1955. (Both, courtesy of the Matsuyama Collection, City of Seaside Archive.)

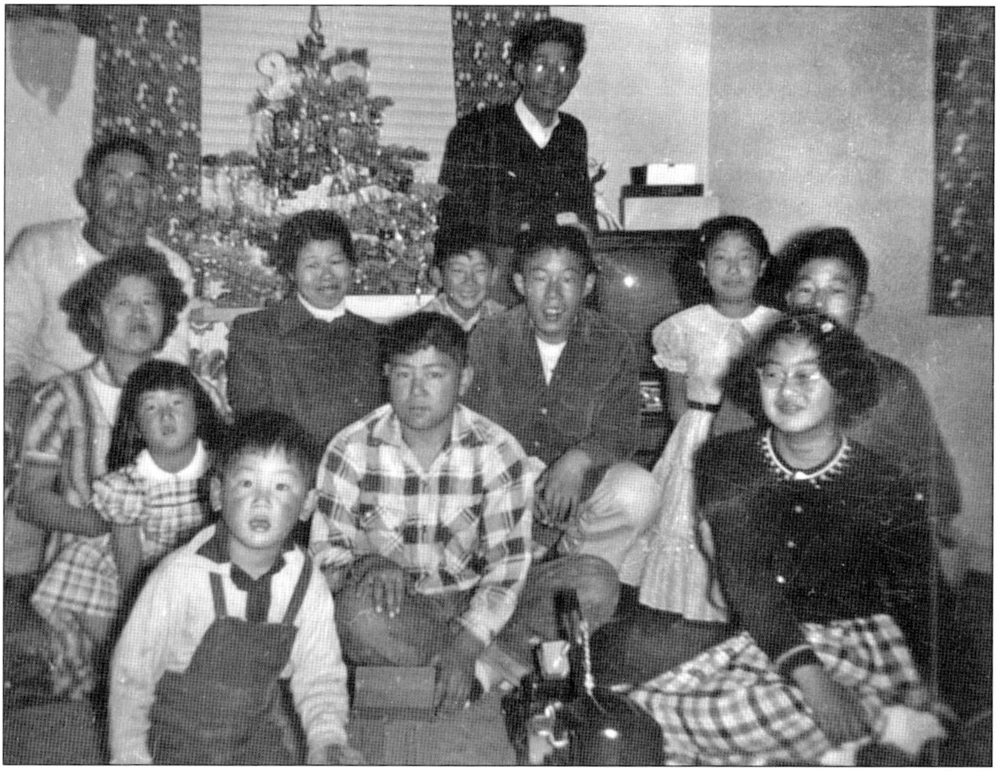

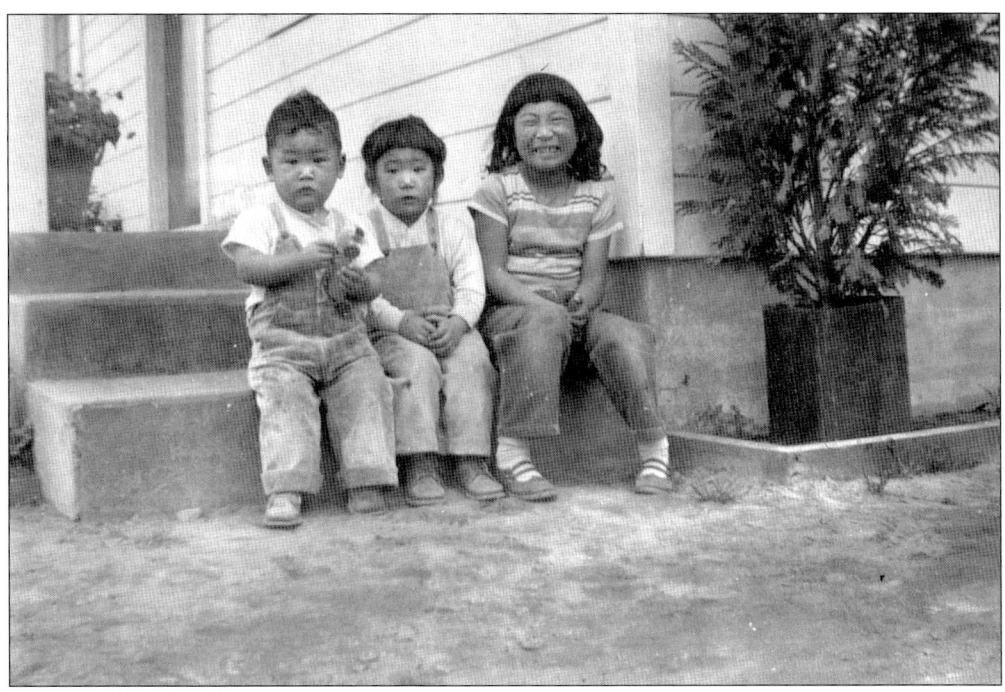

From left to right, Willie Matsuyama, Aiko Matsuyama, and an unidentified child are pictured above. Below, seated from left to right are Tamiya Matsuyama and Sami Matsuyama, with their grandfather Goromatsu Matsuyama (standing at the far left, partially obscured) in 1951. (Both, courtesy of the Matsuyama Collection, City of Seaside Archive.)

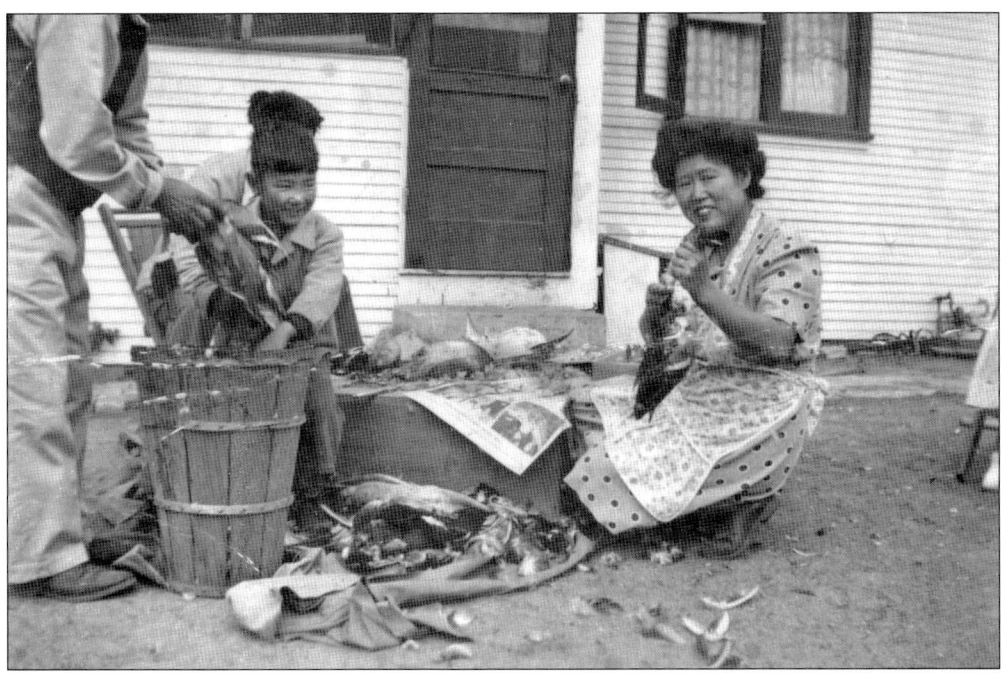

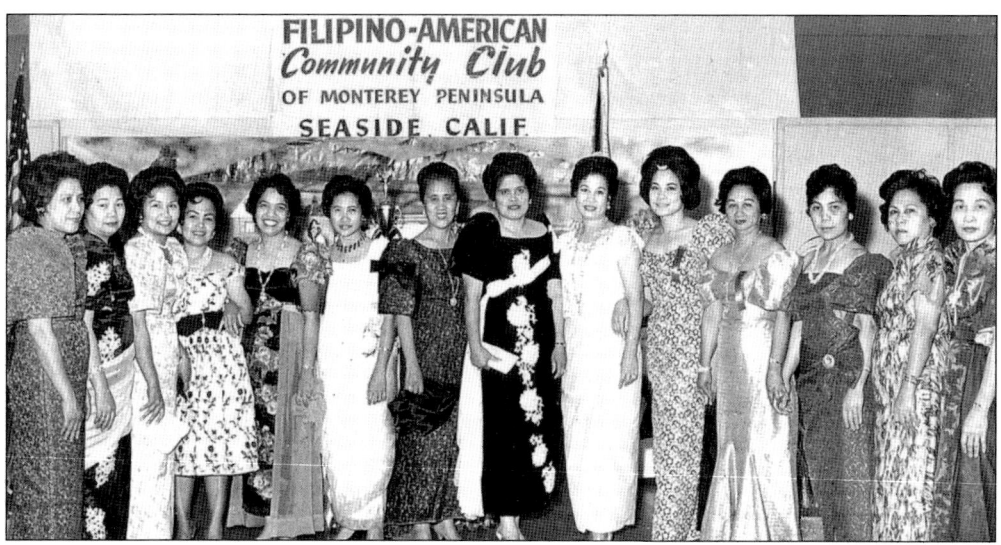

Like the Japanese, Filipinos re-formed in the years following World War II into a visible and distinctive community that was both military oriented and centered in Seaside. Filipinos responded to discriminatory laws and practices in California and in Monterey County in both the prewar and postwar years by organizing unions and becoming pioneers in civil rights. During the 1960s and 1970s, the Filipino community became active in the Catholic church and the military as a new Filipino-American cultural identity was shaped. Filipinos expanded the local Fil-Am Clubs and became leaders in Seaside's St. Francis Xavier Catholic Church. In 1970, three Filipino families, Patrick and Stela McKenzie, Mr. and Mrs. Ramon Nierva, and Mr. and Mrs. Robert Lundholm, organized the International Festival at St. Francis Xavier, an event that occurs annually to the present day. Glenn Olea served as a city councilman from 1971 to 1978 and as Seaside's mayor from 1980 to 1982, the first Filipino mayor in American history. Above, from left to right, are Ofelia Antonio, Lourdes Del Pena, Amy Cosio, ? Grospe, Lucita Nuqui, Eva Sabado, Valentina Medina, Leonarda DaAton, Carmen Cancio, Connie Turquesa, Josie Rogacion, Fely Faller, Rosario Mandolado, and Ciprinana Parcasio. Below is a Filipino parade float in 1962. (Above, courtesy of the Monterey Peninsula Filipino American Clubs; below, courtesy of the City of Seaside Archive.)

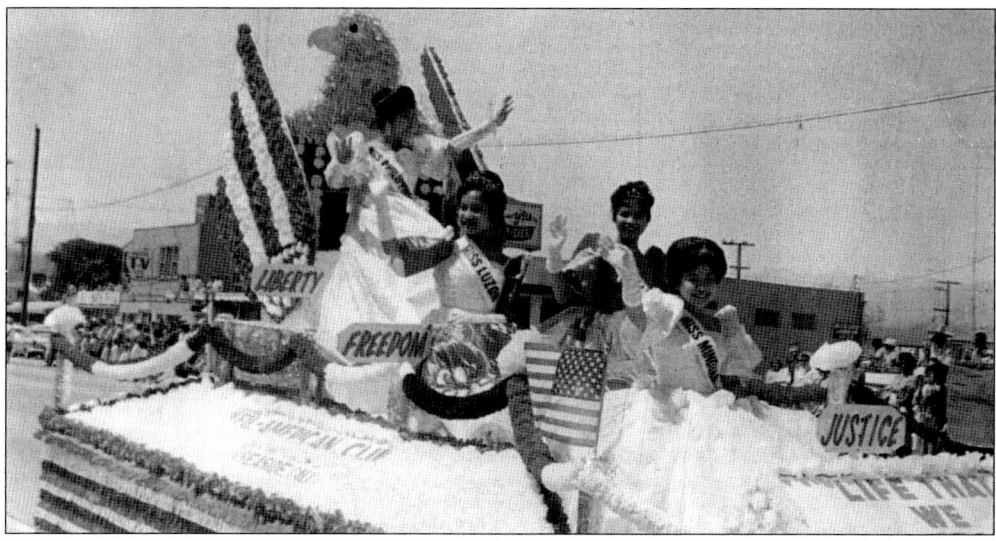

People of Mexican origin had historic roots on the Monterey Peninsula going back to colonial times and a long history as California's largest ethnic minority. They formed a distinctive community in Seaside, working in agriculture, construction, and small businesses. The photographs here depict the extended family of Orancio and Evangelina Perez (pictured at right). The image below is of the Perezes' party on Luzern Street. (Both, courtesy of the Evangelina Perez Collection, City of Seaside Archive.)

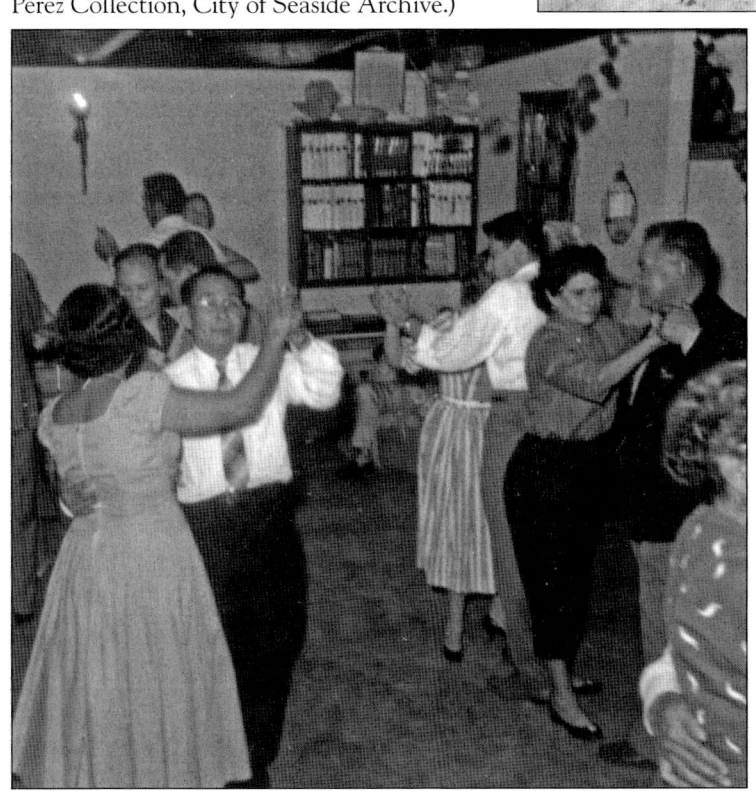

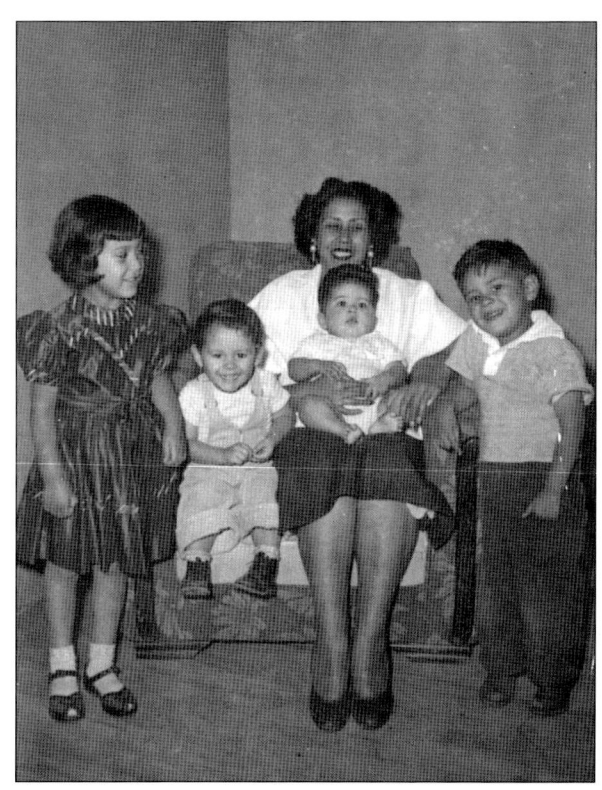

With Filipinos, Mexican-descended people shared a culture and identity shaped by Catholicism. At left are Mary Lou, Richard, Bobby, George, and Evangelina Perez. Below is a 1953 picture of the Perez family. (Both, courtesy of the Perez Collection, City of Seaside Archive.)

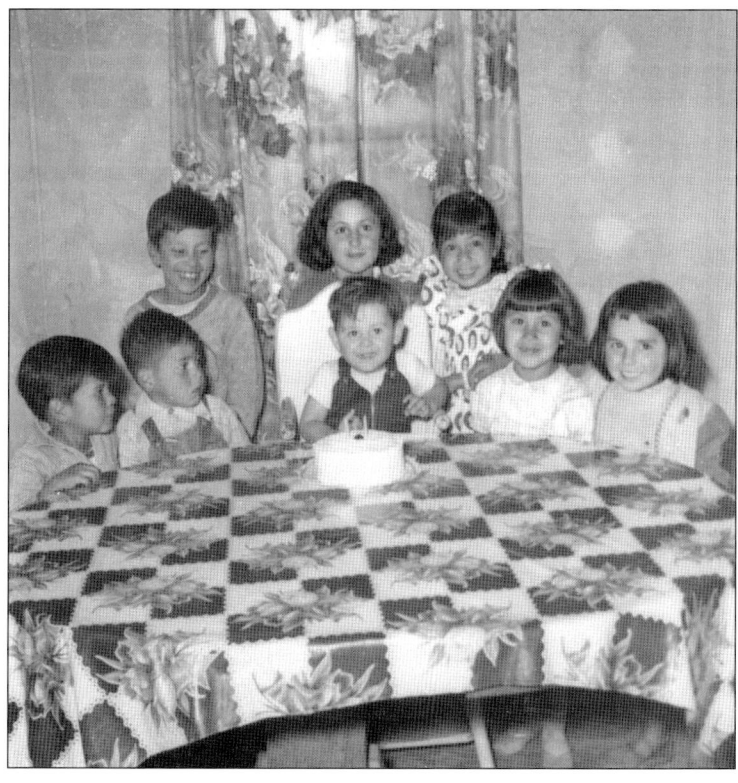

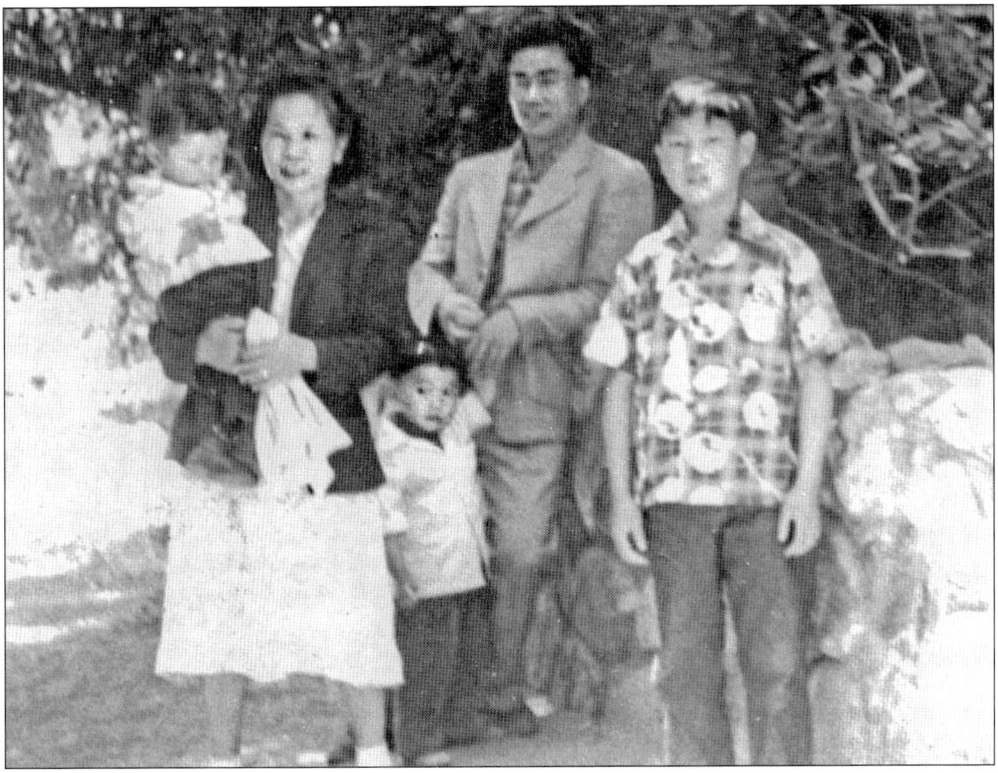

The Chinese settlement in Seaside began in the 1930s. These photographs depict the Quock family. The Asian community expanded throughout the 1940s and 1950s to include Vietnamese and Pacific Islanders, as well as Chinese, Japanese, and Filipinos. They remained at 10 percent of Seaside's population. Above is a Quock family photograph from 1950 at 1221 Elm Street. The image at right is of Kwantani Ito, the owner of the Park in Market. (Both, courtesy of the Lyle Quock Collection, City of Seaside Archive.)

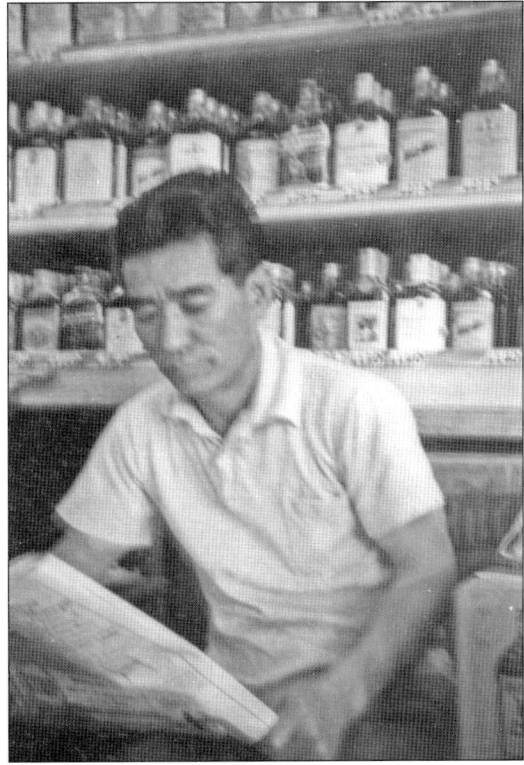

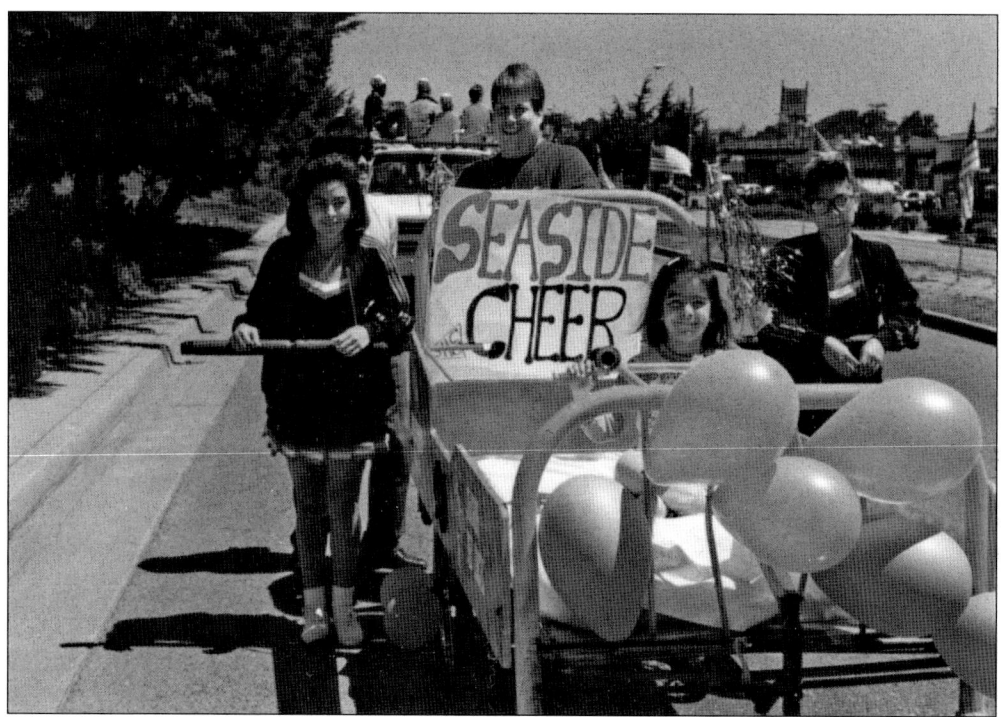

Seaside had always been known for its frequent and unusual parades. Most notable were the Fourth of July parades and the Bed Races, which occurred annually. Above are the Bed Races in 1987, and below are unidentified ladies in a parade in the 1950s. (Both, courtesy of the City of Seaside Archive.)

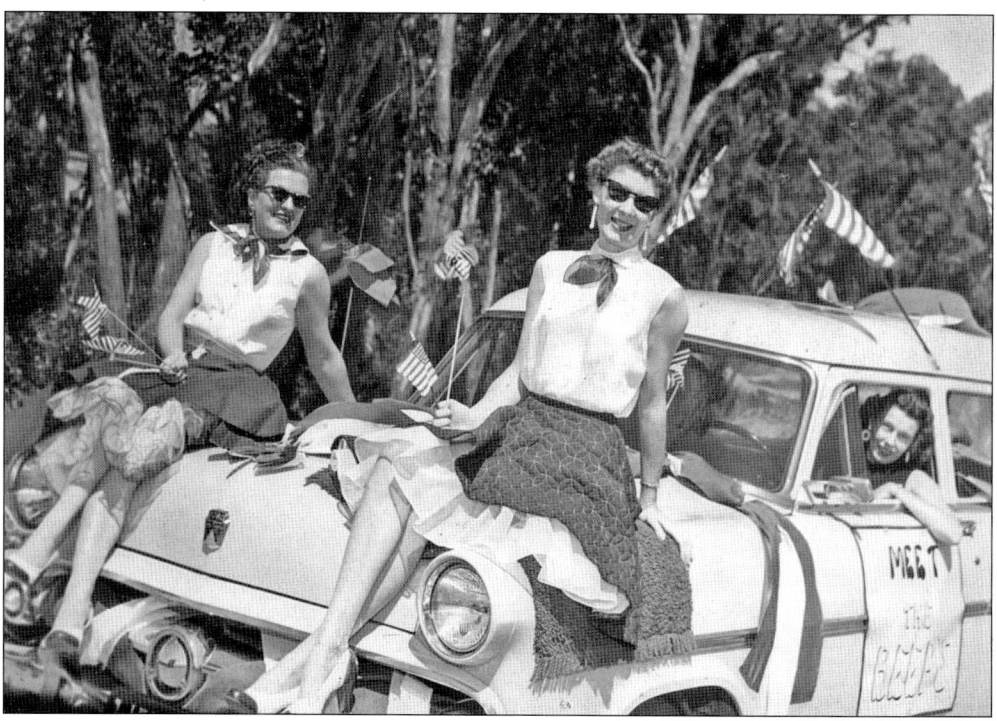

Four
Reinventing Seaside in the 1960s

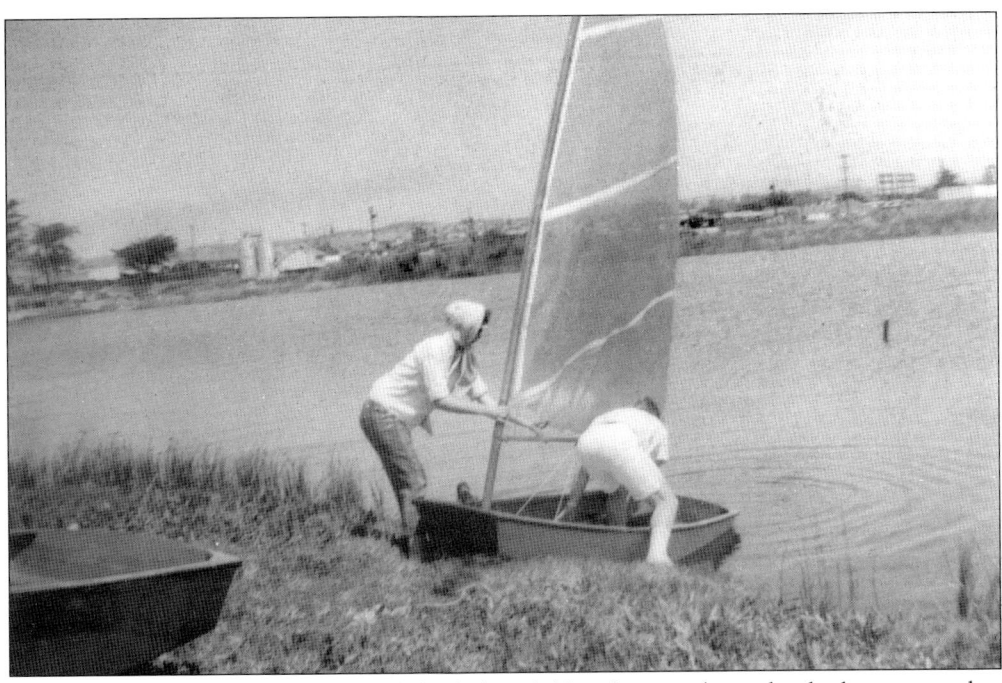

By the beginning of the 1960s, Seaside had identifiable ethnic enclaves that had come together as a community. This image shows unidentified people on Roberts Lake. (Courtesy of the City of Seaside Archive.)

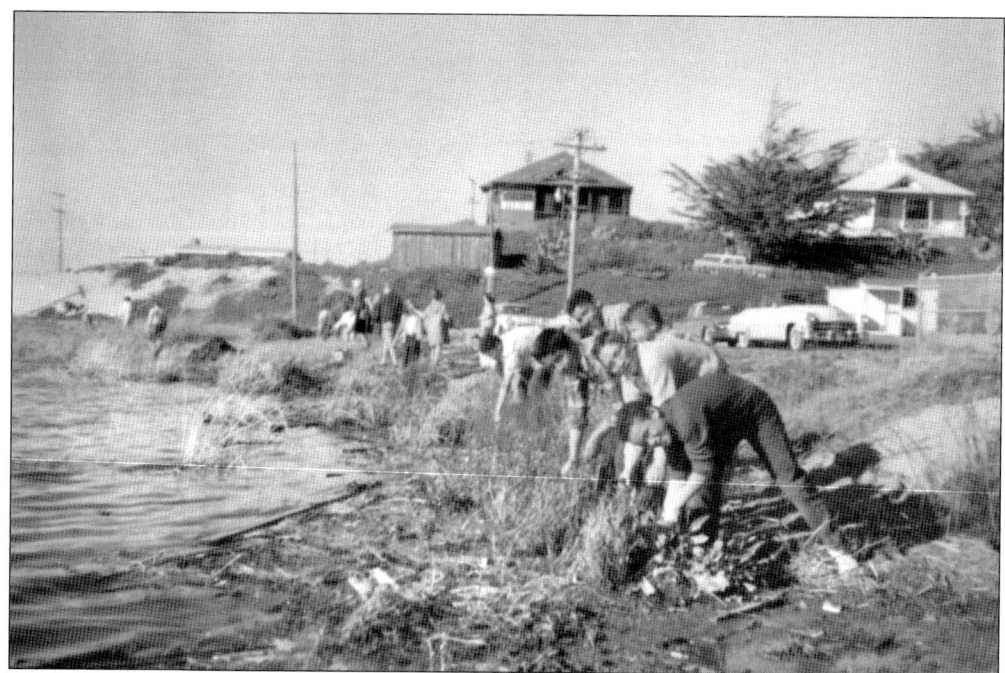

These photographs depict Seasiders at play at one of the most important landmarks in the city, Roberts Lake. The Boy Scout troop shown above in 1958 demonstrates civic pride in their effort to clean the area of litter. Below, Seaside community leaders are shown on the way to Sacramento. (Both, courtesy of the Lenora Bean Collection, City of Seaside Archive.)

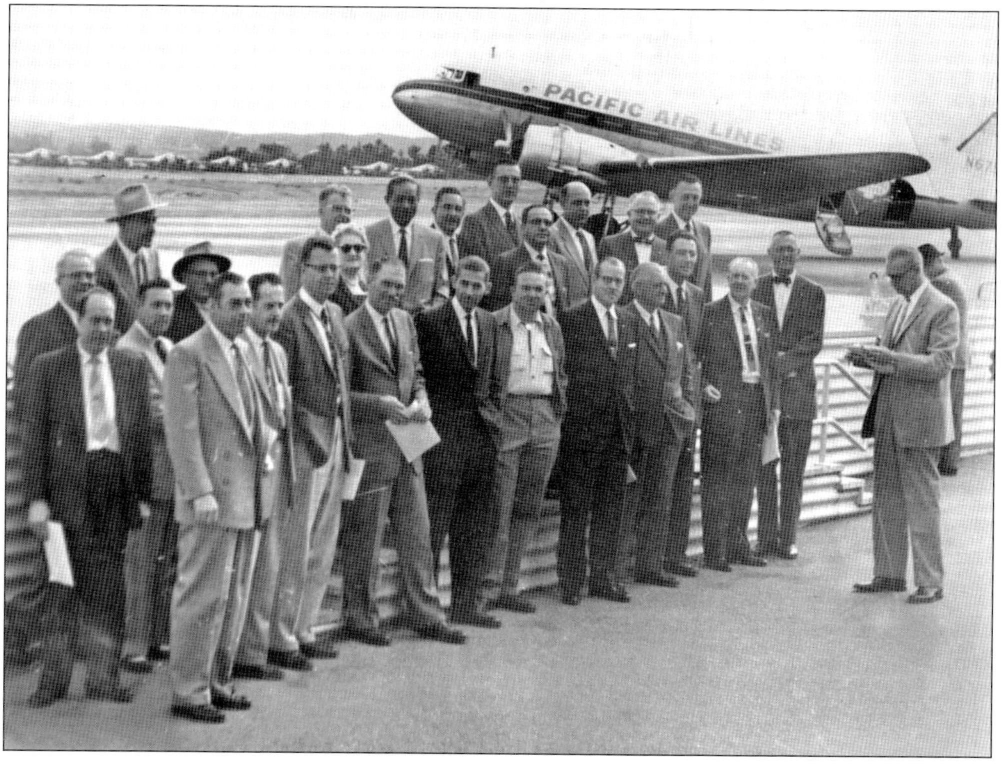

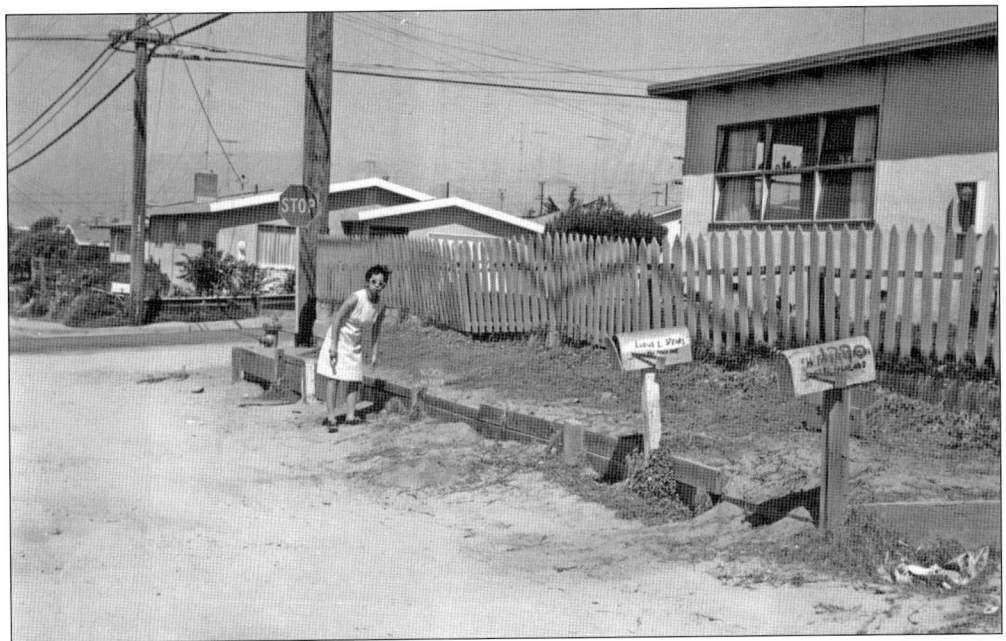

Seasiders emerged from the effort to incorporate eager to create a modern American suburb. The first step was to obtain federal funds needed to create both infrastructure and new housing and commercial development. The above image is of 1600 San Pablo Street in 1964; the image below features unidentified residents in 1969. (Both, courtesy of the City of Seaside Archive.)

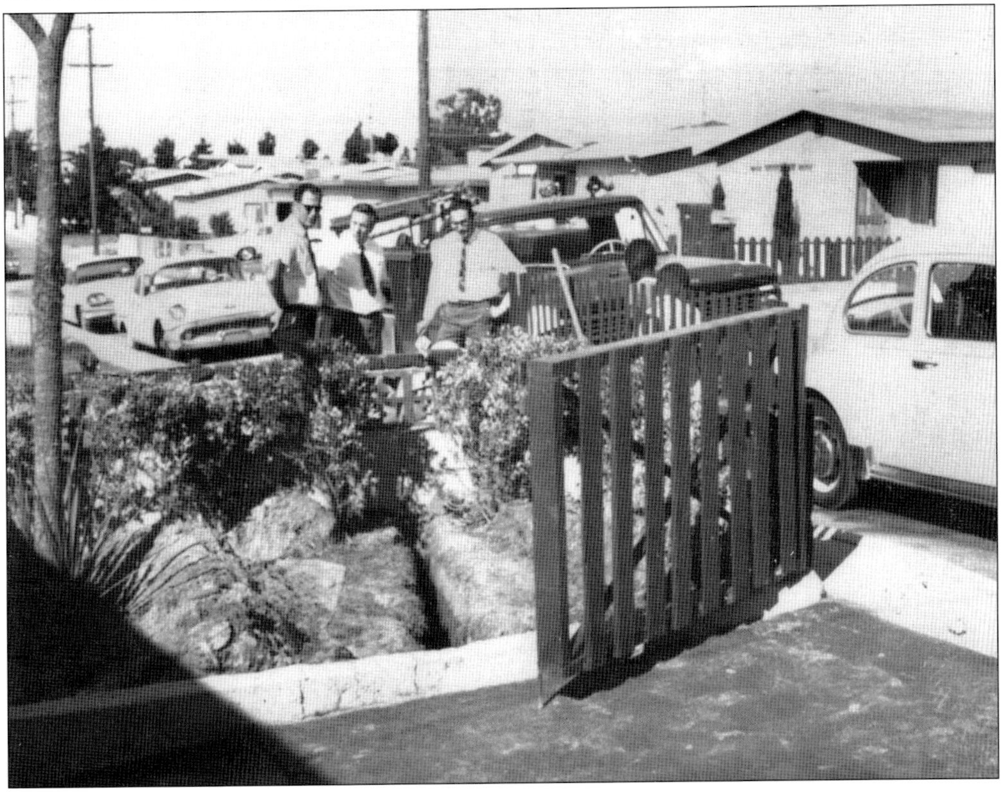

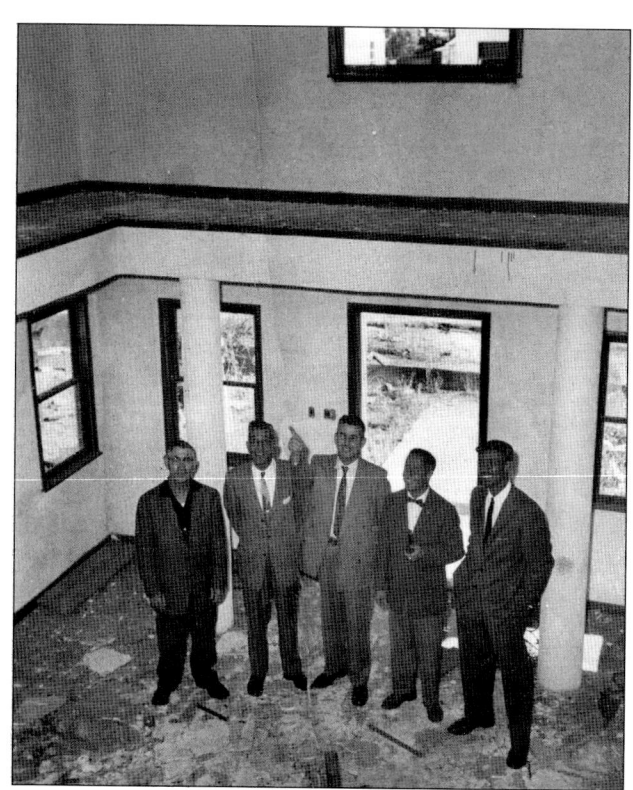

At left is the Noche Buena Project team. Below is more redevelopment plans in Seaside in 1963 on the Noche Buena Project. (Both, courtesy of Richard Joyce Collection, City of Seaside Archive.)

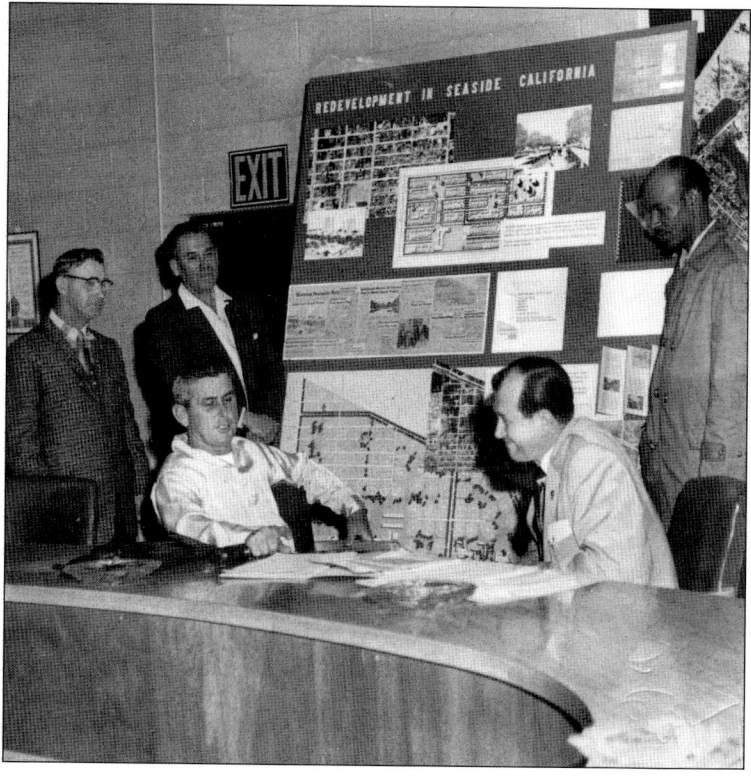

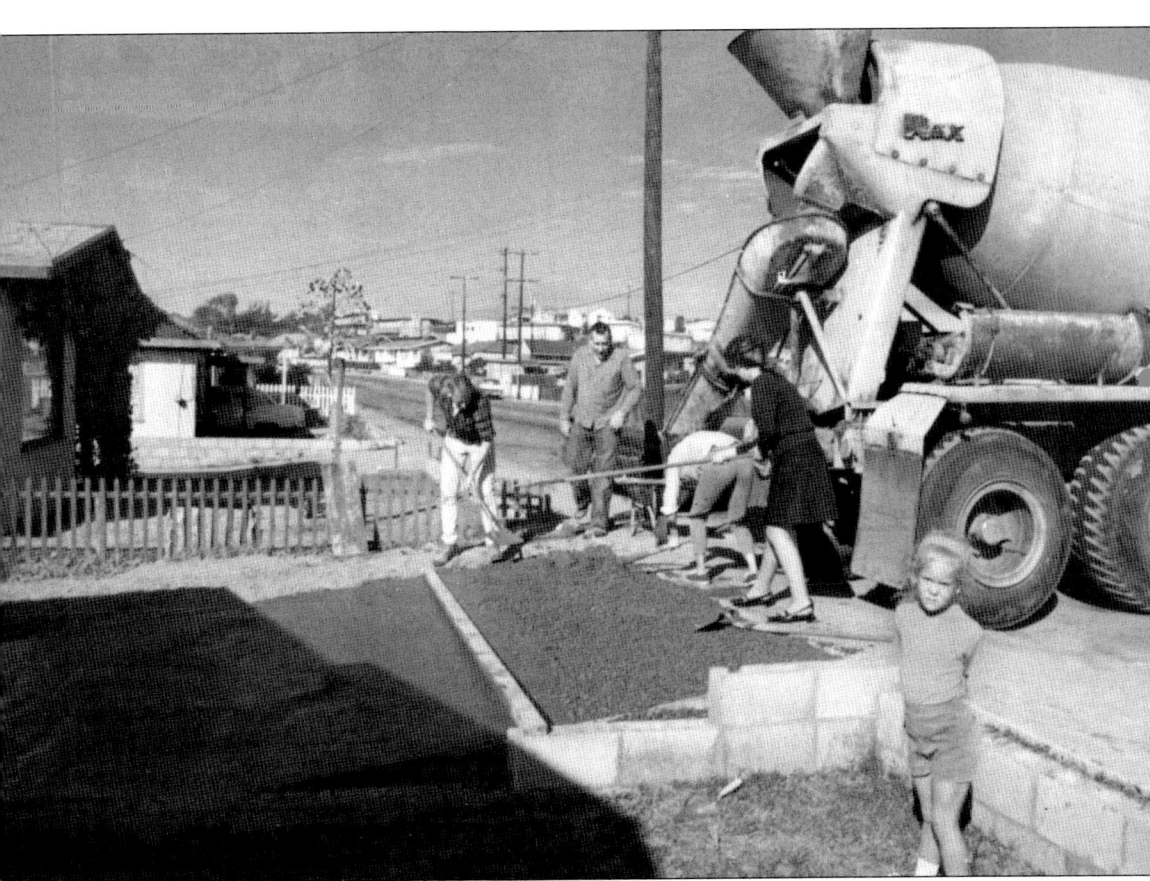

This photograph depicts a home being rehabilitated. According to Redevelopment Agency staff member Carl Williams, Seaside focused far more on refurbishing homes than on demolition. Seaside's urban renewal plans did not include the large apartment complexes of larger urban centers but on building and bringing up to code single-family homes. (Courtesy of the City of Seaside Archive.)

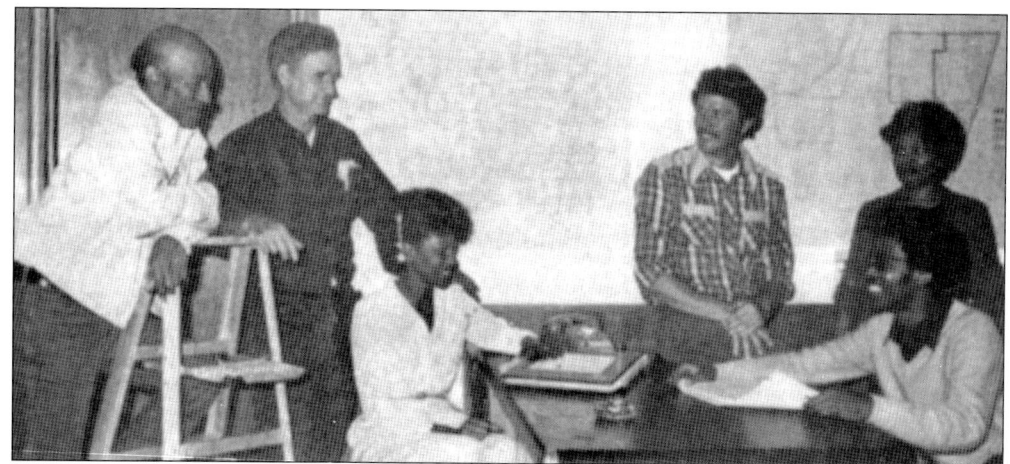

A multiracial Citizens Advisory Committee of 75 members first formed in 1954 and, after a year of study, led to a recommendation adopted in 1956 by the city council that a 22-block area (66 acres) between Soto and Waring Streets and Broadway and Hilby Avenue would be redeveloped and turned into a "garden city of new homes, tower apartments, and landscaping." It would be known as the Noche Buena Project. The city received a Housing and Home Finance Agency loan in 1958 for $949,514. In addition, credit for building additional schools in Seaside and infrastructure such as sewers, storm drains, engineering services, and street improvements amounted to an additional $327,640. The city spent $147,118 of its own money on the project, completed in 1964, and increased the value of the property by 65 percent. In the above image, from left to right, are Richard Joyce, Bob Kline, Vicky Young, Mike Dowling, Mary Claypool, and Jim Claypool in 1981. Below is the design review board—Sabastian Bordonaro (far left), Richard Joyce, Ted Minnis, and Marcel Sedeletzky. (Both, courtesy of the Richard Joyce Collection, City of Seaside Archive.)

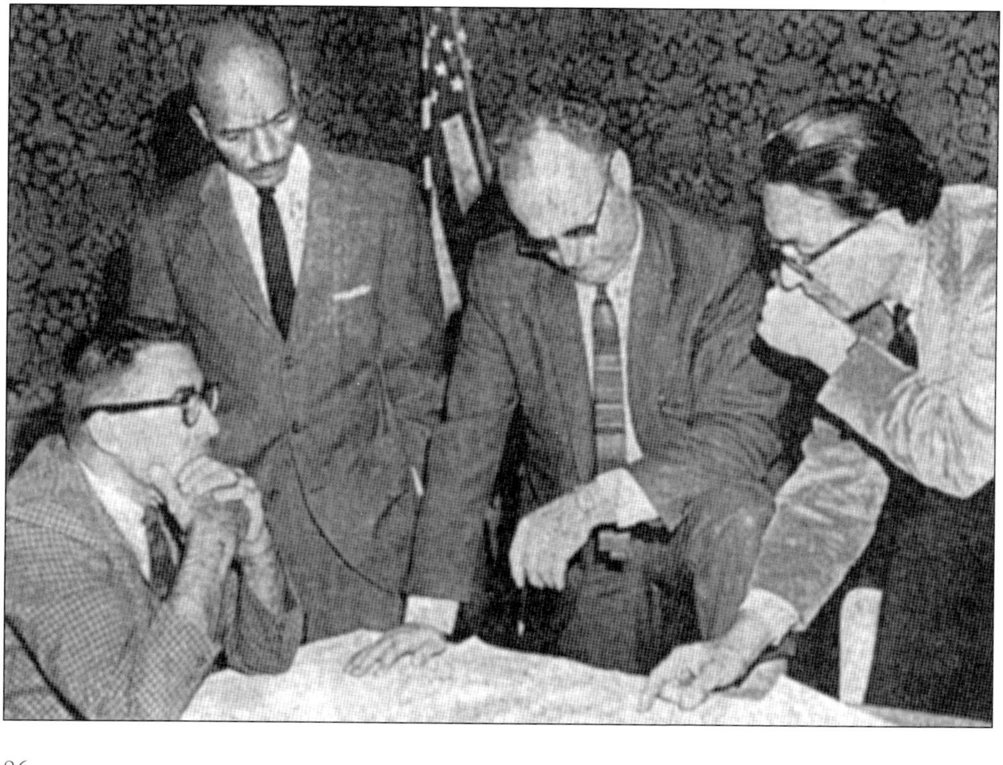

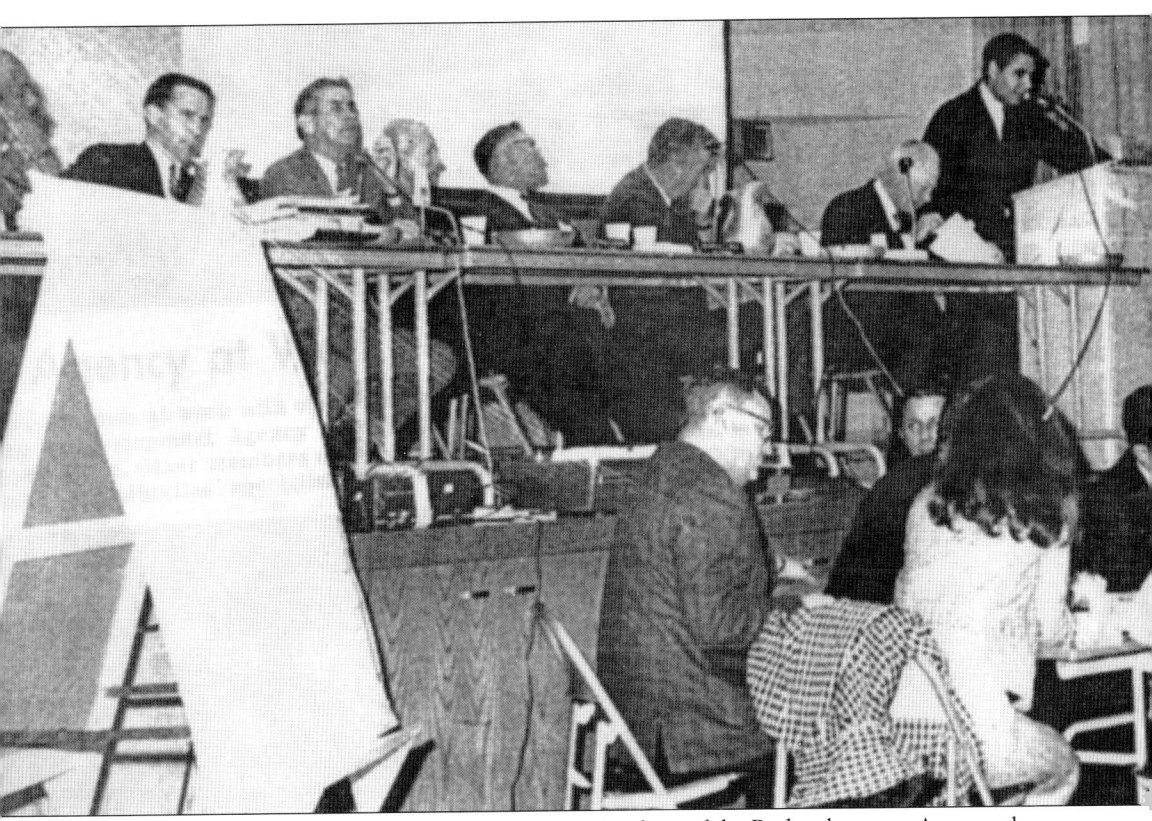

Not everyone in Seaside supported redevelopment. Members of the Redevelopment Agency along with Seaside city attorney Saul Weingarten are shown here at a public forum on redevelopment and urban renewal. Pictured are the Redevelopment Agency members at the public forum, including, from left to right, Richard Joyce, Francis Geary, Michael Heitzenger, Merrild Beck, Saul Weingarten, Russel Hoss, Lewis Wolff, and an unidentified development researcher speaking at the podium. (Courtesy of the Richard Joyce Collection, City of Seaside Archive.)

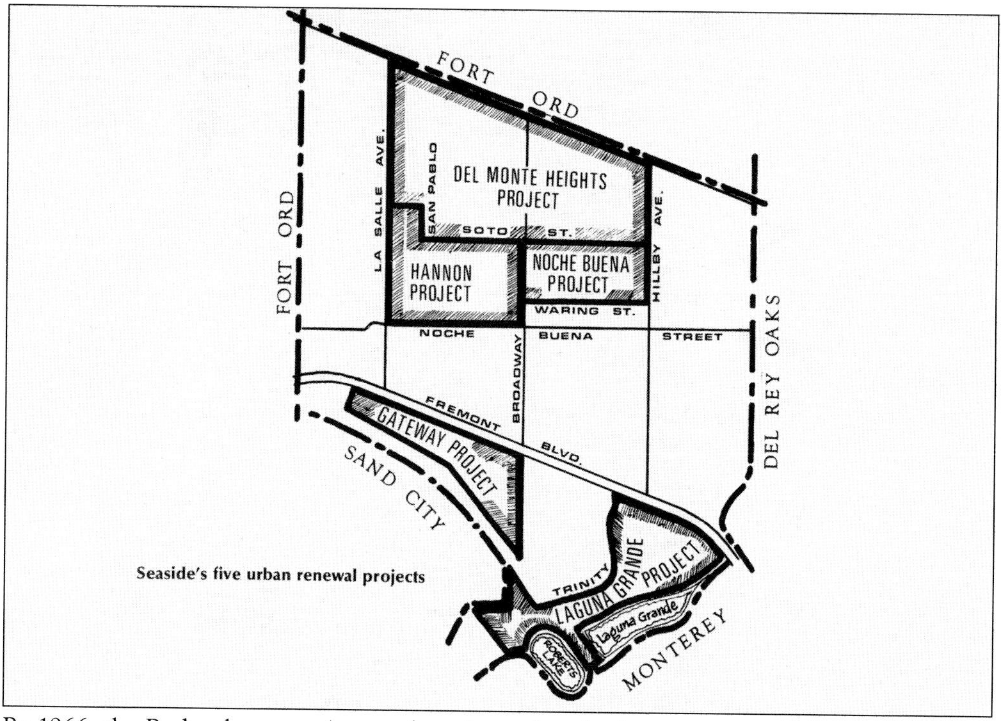

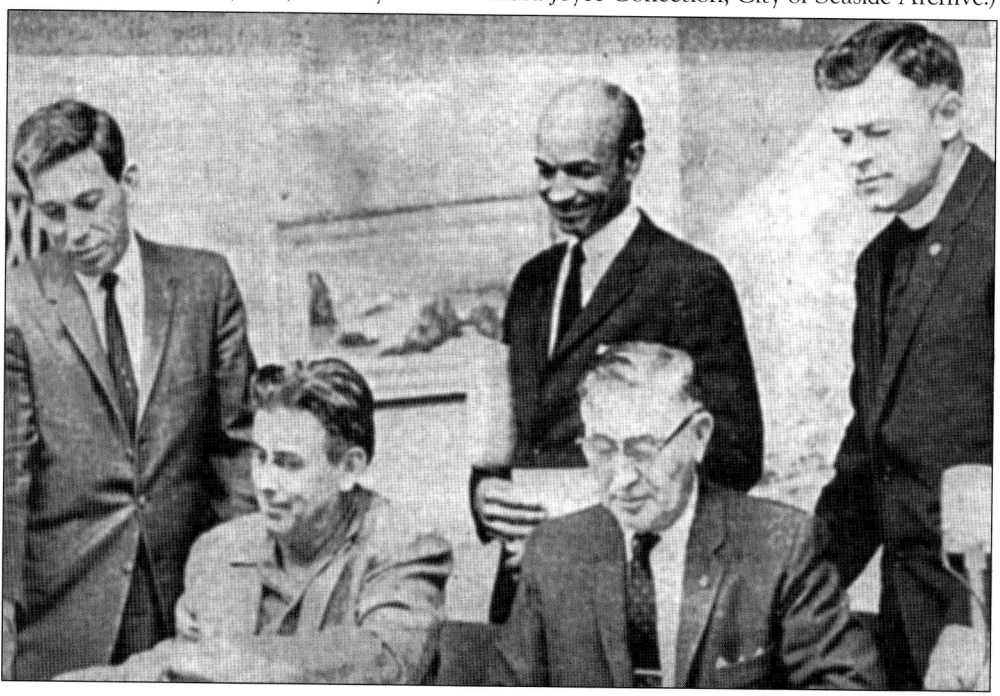

By 1966, the Redevelopment Agency board members had reason to smile, as shown in this photograph. They had successfully gained enough federal funding for three major residential and commercial projects. Noche Buena, Del Monte Heights, and Hannon are shown on the map. The image below shows, from left to right, Bud Houser, Francis Geary, Richard Joyce, Merril Beck, and Rev. Malcom Miner. (Both, courtesy of the Richard Joyce Collection, City of Seaside Archive.)

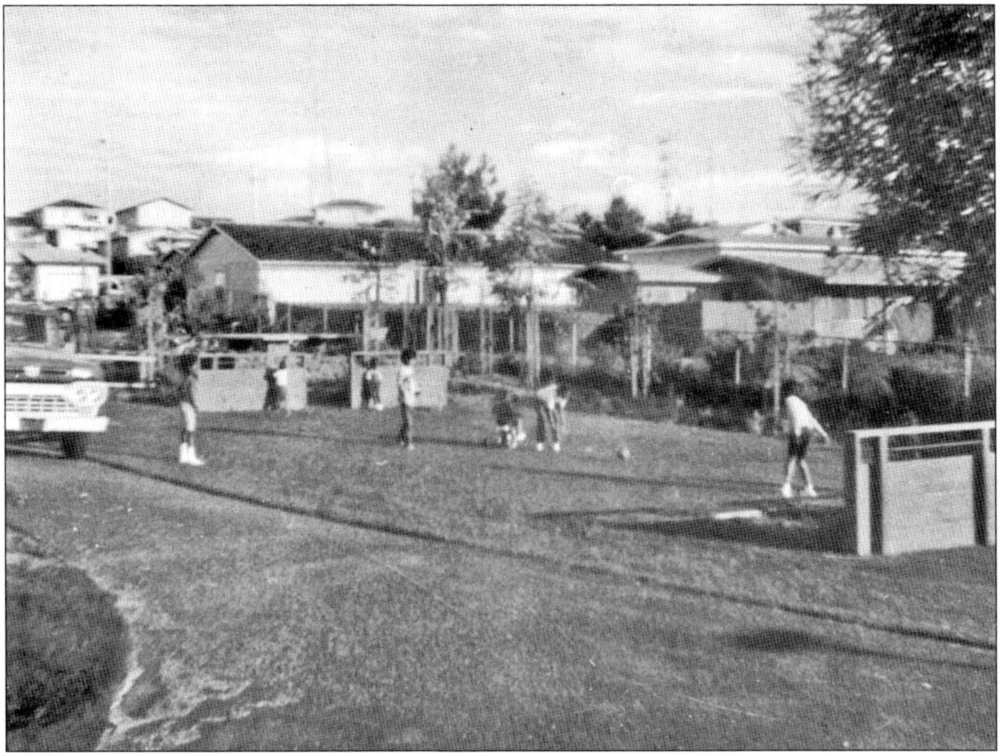

Seaside built numerous parks as an integral part of urban renewal and redevelopment. Shown above are children at play in Soliz Park, and Cutino Park is pictured below. (Both, courtesy of the City of Seaside Archive.)

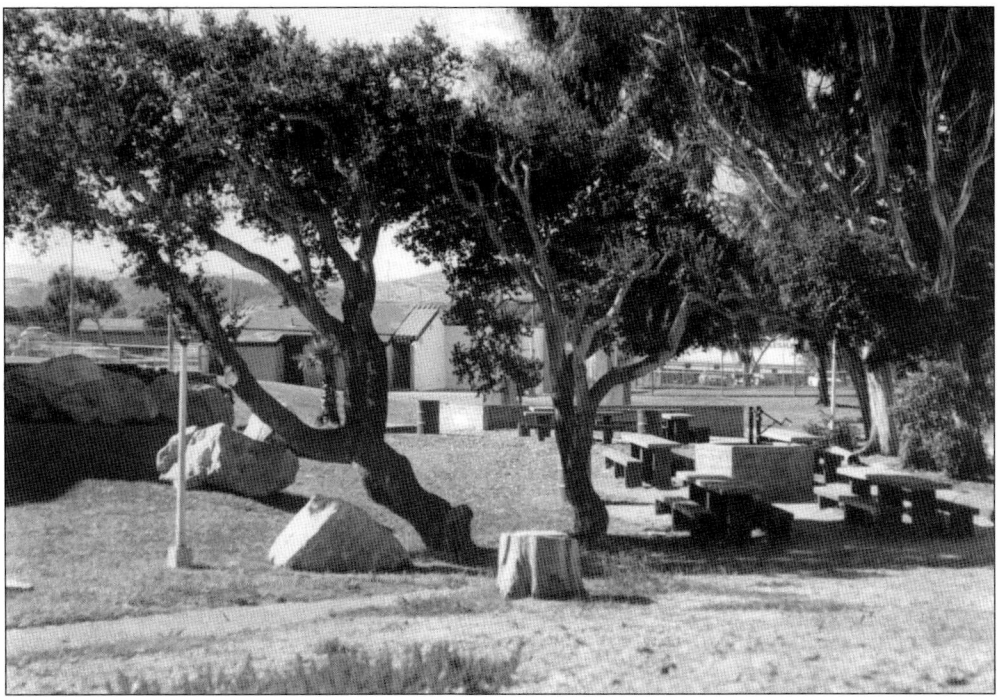

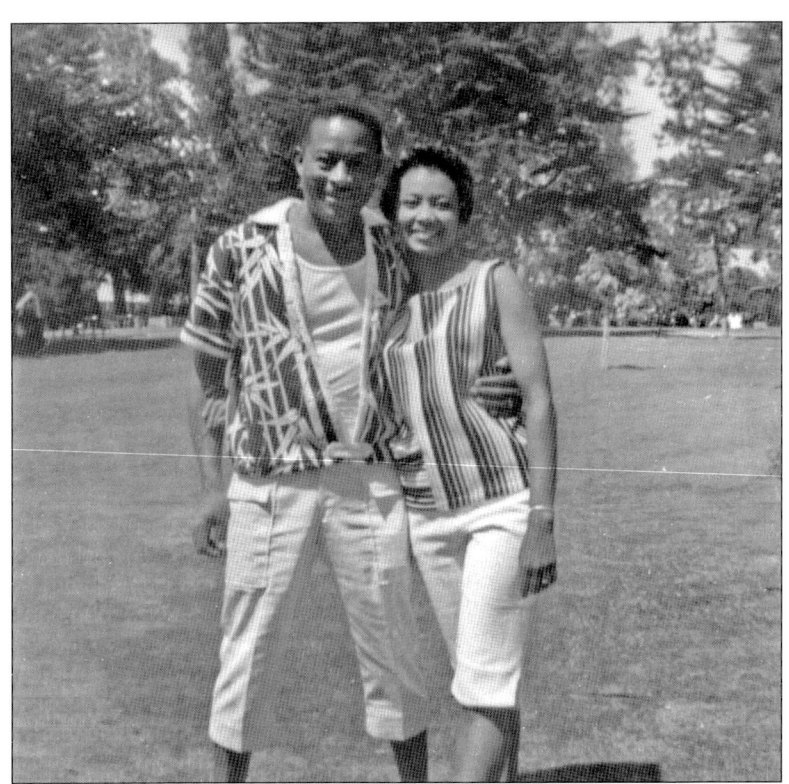

John and Lenora Bean are shown in the image at left at the Seaside Park opening. The picture below is of Kennedy Park. (Left, courtesy of the Lenora Bean Collection, City of Seaside Archive; below, courtesy of the City of Seaside Archive.)

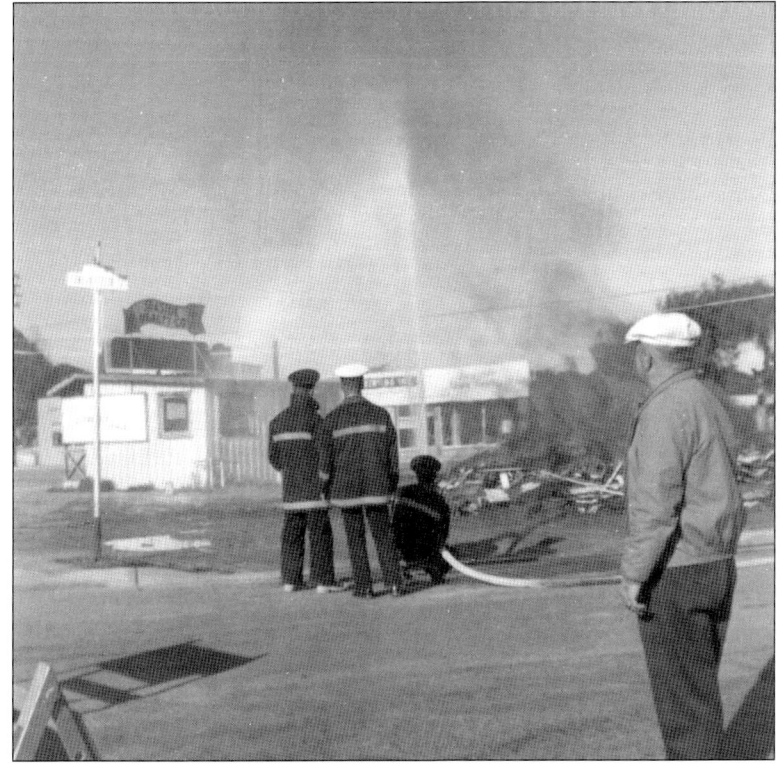

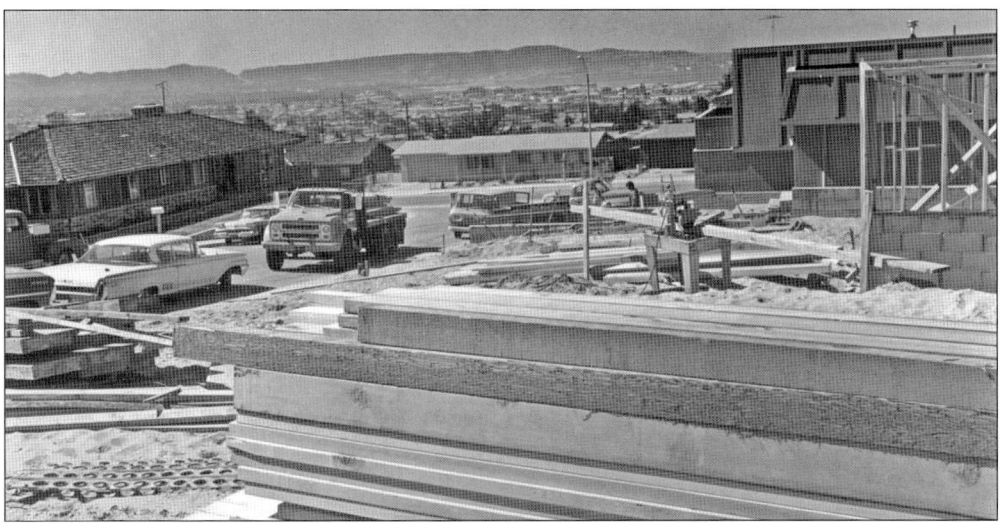

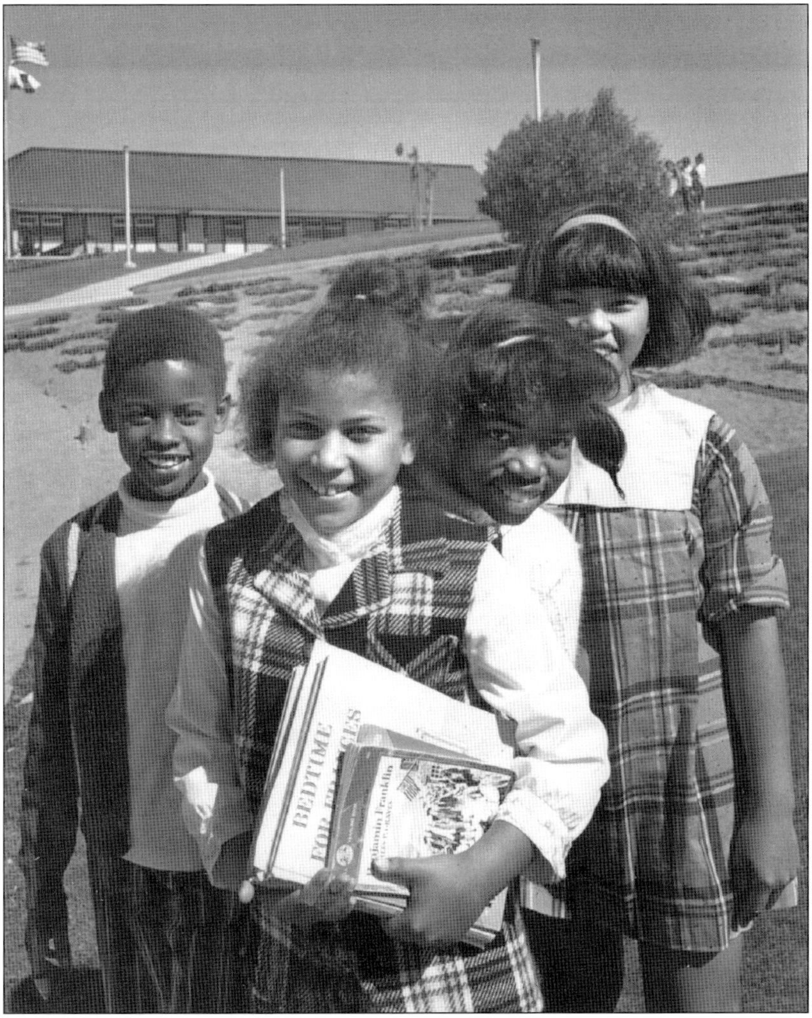

The photograph above depicts construction underway for Del Monte Heights. New schools were an essential part of redevelopment plans. Students at Manzanita Elementary School are shown at right. (Both, courtesy of the City of Seaside Archive.)

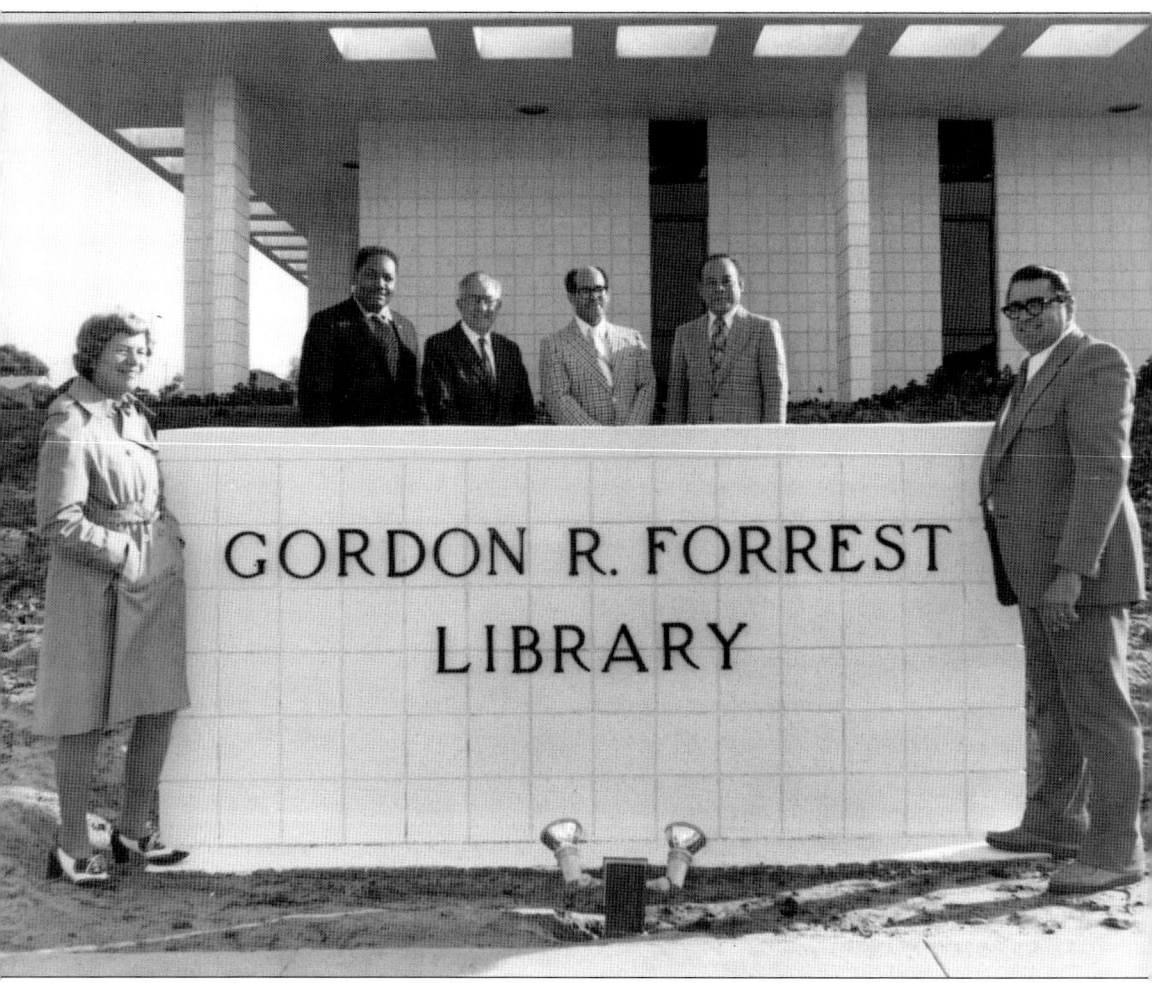

The effort to make a modern suburb out of a helter-skelter community culminated in the construction of two important landmarks in Seaside—the Gordon Forrest Library and the new city hall designed by internationally renowned architect Edward Durrell Stone. Pictured are Mr. and Mrs. Gordon Forrest standing on either side of the library marker. Also shown are, from left to right, councilman Stephen Ross, unidentified, and former Seaside mayors Oscar Lawson and Glenn Olea. (Courtesy of the City of Seaside Archive.)

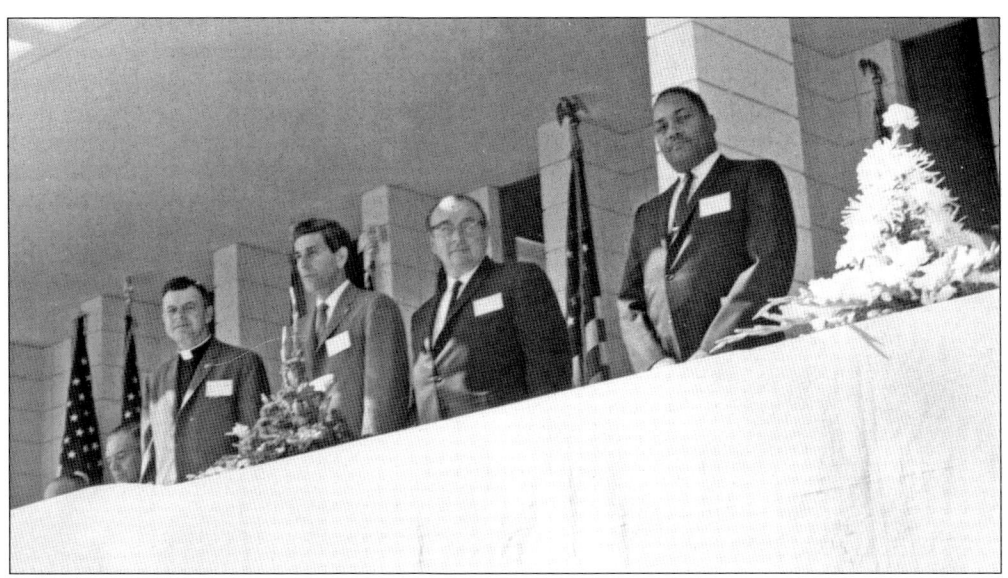

The above picture shows the Seaside City Hall dedication day in 1966. From left to right are Fr. William Scully, city councilman Bud Houser, Emil Schmidt, and councilman Stephen Ross. Below is a picture of the new city hall, which was designed by architect Edward Durrell Stone. (Courtesy of the City of Seaside Archive.)

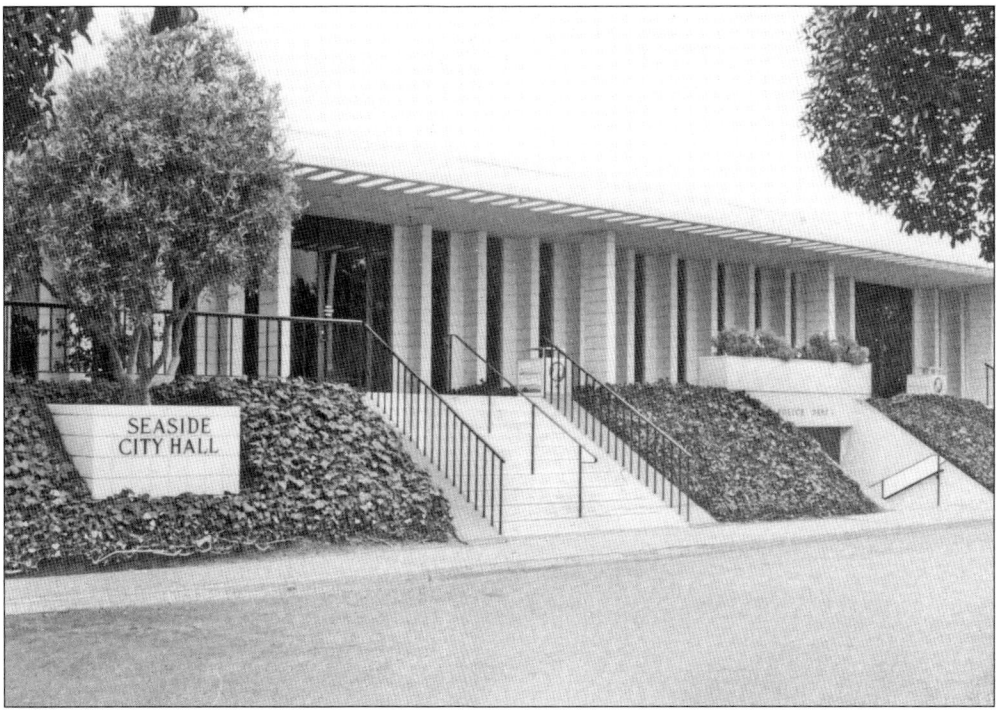

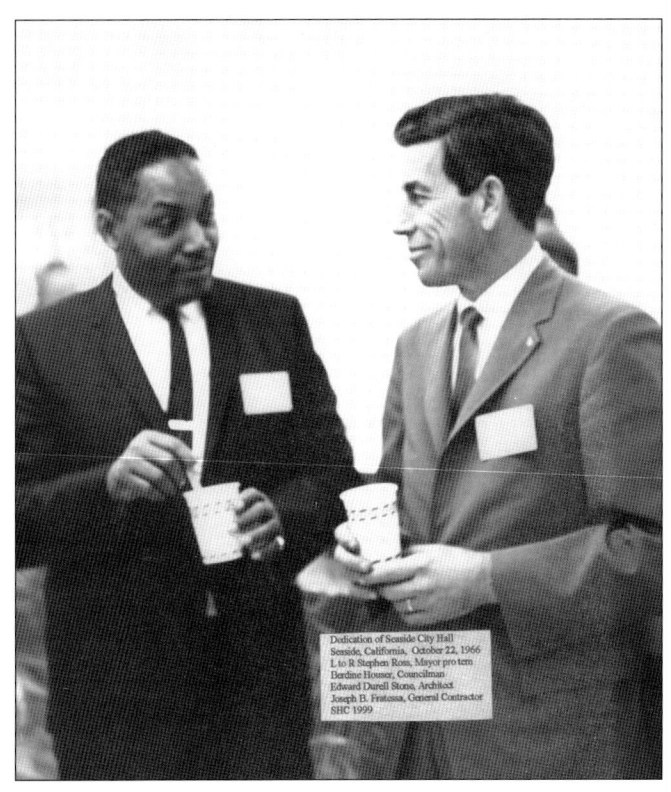

At left is another image from the dedication day in 1966. Pictured are councilman Stephen Ross (left) and Bud Houser. In the photograph below, from left to right, are Rev. G. E. Ellis and former Seaside mayors Andy Anderson and George "Sarge" Cunningham. (Both, courtesy of the City of Seaside Archive.)

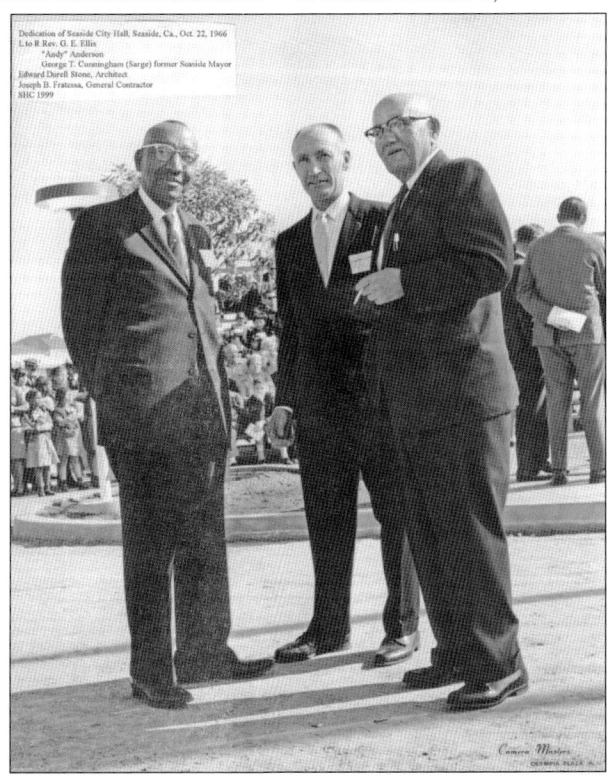

The views of the community show how much the new buildings meant to Seaside residents, who turned out in force and with great enthusiasm for the dedication ceremony and celebration. (Both, courtesy of the City of Seaside Archive.)

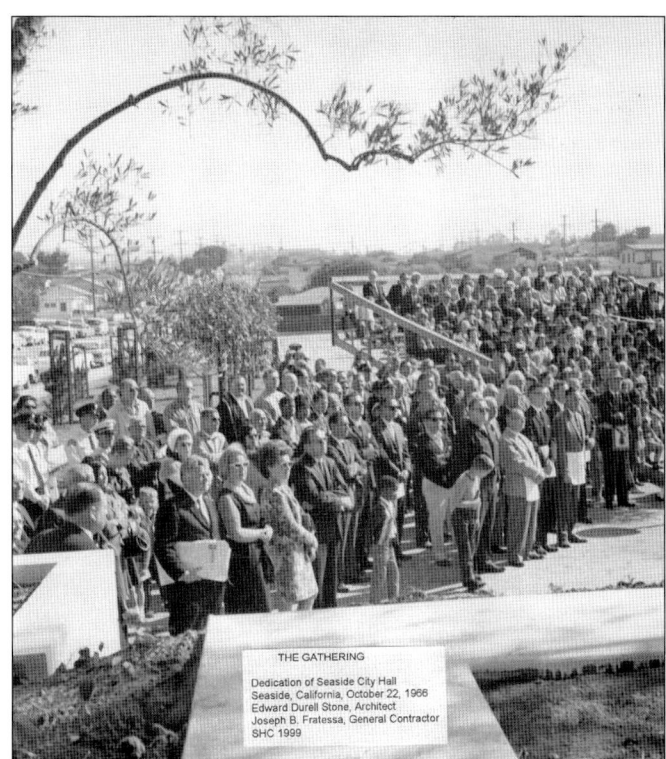

THE GATHERING
Dedication of Seaside City Hall
Seaside, California, October 22, 1966
Edward Durell Stone, Architect
Joseph B. Fratessa, General Contractor
SHC 1999

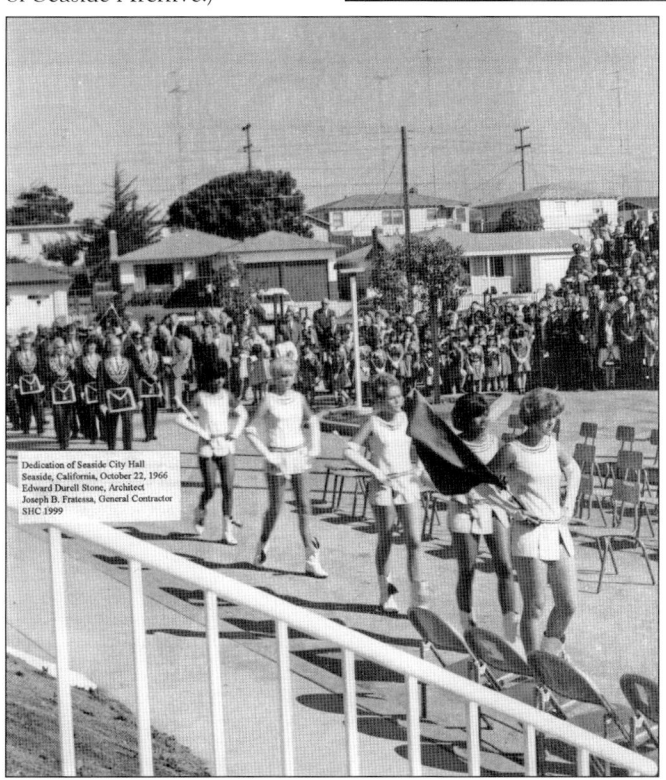

Dedication of Seaside City Hall
Seaside, California, October 22, 1966
Edward Durell Stone, Architect
Joseph B. Fratessa, General Contractor
SHC 1999

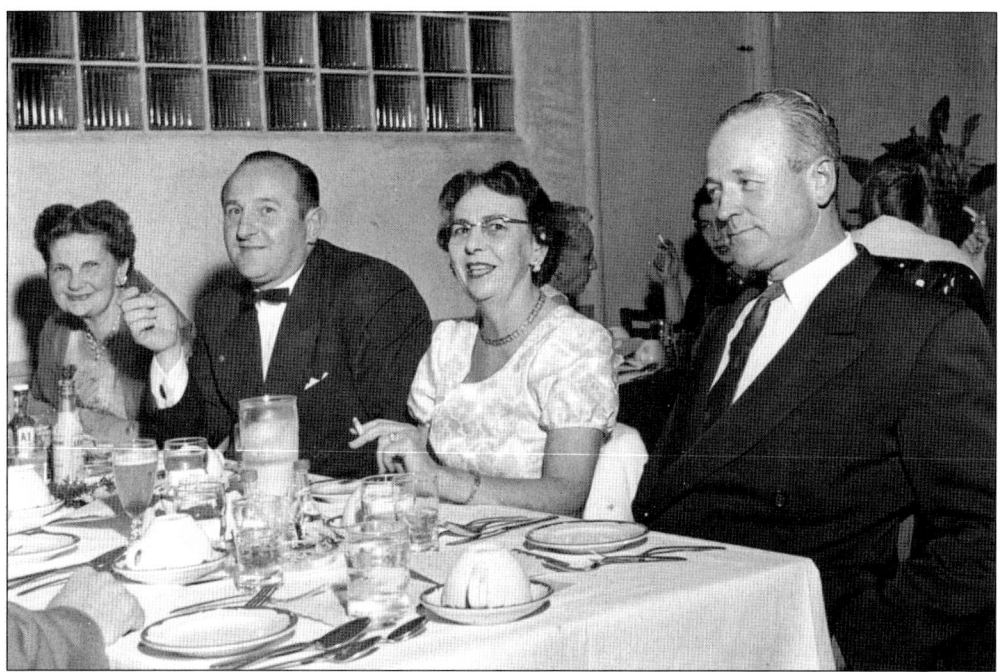

Saul Weingarten, second from left, arrived in Seaside after World War II and established a law practice with Fred Farr, who ran successfully for state assembly in 1955 with Weingarten as his campaign manager. Weingarten was enormously influential in Democratic politics and was responsible for drafting the legislation that allowed Seaside to annex parts of Fort Ord in 1968, doubling Seaside's population and adding substantially to its tax base. Weingarten drove much of the funding at the federal level that allowed for Seaside's redevelopment projects. (Courtesy of the City of Seaside Archive.)

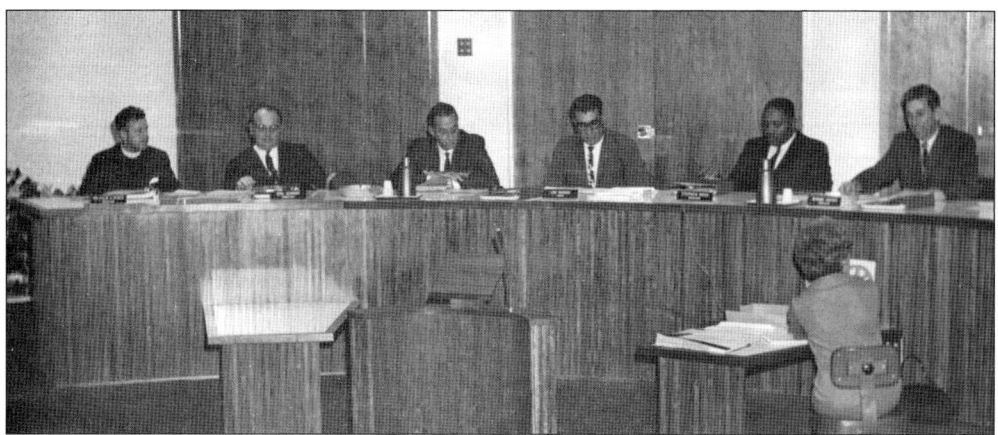

Mayor Lou Haddad (fourth from left) presides over a city council meeting at the new Seaside City Hall. Haddad served as mayor from 1966 to 1972 and on the city council until he was recalled in a contentious and racially charged campaign in 1980. Haddad's tenure in office coincided with one of the most successful civil rights efforts in California cities in the 1960s. From left to right are councilmen Rev. Malcom Miner, Emil Schmidt, unidentified, Haddad, Stephen Ross, and Bud Houser. (Courtesy of the City of Seaside Archive.)

Five

CIVIL RIGHTS!

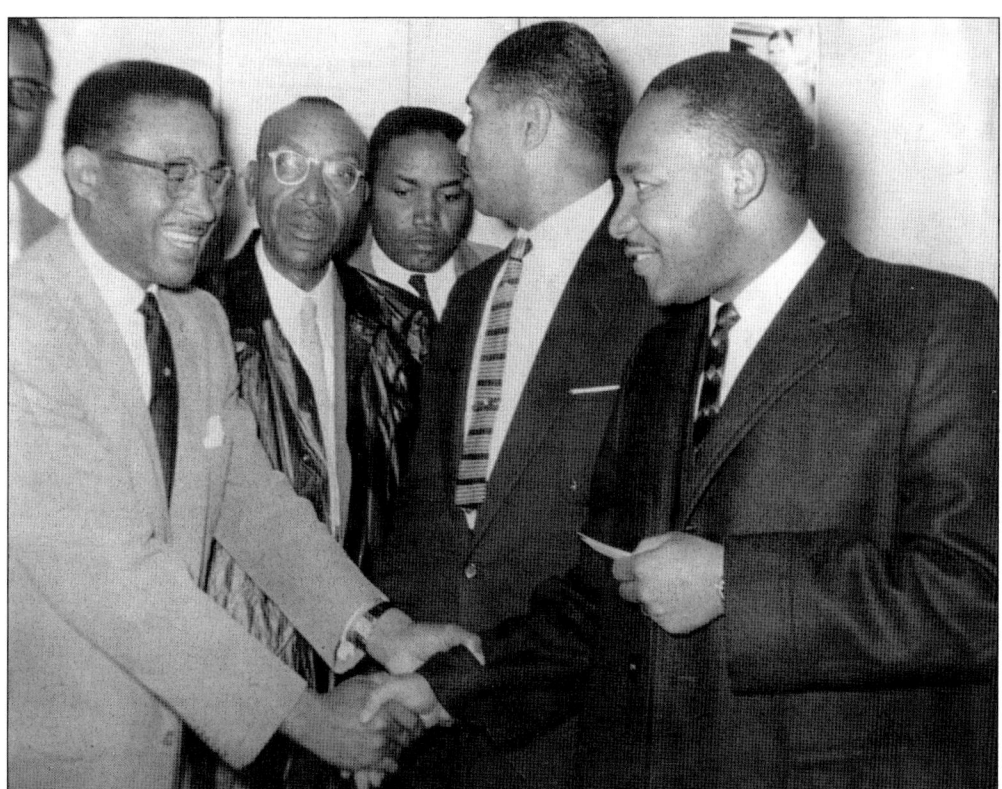

Dr. Martin Luther King Jr. visited Seaside and the Monterey Peninsula in 1962. From left to right are John Bean, Rev. G. E. Ellis, Stephen Ross, Rev. C. Lewis McFadden, and Dr. Martin Luther King Jr. In a 1968 editorial, Sherman Smith argued for a new kind of community in Seaside: "We in Seaside have a special problem, and a special opportunity. Our population is one of the most cosmopolitan in the state; we have a tremendous variety of racial, ethnic and cultural strains, all of which have been woven into our way of life. When a newcomer arrives from the East or West, one of his first chores is to become accustomed to our street names, because so many of them are of Spanish derivation. Our challenge is to see that this new way of life . . . [is] the truly American way of life . . . in which each man is accepted on his own merit . . . or rejected on his own shortcoming . . . not because of his color or his accent, or by the name he calls his God." African Americans such as Sherman and Elizabeth Smith gave Seaside a legacy of social, political, and economic justice, and the strategy of coalition building across racial lines to achieve it. (Courtesy of the Lenora Bean Collection, City of Seaside Archive.)

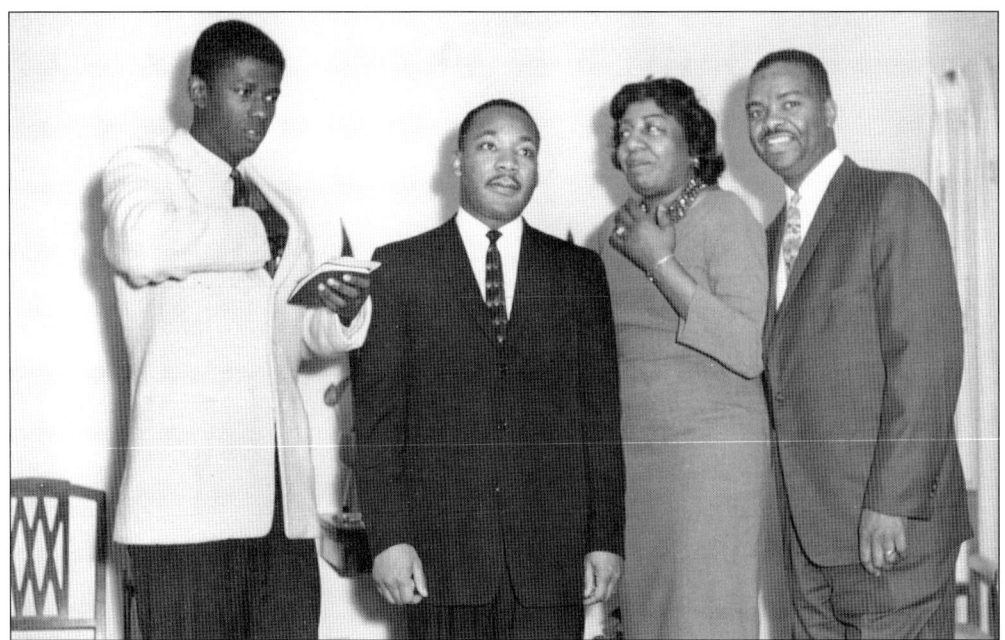

As a result of the activism and leadership of African Americans, Seaside became nationally known as a center for civil rights. In the above 1962 image is, from left to right, an unidentified assistant, Dr. Martin Luther King Jr., and Mary and William Story. The photograph below shows, from left to right, Theron Polite, Rosa Parks, and Ruthie Watts. (Above, courtesy of the Mary Story Collection, City of Seaside Archive; below, courtesy of the Ruthie Watts Collection, City of Seaside Archive.)

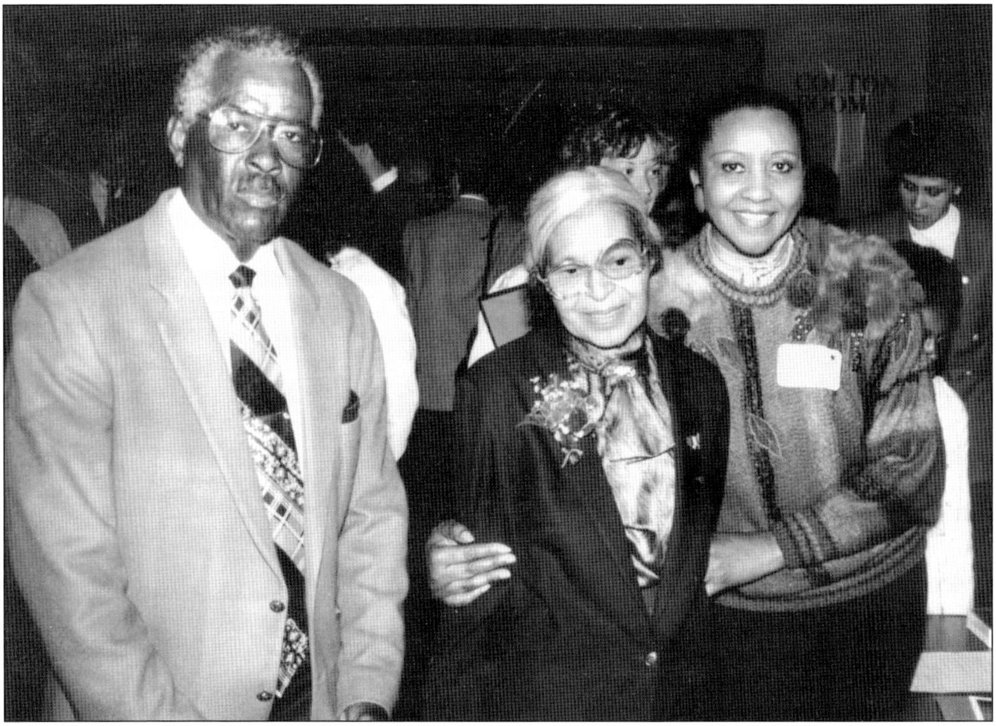

Many important activists and politicians visited Seaside, including Angela Davis and Los Angeles mayor Tom Bradley when he ran for governor of California. At left, Angela Davis is pictured at Monterey Peninsula Community College. Below, from left to right, are Monterey Peninsula Community College board member Sherman Smith, Seaside mayor Stephen Ross, and Los Angeles mayor Tom Bradley. (Both, courtesy of the Smith Collection, City of Seaside Archive.)

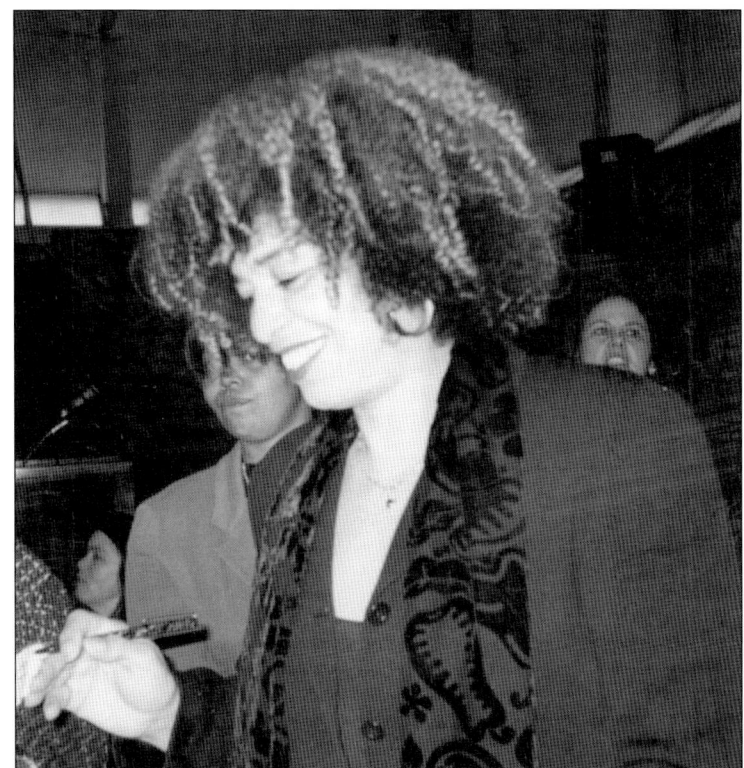

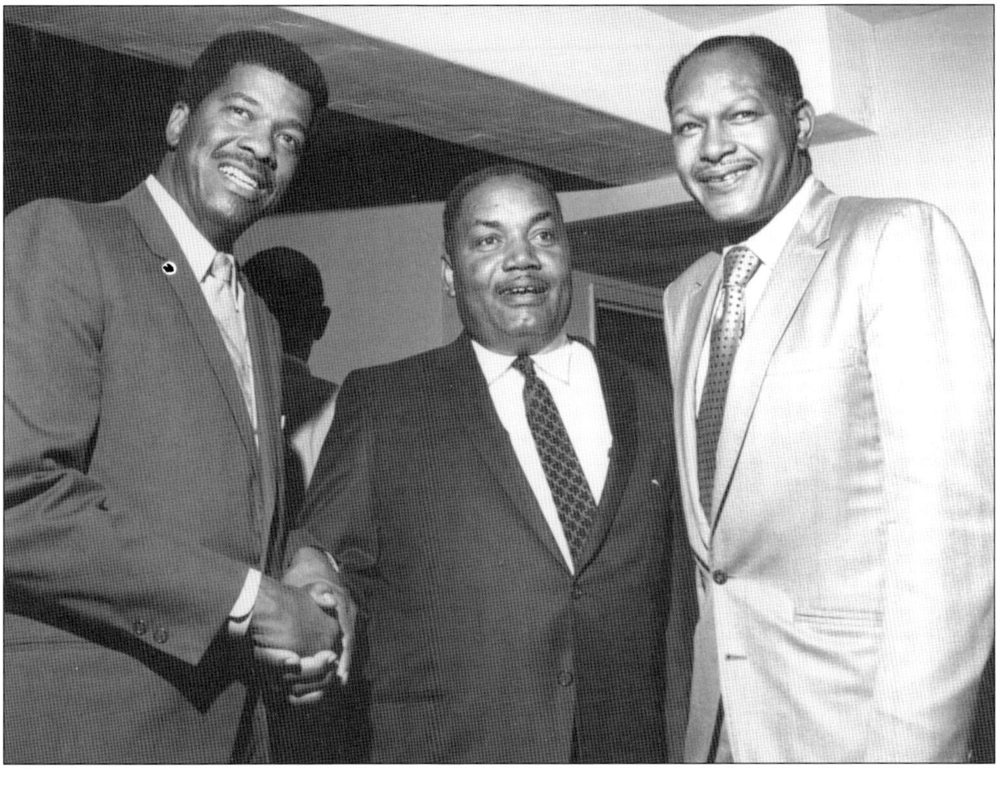

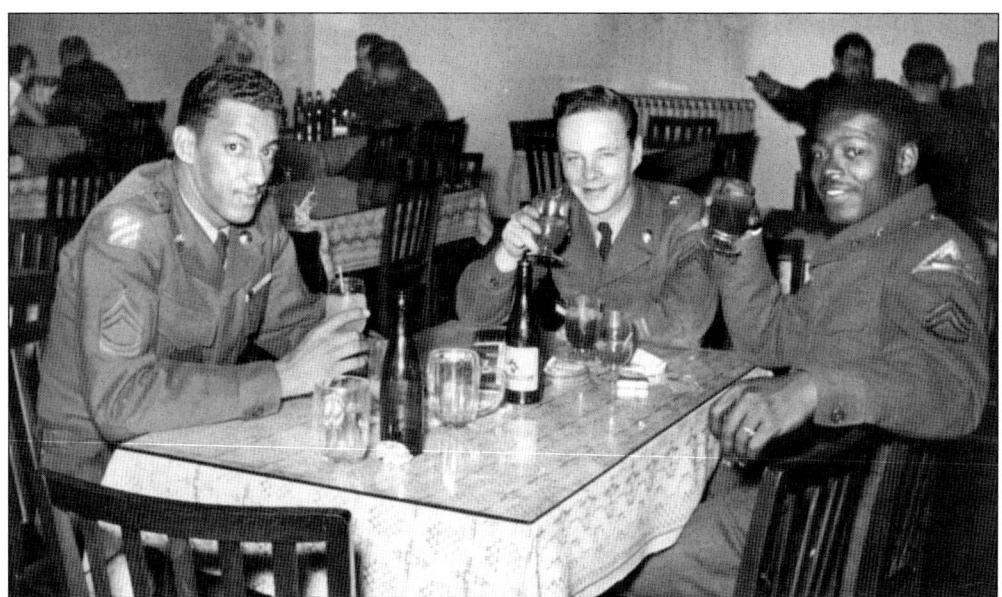

Pres. Harry S. Truman signed Executive Order 9381, which desegregated the military "with equality for all people," and Fort Ord became an integrated training base practically overnight. It is important to appreciate fully the impact of Executive Order 9381 on the political consciousness of both black and non-black servicemen and their families who settled Seaside from 1948 on. Both groups had positive experiences with integration, which they carried with them when they settled in Seaside. (Both, courtesy of the Sherman and Elizabeth Smith Collection, City of Seaside Archive.)

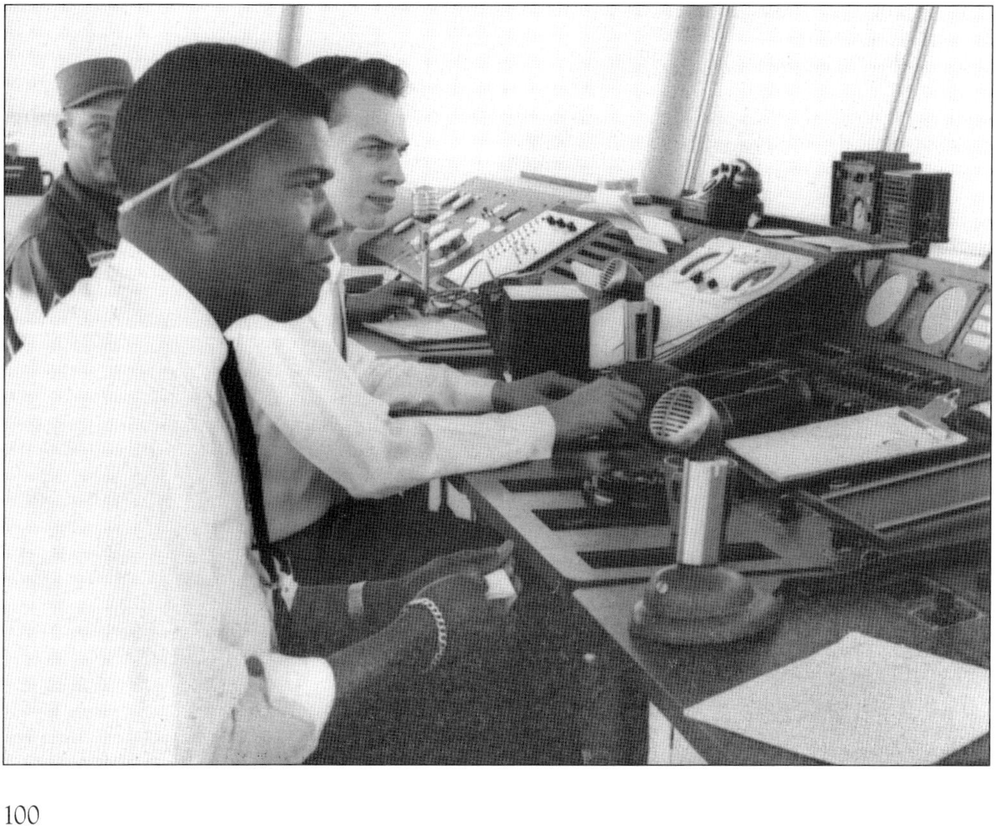

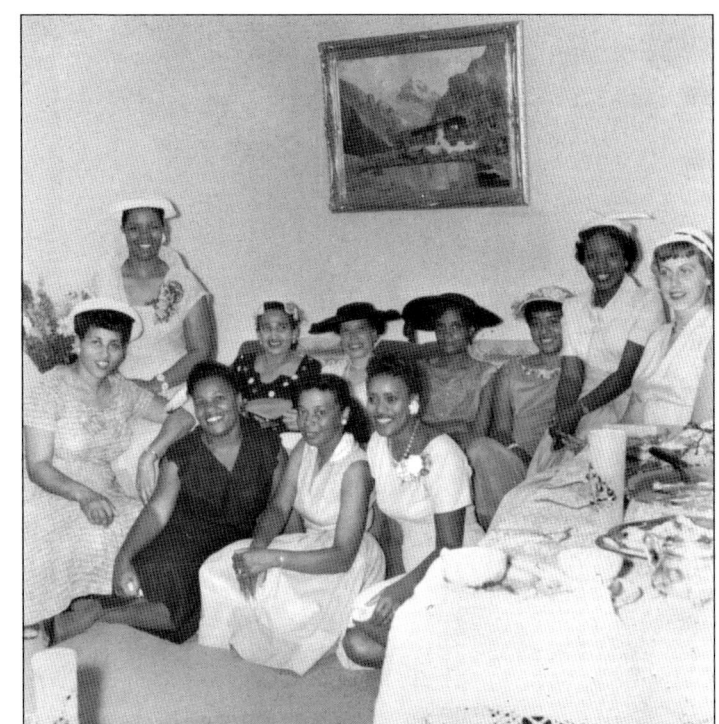

The African American men, women, and children who were part of the military became experienced travelers, as men were stationed in all parts of the world and women and children joined them. (Both, courtesy of the Sherman and Elizabeth Smith Collection, City of Seaside Archive.)

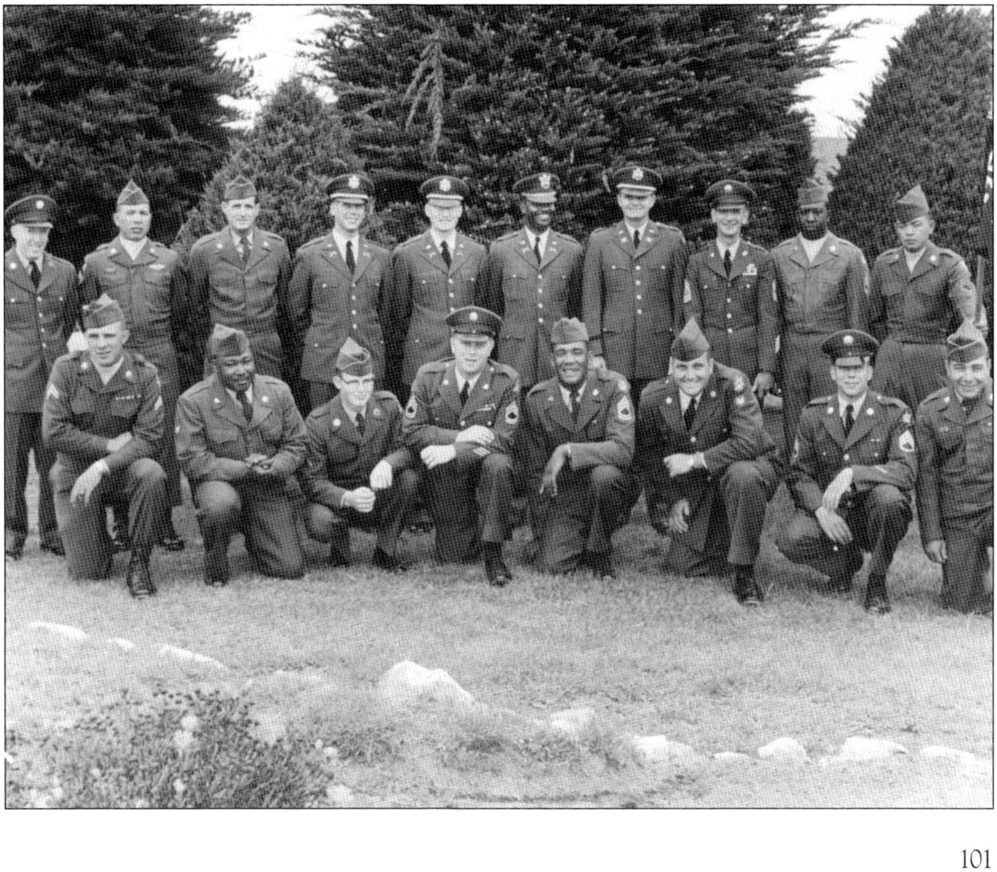

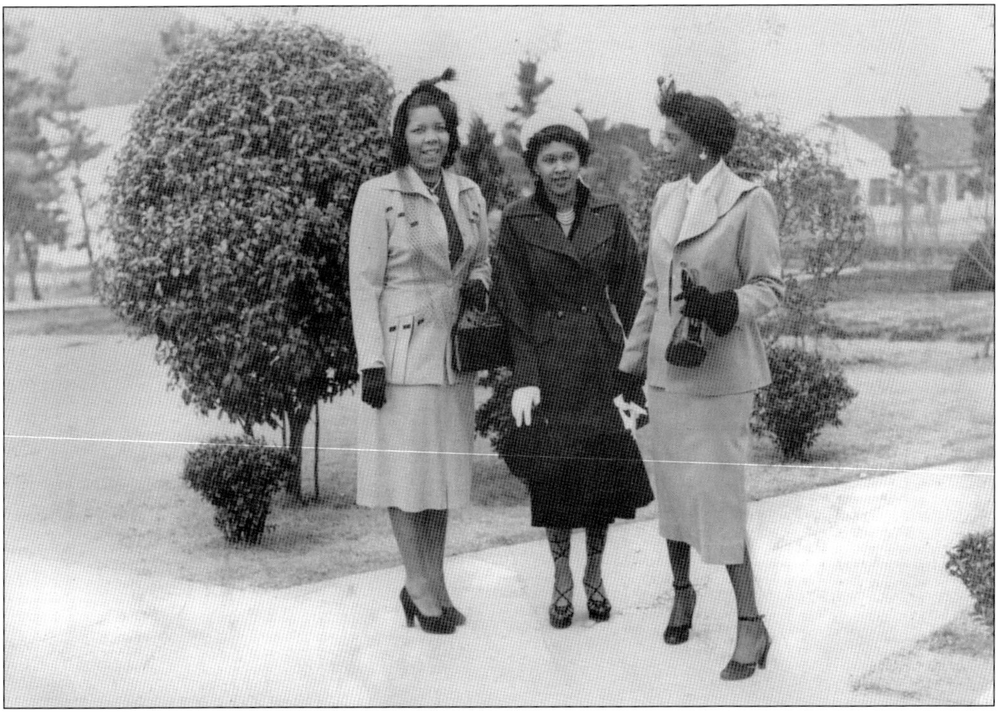

Well educated and from the ranks of officers and higher-level enlisted men, African American families brought a level of sophistication and worldliness to Seaside, and initiated a new era of successful civil rights activism throughout the Monterey Peninsula. (Both, courtesy of the Sherman and Elizabeth Smith Collection, City of Seaside Archive.)

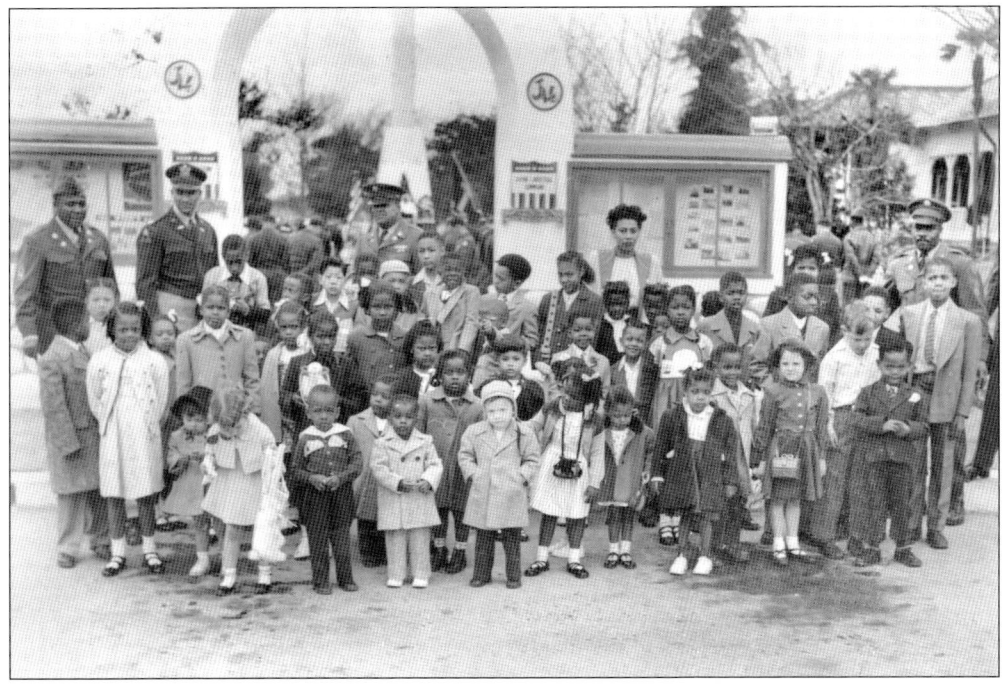

During both World War II and the Korean War, African American soldiers, like their white counterparts, sometimes married women from the communities where they were stationed. Seaside became known not only as a minority community, but also as a mixed-race community. Women from Germany, France, Japan, Korea, and Vietnam added another level of diversity to the population and a twist in racially restricted housing because many of the women were able to buy homes in areas designated for whites only. (Both, courtesy of Rev. Welton McGee, City of Seaside Archive.)

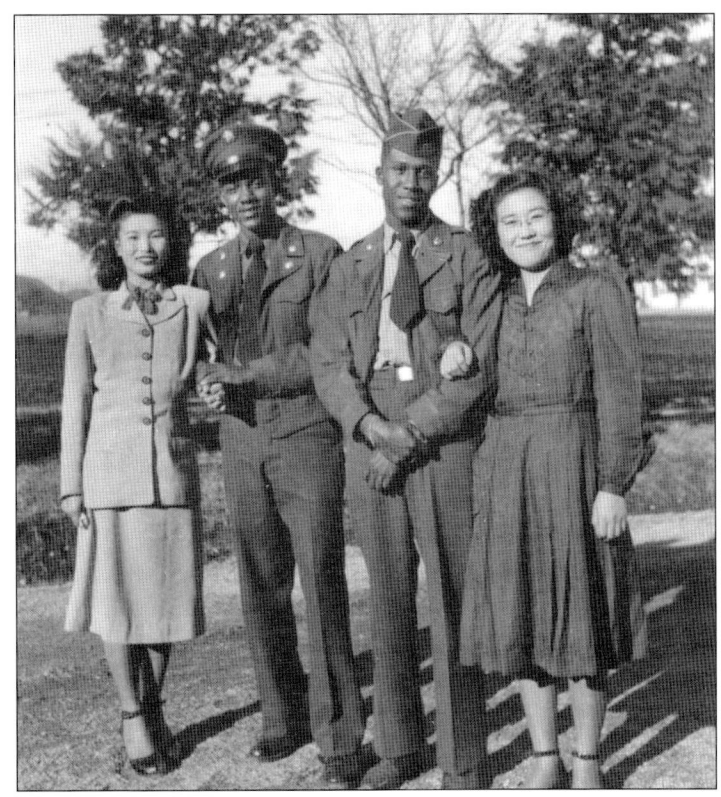

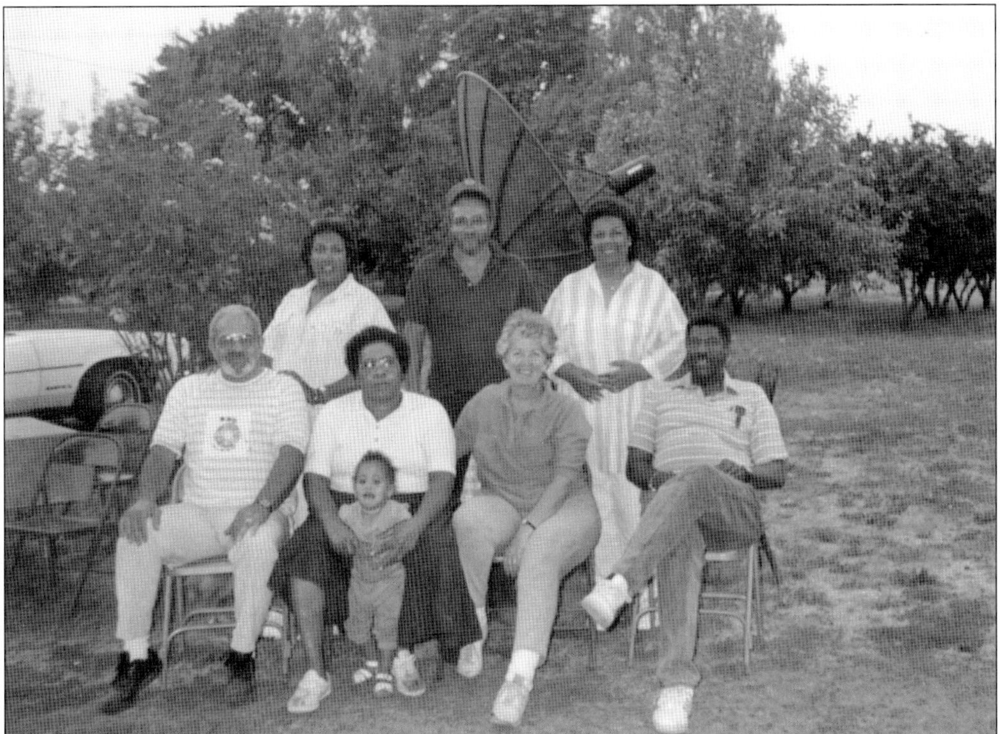

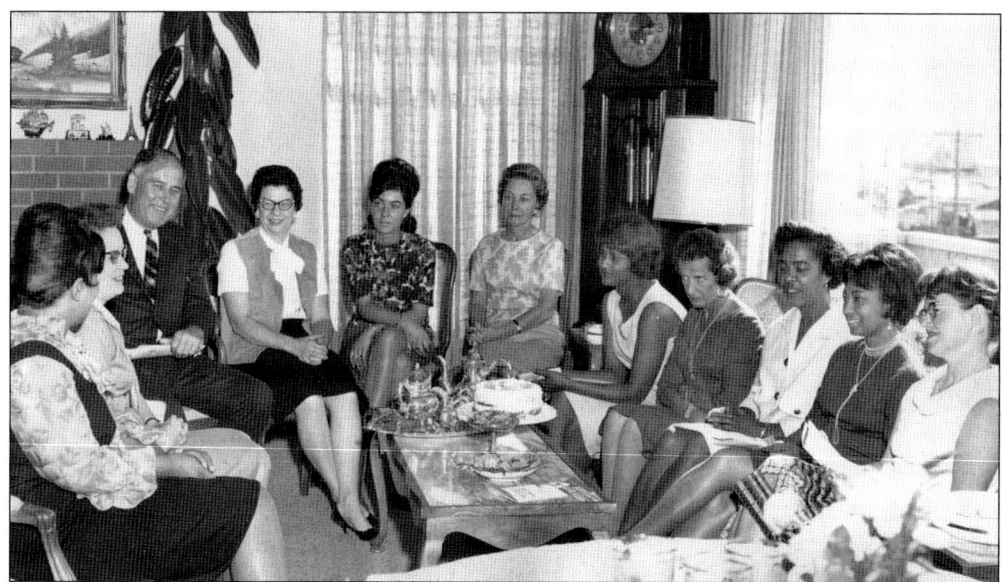

African Americans not only participated in Seaside politics; they led them. The Monterey County Democratic Women's Club (above, with Sen. Fred Farr) is an example of the ways in which blacks worked with other groups to ensure city building, civil rights, and social justice. The NAACP, at the forefront of challenging discrimination during the 1960s, had a membership of more than 1,000 people at that time. The organization focused on employment on the peninsula. The service industries in particular had a history of excluding blacks both in employment and as hotel guests. The NAACP threatened to take motel owners on the Monterey Peninsula to court in 1962 to force them "take down racial barriers." They complied. Representatives of the NAACP met with business owners and bank managers to encourage the hiring of African Americans. According to NAACP president Henry Hopkins, writing for the *Seaside Post News-Sentinel* in 1978, "Since the beginning of 1977, our membership has increased over 100 percent. . . . Now 70 percent of the members are residing in Seaside." (Above, courtesy of the Lenora Bean Collection, City of Seaside Archive; below, courtesy of the Ruthie Watts Collection, City of Seaside Archive.)

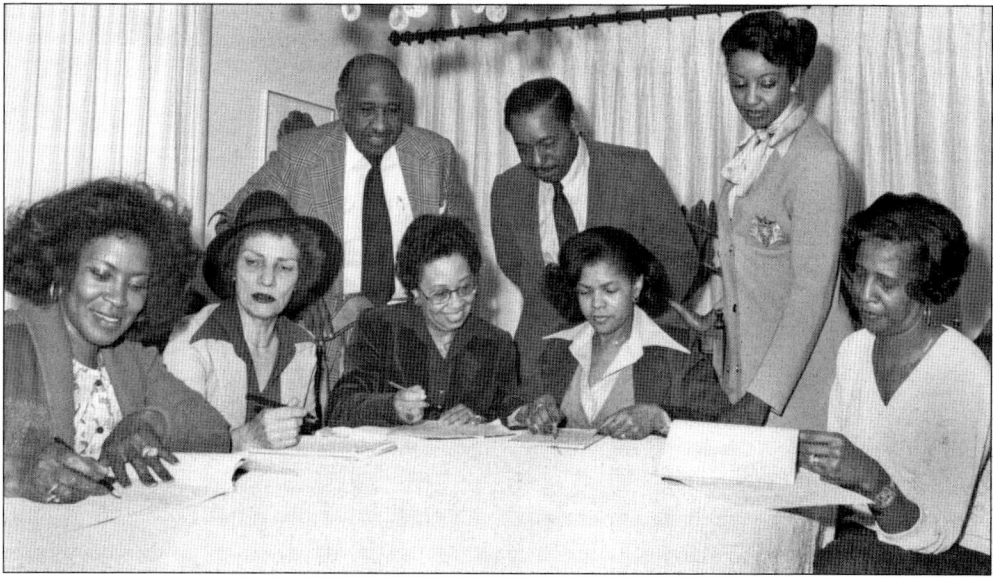

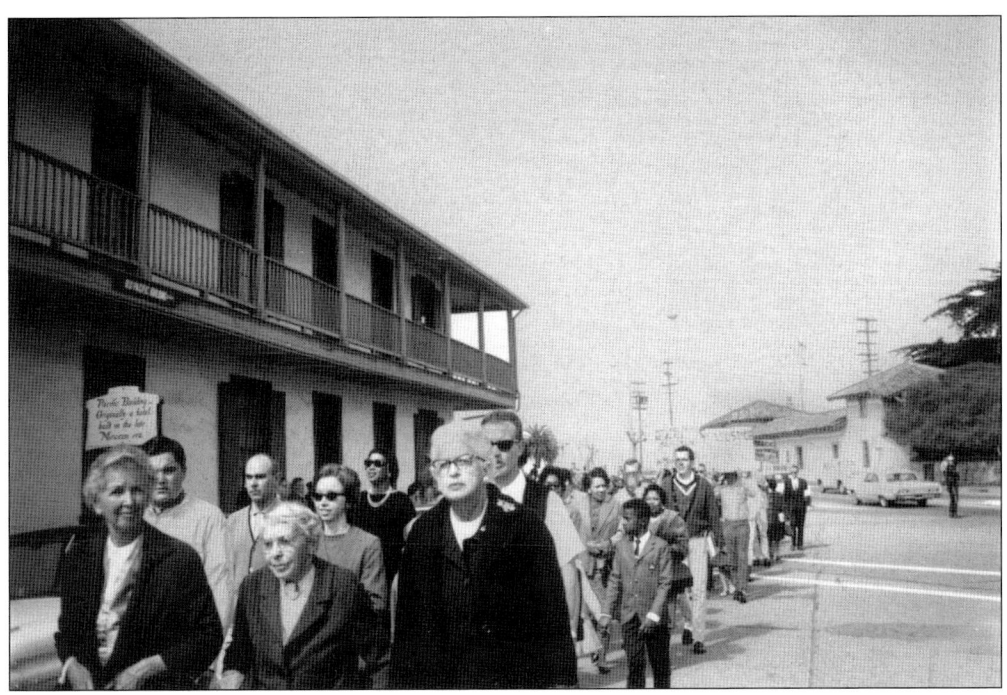

The above picture shows a 1960s NAACP march. Below is a photograph taken in 1983 of the annual Martin Luther King Day march in Seaside down Broadway. This march included thousands of citizens from across the county and continues to the present day. (Above, courtesy of the Sherman and Elizabeth Smith Collection, City of Seaside; below, courtesy of Vern Fisher, *Monterey County Herald*, City of Seaside Archive.)

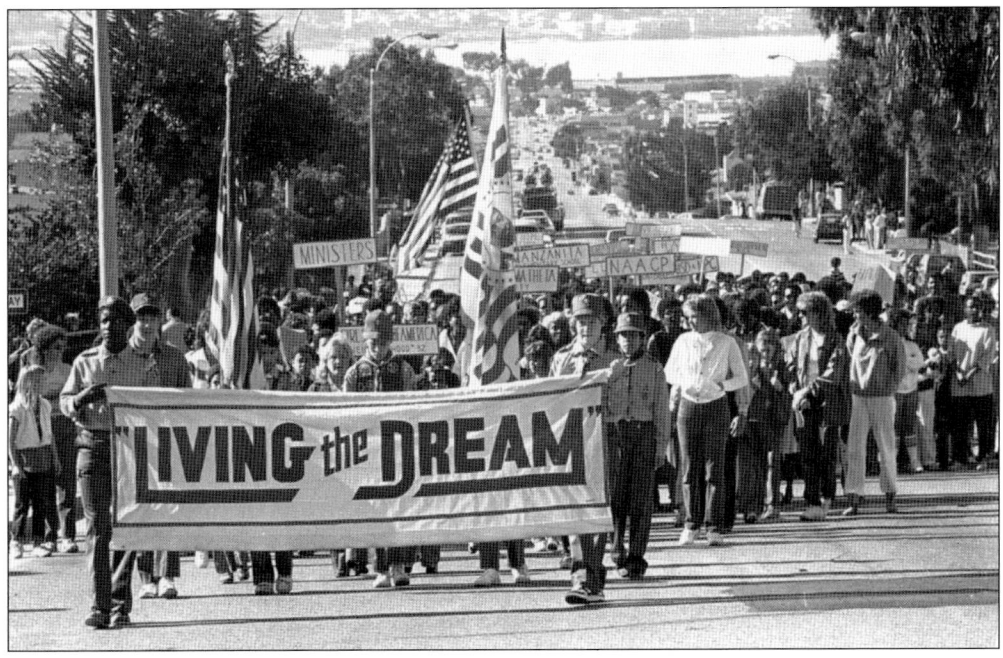

105

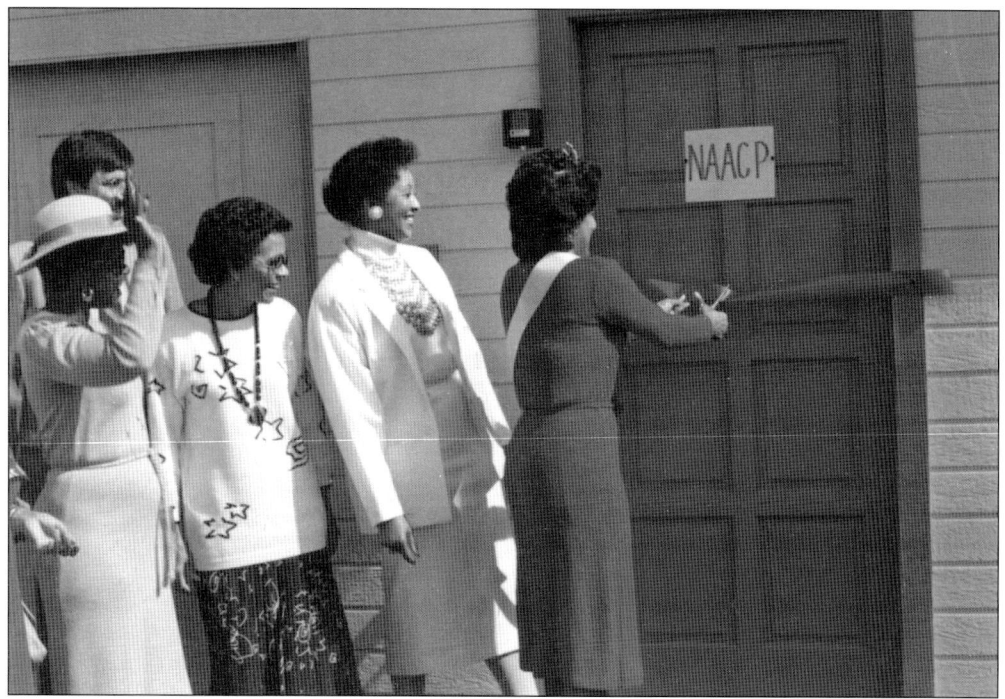

Pictured is the opening of the new NAACP office in Seaside. From right to left are Marcella Mitchell, Mrs. NAACP; Ruthie Watts; Parniest Glover; Frances Armstrong; and Judge Michael Fields. Below is another NAACP event. (Both, courtesy of the Ruthie Watts Collection, City of Seaside Archive.)

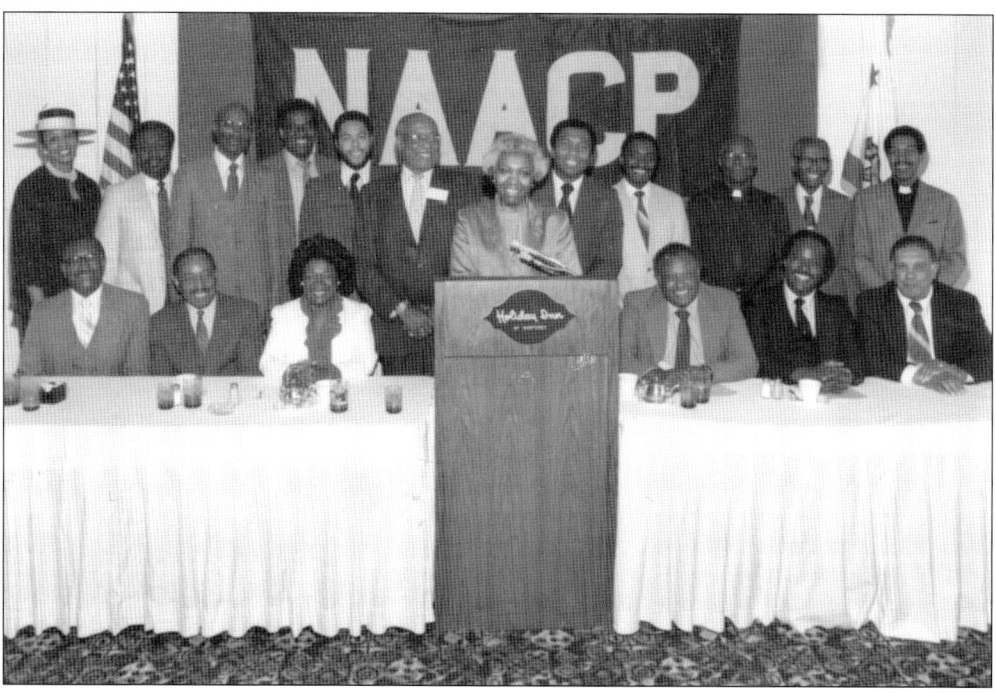

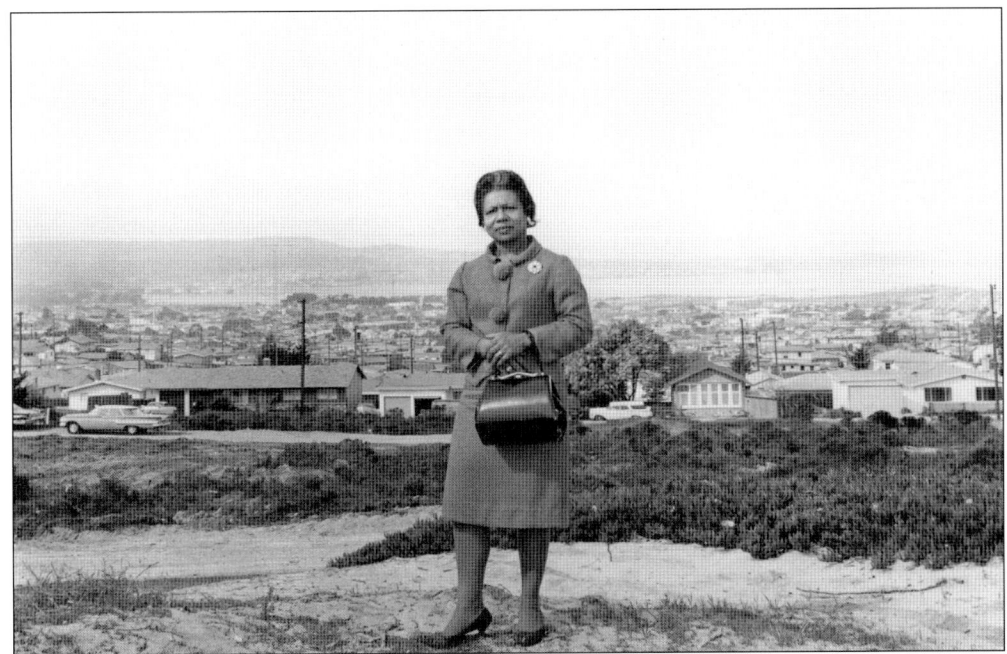

Pearl Carey was described as "Seaside's Rosa Parks, Martin Luther King—everyone was embodied in that woman." Seaside's first African American city councilwoman, Carey arrived in 1952 as a military wife. Carey remained a vital part of successful efforts to contest the gerrymandering of county supervisor districts 20 years later in Seaside politics and remained a force in Democratic politics for many years. She was elected as a delegate to the Democratic National Convention in 1972 and was the first person in Monterey County of any color to serve on a committee of a national political party. However, it cost her a state job as an advocate for minorities seeking employment in federally funded projects. She challenged the Hatch Act, which her firing was based on, but lost at the Supreme Court level. The fight was a testament to her strength, perseverance, and faith in social justice. Pictured at right are Dr. Charlie Mae Knight (left) and Pearl Carey. (Both, courtesy of the Pearl Carey Collection, City of Seaside Archive.)

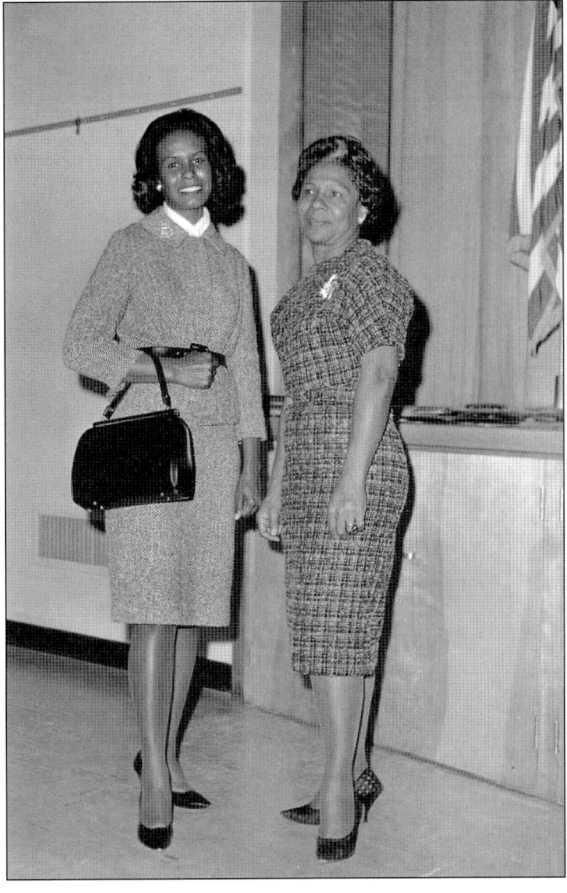

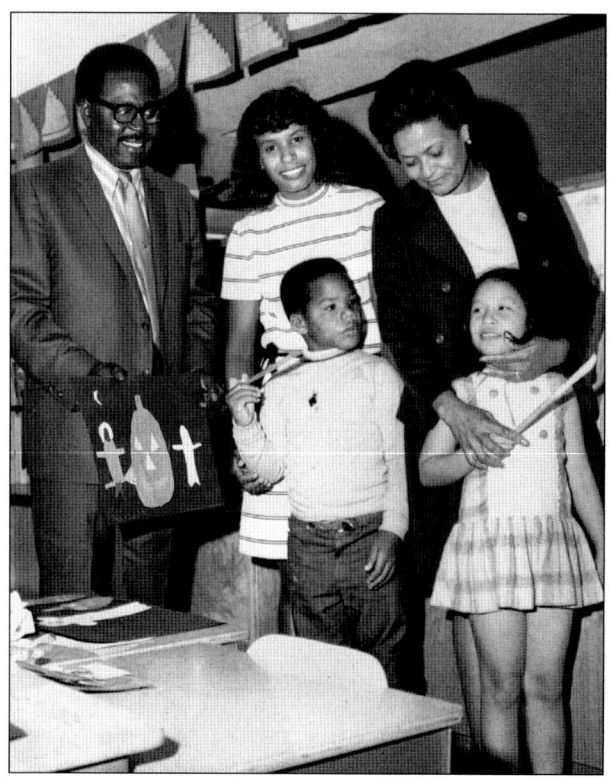

Dr. Charlie Mae Knight, an African American fourth-grade teacher at the mostly black Highlands Elementary School in 1965, single-handedly integrated the faculty of the Monterey Peninsula School District, making it a model for every other district in California by 1970. Dr. Knight visited more than 125 black colleges in the South to recruit nearly 70 African American teachers and administrators in a little over three years. These individuals included Dr. Henry Hutchins, Bertha Hutchins, Dr. Billy DeBerry and his wife, Rose, Helen Rucker, and Bettye Lusk, all of whom remain prominent both in Seaside and Monterey County. Dr. Charlie Mae Knight is pictured in the center. (Courtesy of the City of Seaside Archive.)

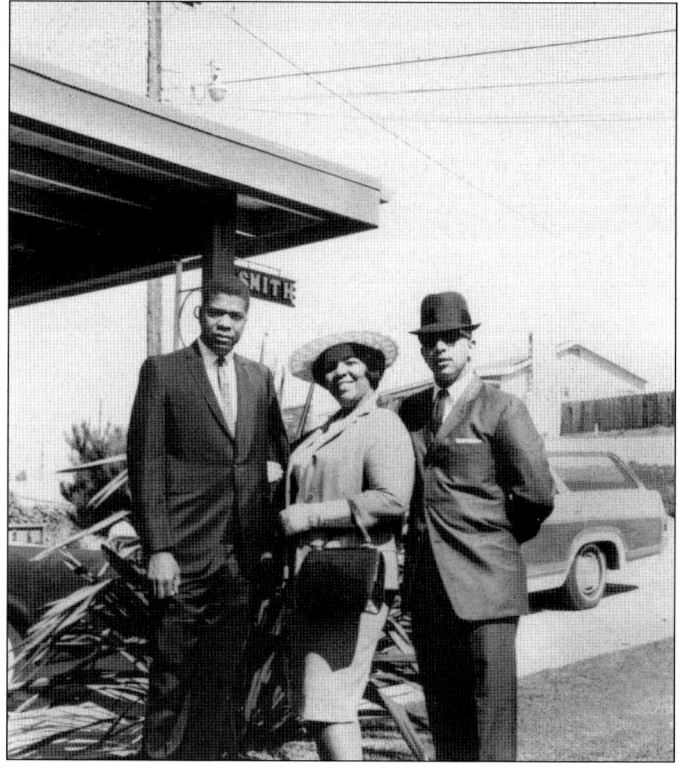

Sherman Smith, a retired army major who, together with his wife, Elizabeth, successfully forced the integration of the Ord Terrace Development, served as president of the Human Rights Commission in Seaside and was the first African American elected to the Monterey Peninsula Community College Board in 1964. As the longest serving trustee in the state of California, Smith served on the board for 33 years. Sherman and Elizabeth Smith are pictured with an unidentified man in front of their newly purchased home in Ord Terrace in 1966. (Courtesy of the Sherman and Elizabeth Smith Collection, City of Seaside Archive.)

The photograph here is of Stephen E. Ross. Ross served 16 consecutive years on the Seaside City Council and as mayor pro-tem and mayor from 1978 to 1980. Originally from Texas, Ross graduated from Antioch College in California with a bachelor's degree and a master's degree in urban studies and urban planning. He also did advance studies at the University of California, Berkeley. (Courtesy of the City of Seaside Archive.)

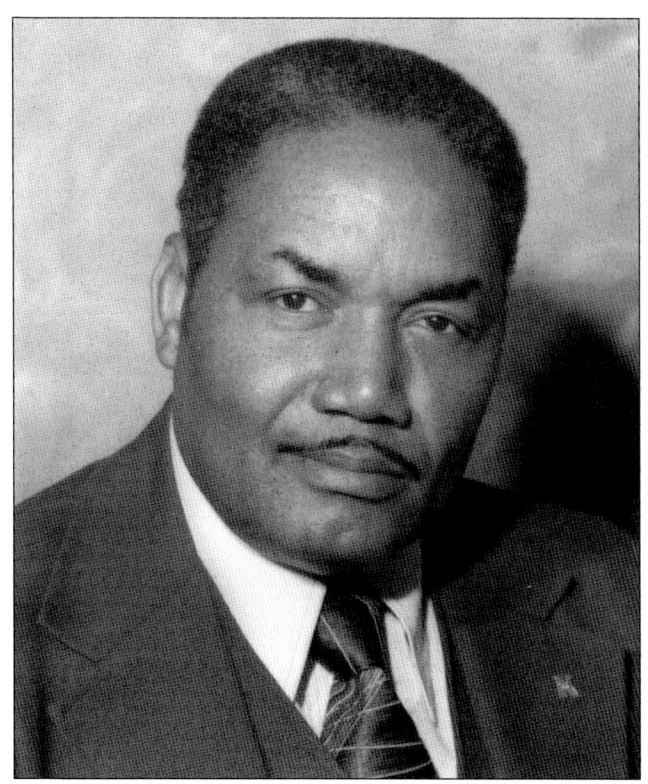

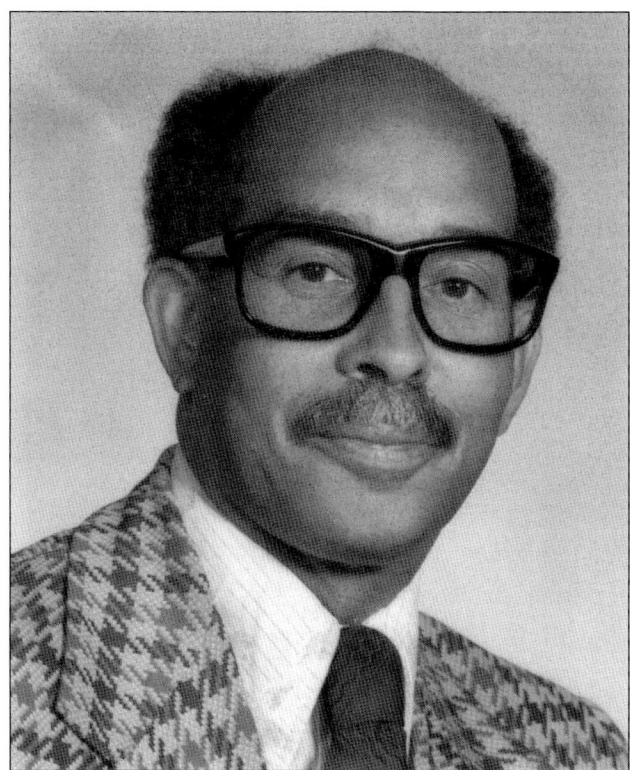

Mayor Oscar Lawson is shown here. Lawson served on the city council from 1972 to 1976, was mayor pro-tem from 1974 to 1976, and served as the first black mayor of Seaside from 1976 to 1978. From 1976 until the recent election of Ralph Rubio in 2004, all of Seaside's mayors were African American. (Courtesy of the City of Seaside Archive.)

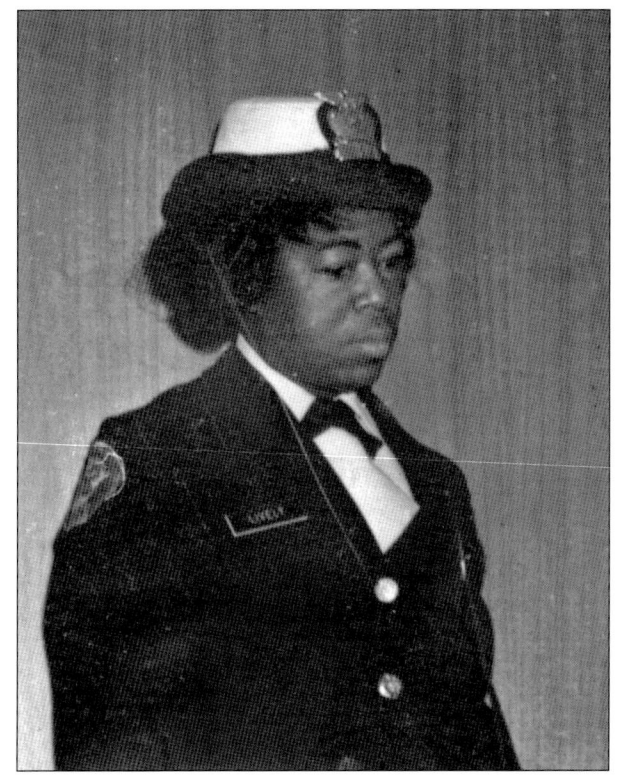

Ira Lively, shown at left, was the first African American woman to serve on the City of Seaside police force in 1956 and also became a city council member in 1984, serving throughout the 1980s. Helen Rucker arrived in Seaside as part of a contingent of black teachers recruited by Dr. Charlie Mae Knight to integrate the Monterey Peninsula School faculties. A librarian, Rucker became a community activist and was elected to the city council first in 1994 and as mayor pro-tem in 1996. She is currently a trustee on the Monterey Peninsula School Board. Below are Helen Rucker and James Rucker, her son. (Both, courtesy of the City of Seaside Archive.)

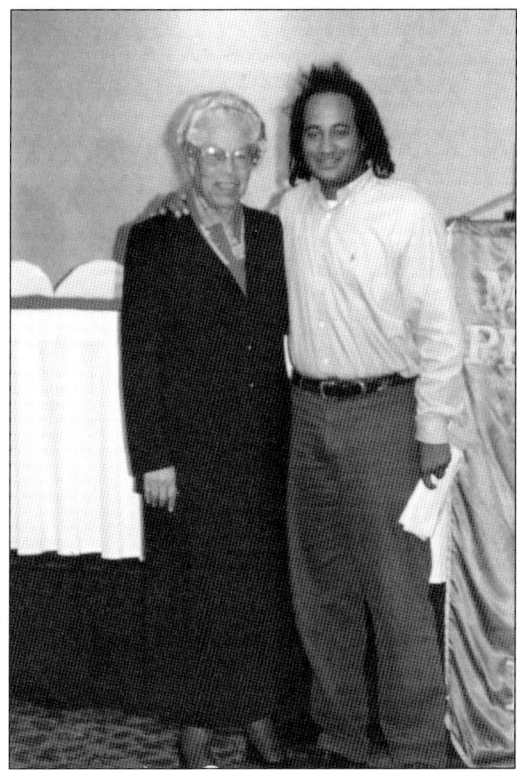

Cecil Bindel joined the NAACP in 1951 at the behest of his friend realtor John Bean. In 1962, he became president and served two terms. Bindel and the NAACP focused on equality issues, especially employment on the peninsula. The service industries in particular had a history of excluding blacks both in employment and as hotel guests. Bindel threatened to take motel owners on the Monterey Peninsula to court in 1962 to force them "take down racial barriers." The photograph at right is of a 1960s NAACP event. On the far left is Cecil Bindel and far right is Lenora Bean; the rest are unidentified. (Courtesy of the City of Seaside Archive.)

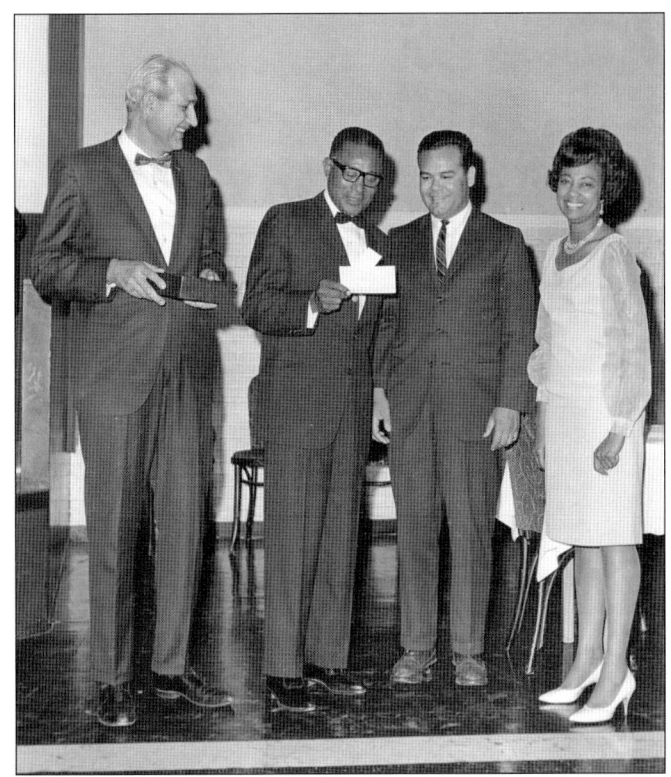

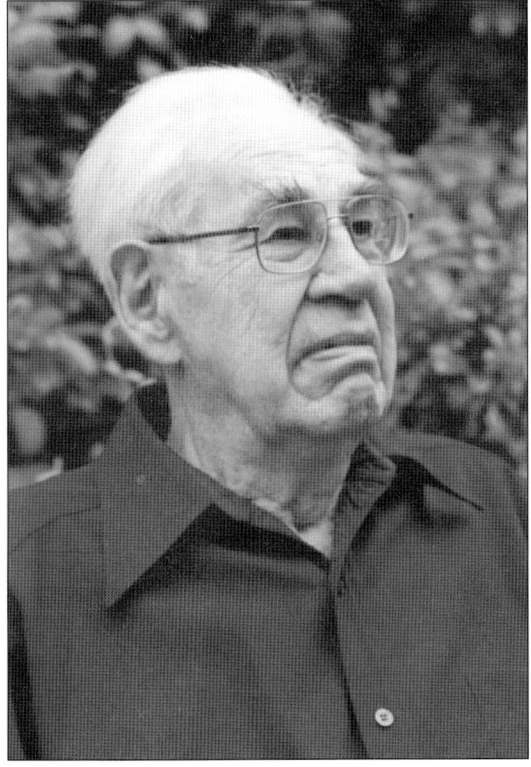

Richard Criley (pictured at left) served as executive director of the Monterey County chapter of the American Civil Liberties Union from 1981 and was responsible for reviving the organization and bringing in hundreds of new members. He was tremendously influential in supporting and leading civil rights actions in Seaside and throughout the peninsula. (Courtesy of the City of Seaside Archive.)

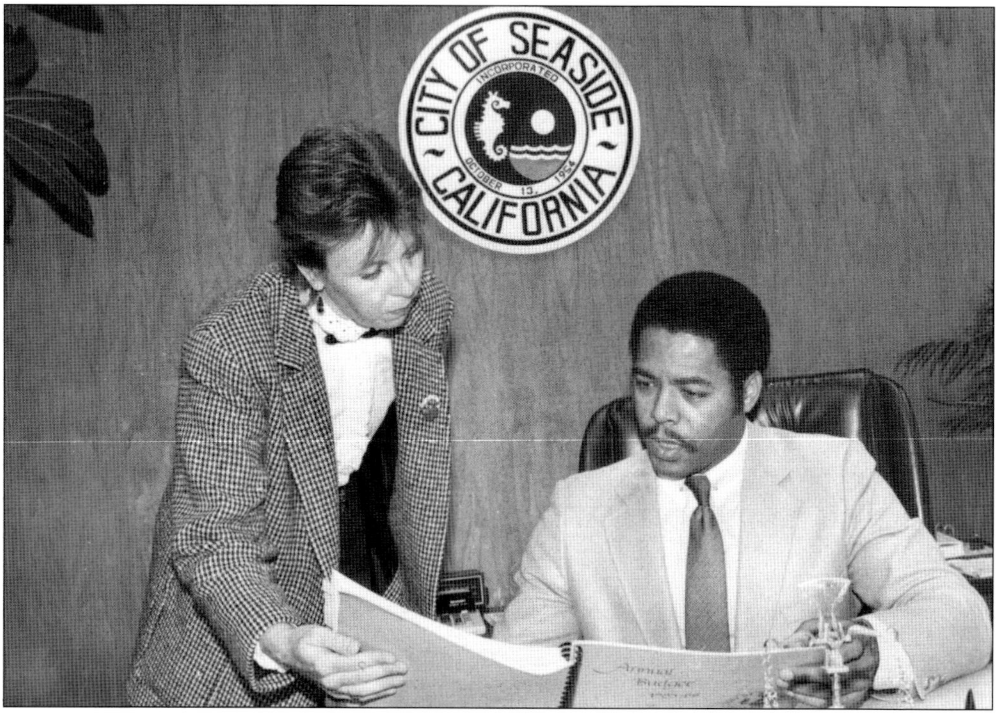

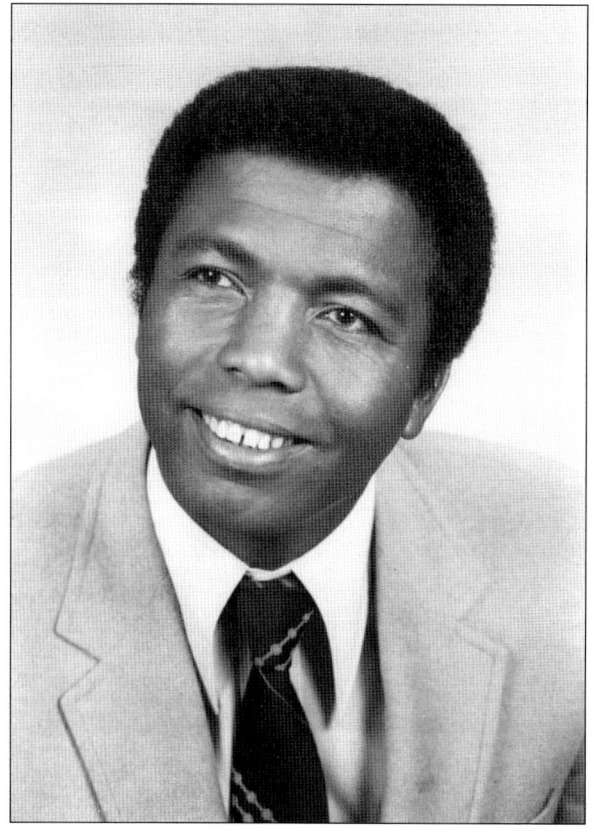

Charles McNeely was city manager from 1983 to 1993 and was praised for development programs and economic recovery, strong leadership, and the expansion of the auto mall. Lance McClair was 39 years old in 1982, the youngest mayor in the city's history. As a leading figure in the African American social and political community of Seaside, his candidacy marked the culmination of the shift begun in the 1970 election that firmly established African Americans as the dominant political power. McClair would serve as Seaside's mayor for four consecutive two-year terms, from 1982 until 1994. (Both, courtesy of the City of Seaside Archive.)

Don Jordan originally won a place on the Seaside City Council in 1991. He served two terms as mayor from 1994 to 1998 and remains a city councilman in 2008. As mayor and together with then–city manager Tim Brown, Jordan was responsible for the acquisition of Bayonet and Blackhorse golf courses from the army, as well as a number of development projects that marked Seaside's transition from a military town after the closure of Fort Ord in 1994. The picture below is of Julian Bond and an unidentified person. When he visited Seaside, Bond, a famous civil rights activist and leader, founded the Student nonviolent Coordinating Committee in the 1960s. Although he was elected to the Georgia state legislature in 1965, he was prevented from taking his seat by segregationists until the U.S. Supreme Court ruled in his favor. He served in the legislature for 20 years. (Both, courtesy of the City of Seaside Archive.)

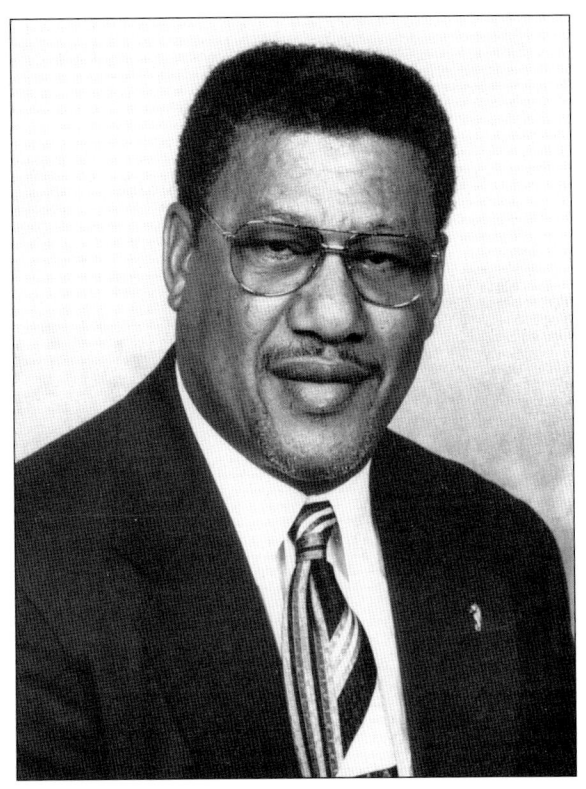

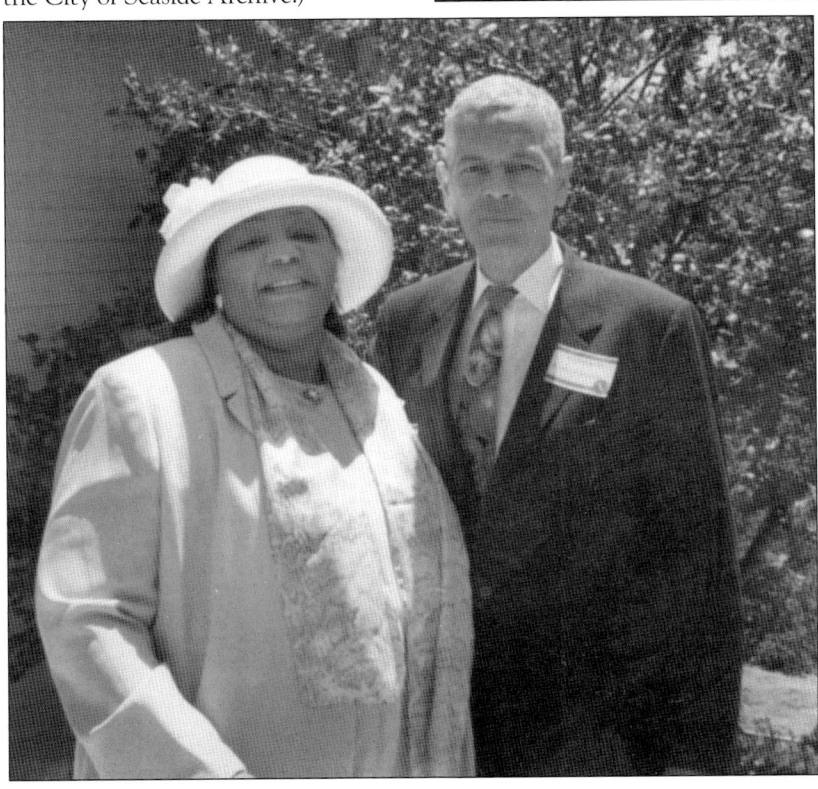

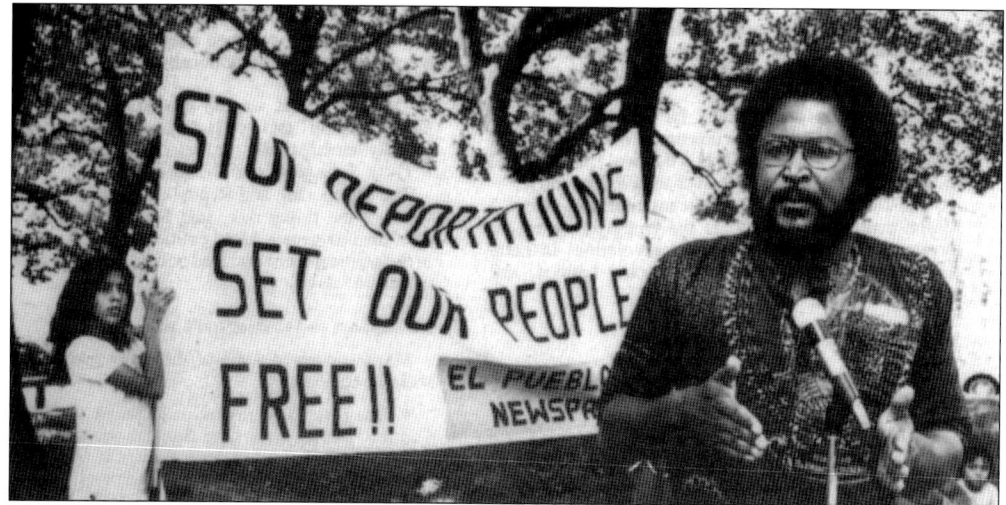

Mel Mason came to Seaside from Kentucky in 1956. He became an internationally recognized activist who fought for social justice. Most notably, he created partnerships with other minority groups, particularly Latinos, through the United Farm Workers. He is a former member of the Black Panther Party, a former Seaside city councilman, and a former Socialist Workers Party candidate for governor of California in 1982 and president of the United States in 1984. He is the immediate past president of the Monterey Peninsula Branch of the NAACP and was recently elected third vice president of the California state NAACP. Dr. William Melendez (pictured below) arrived from New York to teach in Salinas schools in 1970 and became president of LULAC (League of United Latin American Citizens), serving throughout the 1980s. He fought for bilingual education in the schools and was instrumental in building coalitions with African American organizations such as the NAACP to bring about social justice for minority groups. (Above, courtesy of the City of Seaside Archive; below, courtesy of the William Melendez Collection.)

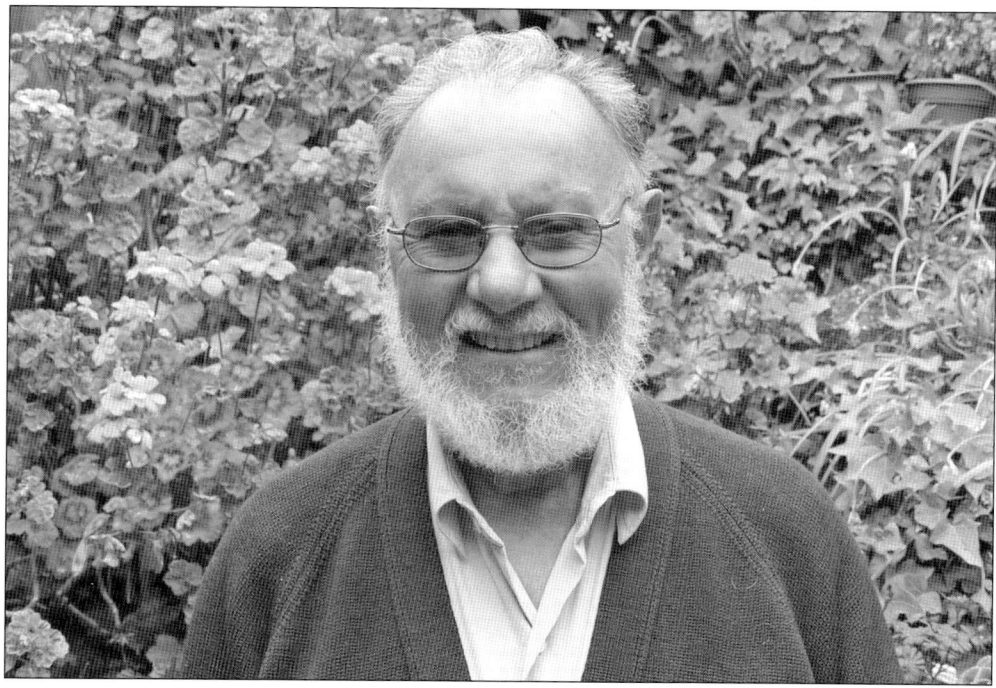

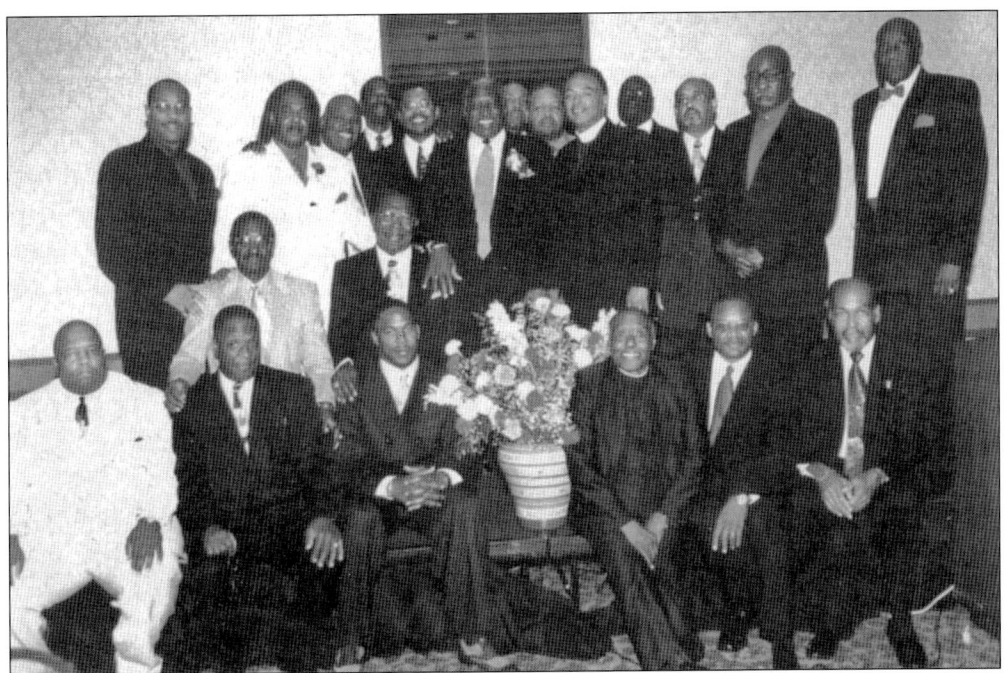

Pictured above are members of the Ministerial Alliance. The Ministerial Alliance formed in 1948 to promote civil rights through political activism under the leadership of black ministers in Seaside. It was a powerful organization that sustained African American political and social work throughout the 1960s and into the present day. E. Walker James, one of Seaside's most prominent leaders in civil rights, together with Morris McDaniel and other activists, formed the Citizens League for Progress and the Yellow Jackets, a citizens' group against crime. He is shown below with his fellow Buffalo Soldiers and the Tuskegee Airmen. From left to right are E. Walker James, George William, Thomas Gaines, Frank Steele, and Sherman Smith. (Both, courtesy of the E. Walker James Collection, City of Seaside Archive.)

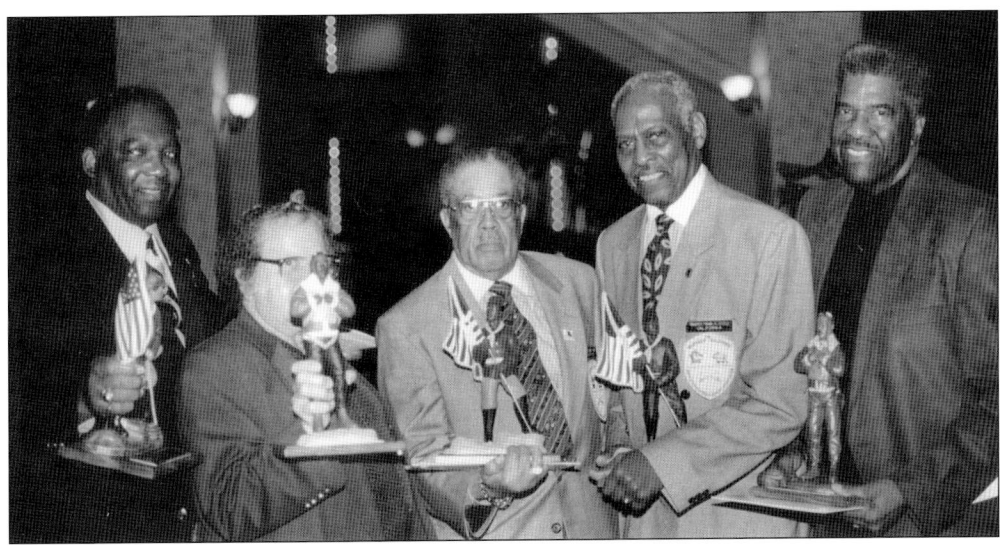

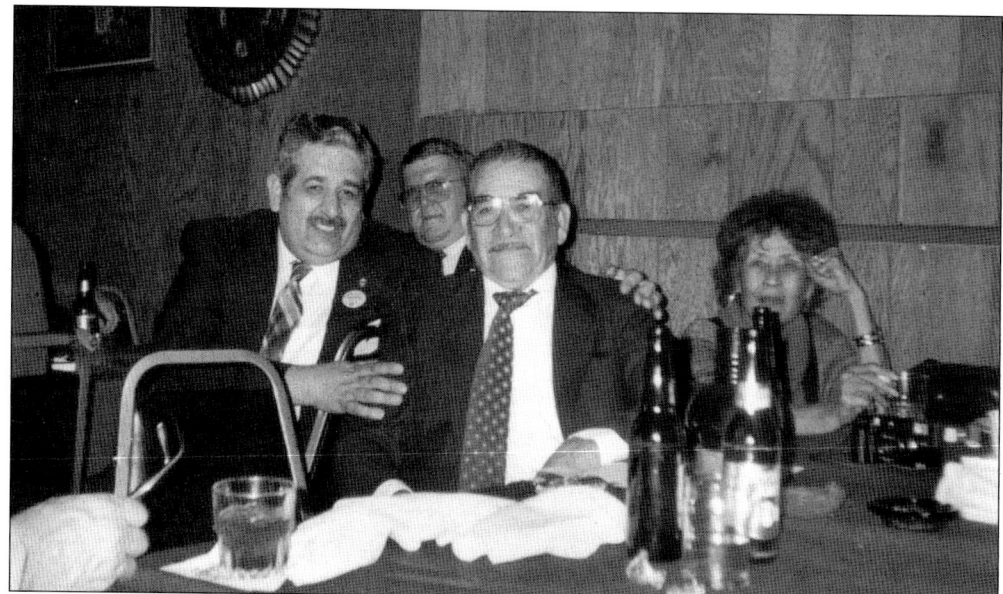

The Veterans of Foreign Wars and the American Legion are organizations reflective of the ways in which Seaside blended the military with the civil rights movement and politics. The two organizations are the backbone of Seaside's political, social, and cultural life. These photographs show VFW members participating in the annual Martin Luther King march in Seaside through a gathering of local politicians at the VFW. Pictured above is Orancio Perez, known as Mr. VFW, at an event with a friend. Evangelina Perez is seated at right. In the photograph below, standing from left to right, are Mayor Jerry Smith and city council members Ralph Rubio and Tom Mancini. Seated in front of them, from left to right, are three unidentified members of the American Legion, Merrilyn Mancini, and Byrl Smith. (Above, courtesy of the Perez Collection, City of Seaside Archive; below, courtesy of the Veterans of Foreign Wars Collection, City of Seaside Archive.)

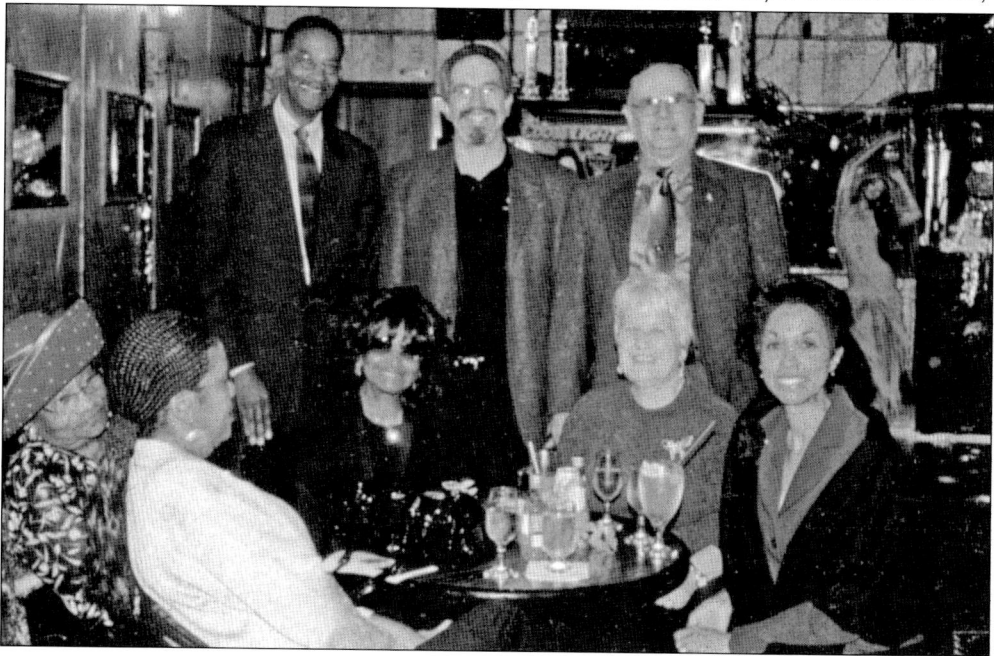

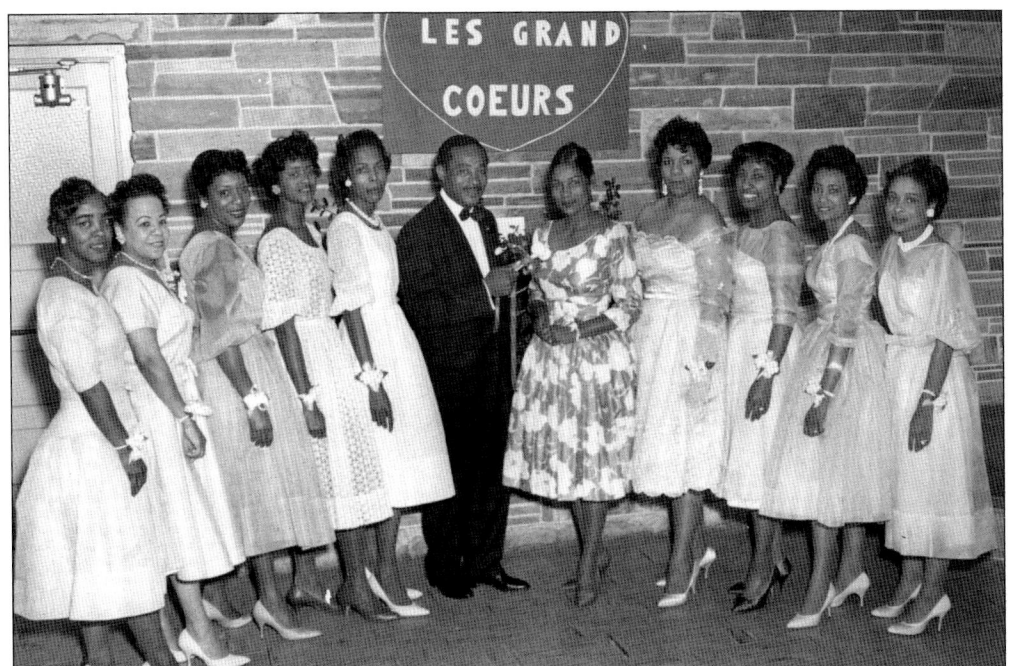

The vibrant, middle-class African American community came to define Seaside from the post–World War II era through the 1990s. The photographs here depict some of the aspects of African American social life that focused on the arts and on the important social organizations that made up the community's culture, such as Les Grande Coeurs; African American sororities and fraternities; the Links, Inc.; and the Seaside Blues Festival, as well as many others. (Both, courtesy of the Lenora Bean Collection, City of Seaside Archive.)

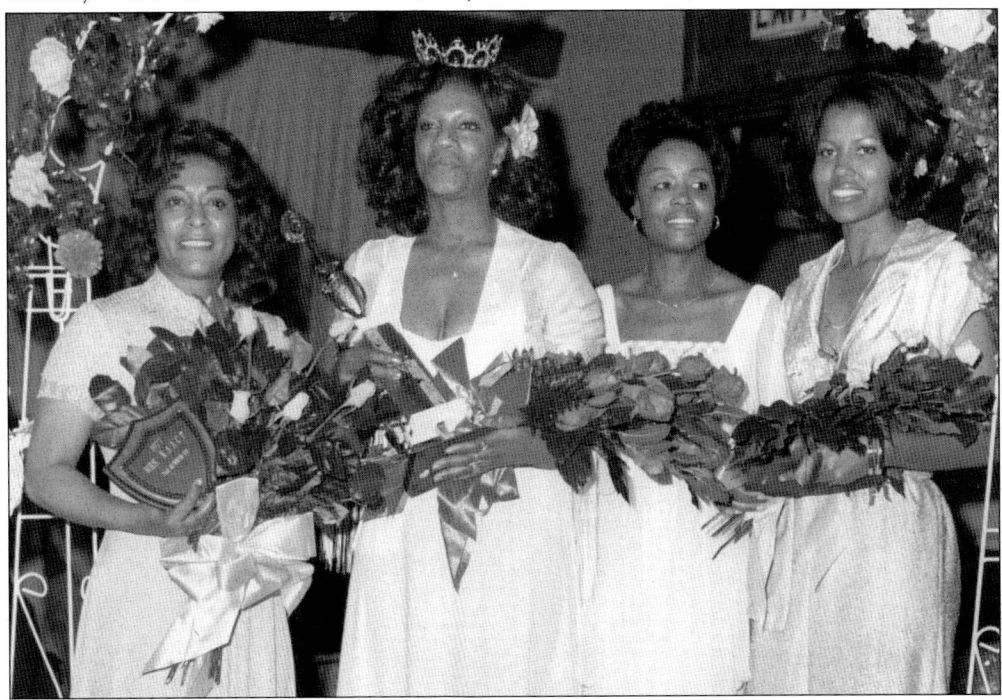

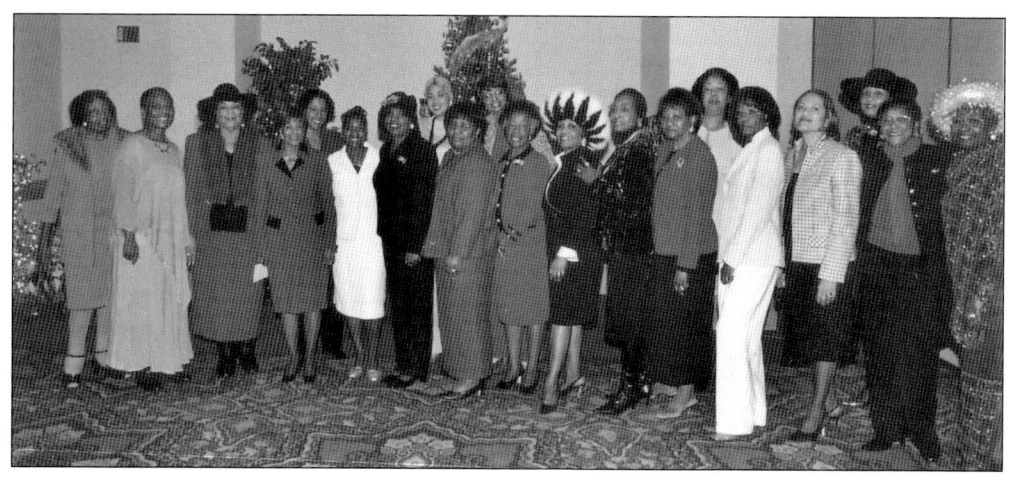

All of these groups had the dual purpose of community spirit and community service, raising funds for everything from scholarships for youth, support for the schools and school programs, and for the Red Cross, American Heart Association, and other worthy organizations. Above is a Links, Inc., event in Monterey, while the first Blues Festival board members are pictured below. Below, from left to right, are (first row) Augustina Lewis, treasurer; Sam Karas; Franklin Washington; Josh Stewart, vice president; and Rubin Simpson. Directors not shown are Dr. Henry Hutchins, Otis and Atty Jones, and Warren Robbins; (second row) Morris McDaniels, president; Martien Puentes, secretary; Evella Brandon; James Manning, financial secretary; Bill Jackson; and Billy De Berry. (Both, courtesy of the City of Seaside Archive.)

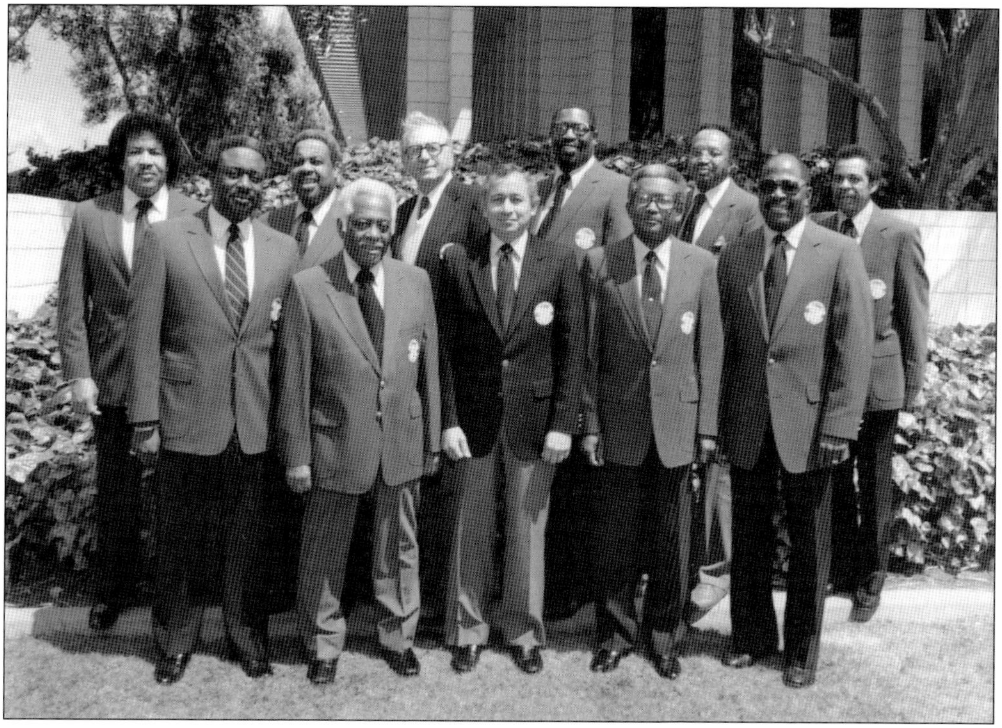

Six
From Military Town to Budding Resort

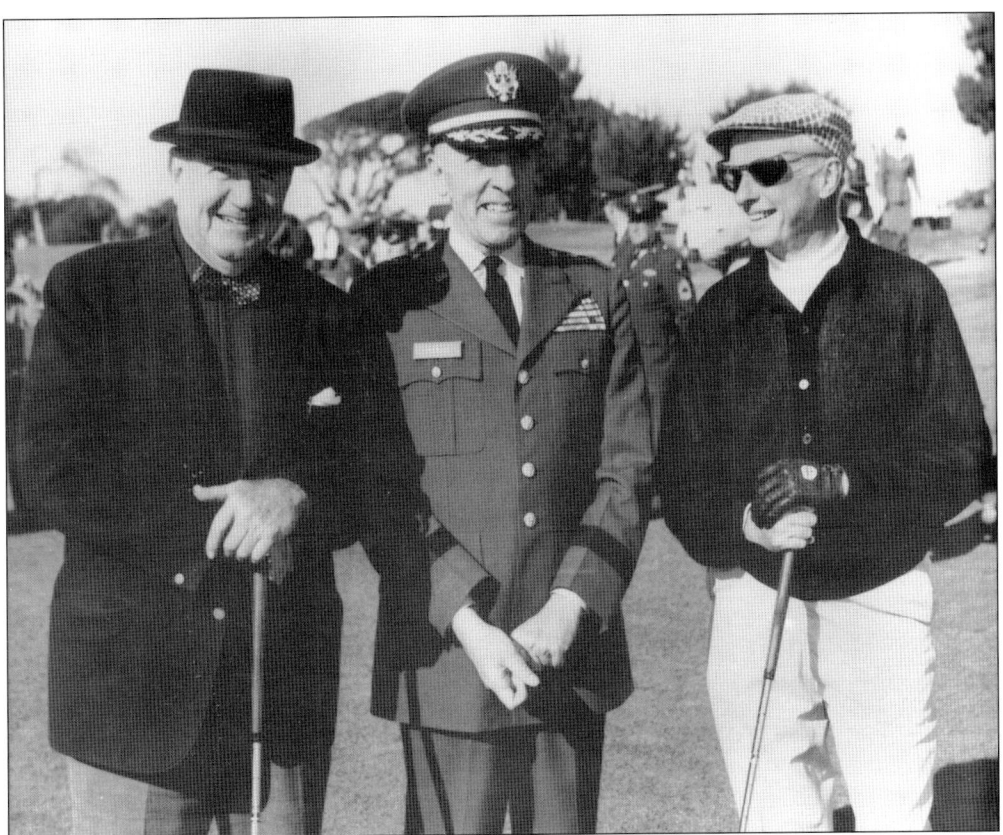

Between 1991 and 1994, the U.S. government closed Fort Ord as an active-duty base. The consequences for Seaside were dramatic as the city changed its identity from military town to resort destination. Pictured in December 1967 are, from left to right, Maj. Gen. Robert McClure; Maj. Gen. Thomas Kenan, commanding general of Fort Ord; and Maj. Gen. Edwin Carns at the opening of the new nine-hole golf course at Ford Ord. (Courtesy of the Bayonet and Blackhorse Collection, City of Seaside Archive.)

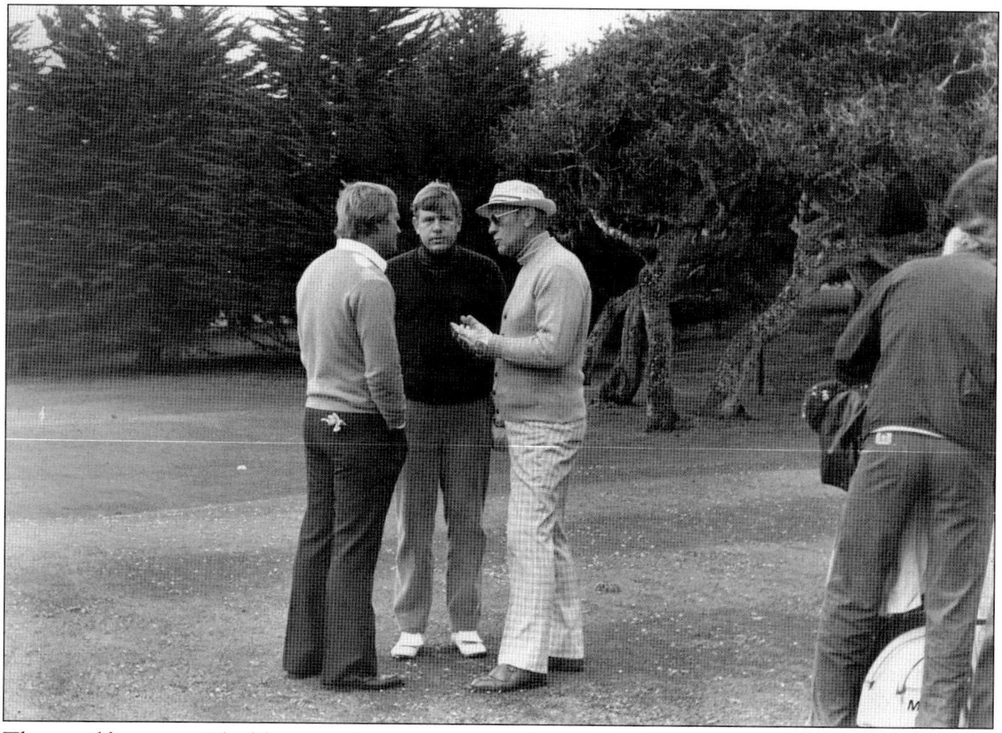

These golf courses, Blackhorse and Bayonet, and the view of Seaside and the water from them were transferred to the City of Seaside from the U.S. Army. Many of the world's most famous golfers and dignitaries played here, including former U.S. president Gerald Ford, pictured above standing on the far right. (Both, courtesy of the Bayonet and Blackhorse Collection, City of Seaside Archive.)

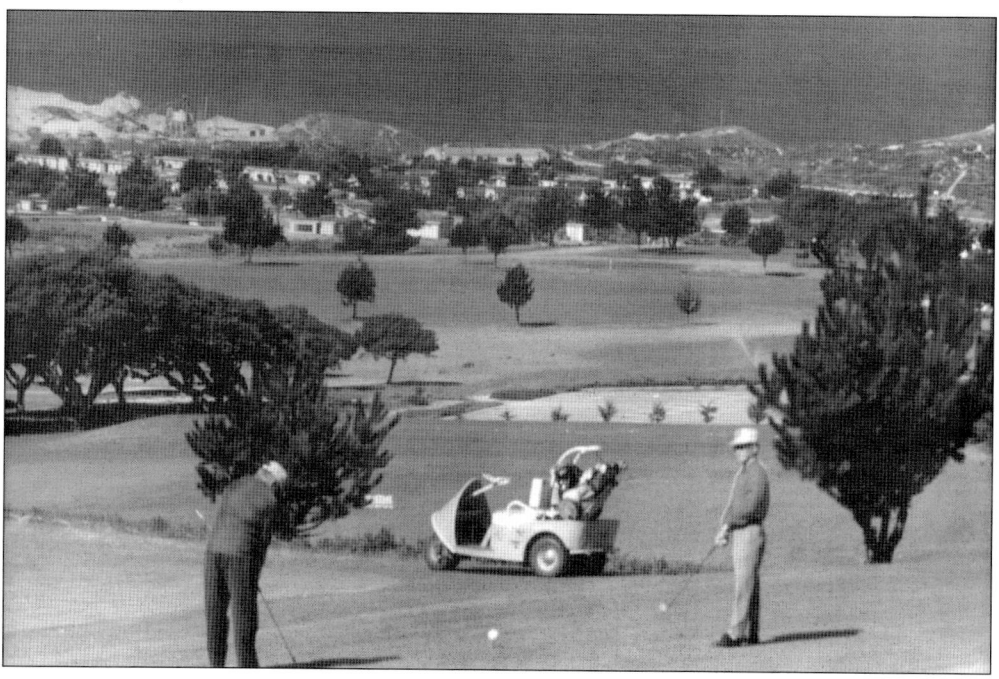

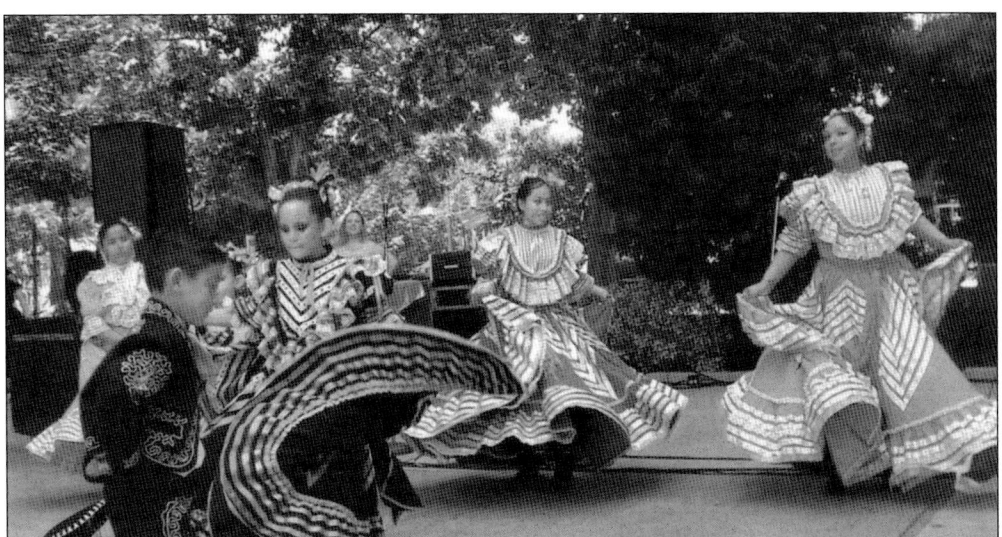

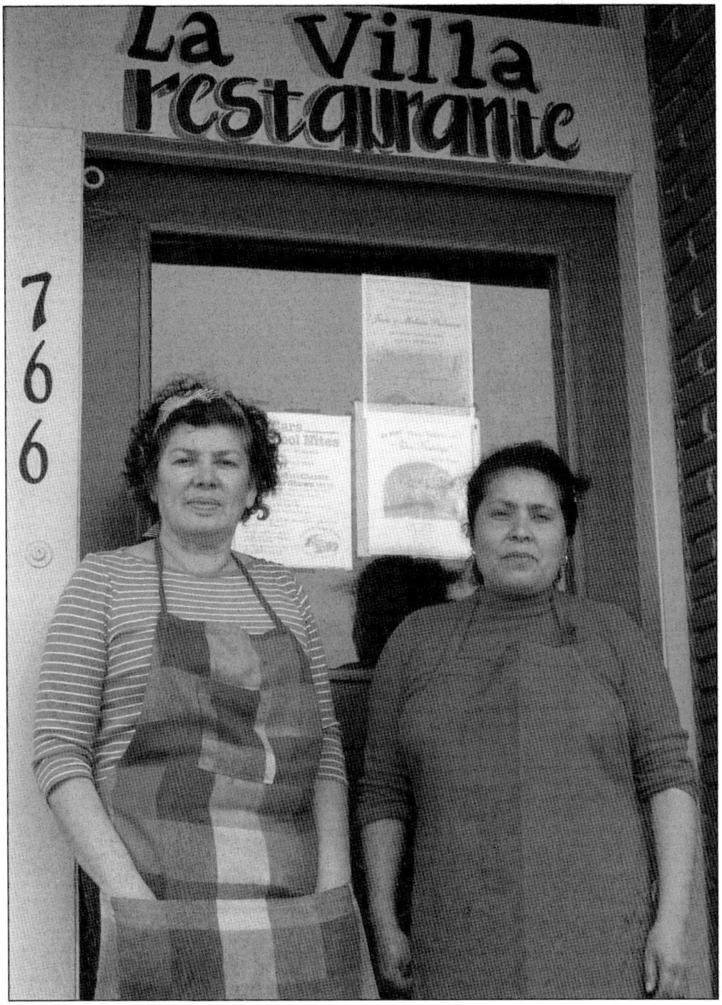

As Seaside entered the last decade of the 20th century and the first decade of the new millennium, it experienced a sweeping demographic shift. A new population of people of Mexican origin arrived in the late 1980s and early 1990s, which created a visible Latino minority/majority in Seaside reflected in new businesses that catered to the new population. In the above photograph are Folklorico Dancers at Laguna Grande Park. Pictured at right are Rosa Sanchez (left), owner of La Villa Restaurante, and Maria Luisa Diaz. (Above, courtesy of the Villalobos Collection; right, courtesy of the Sanchez Collection, City of Seaside Archive.)

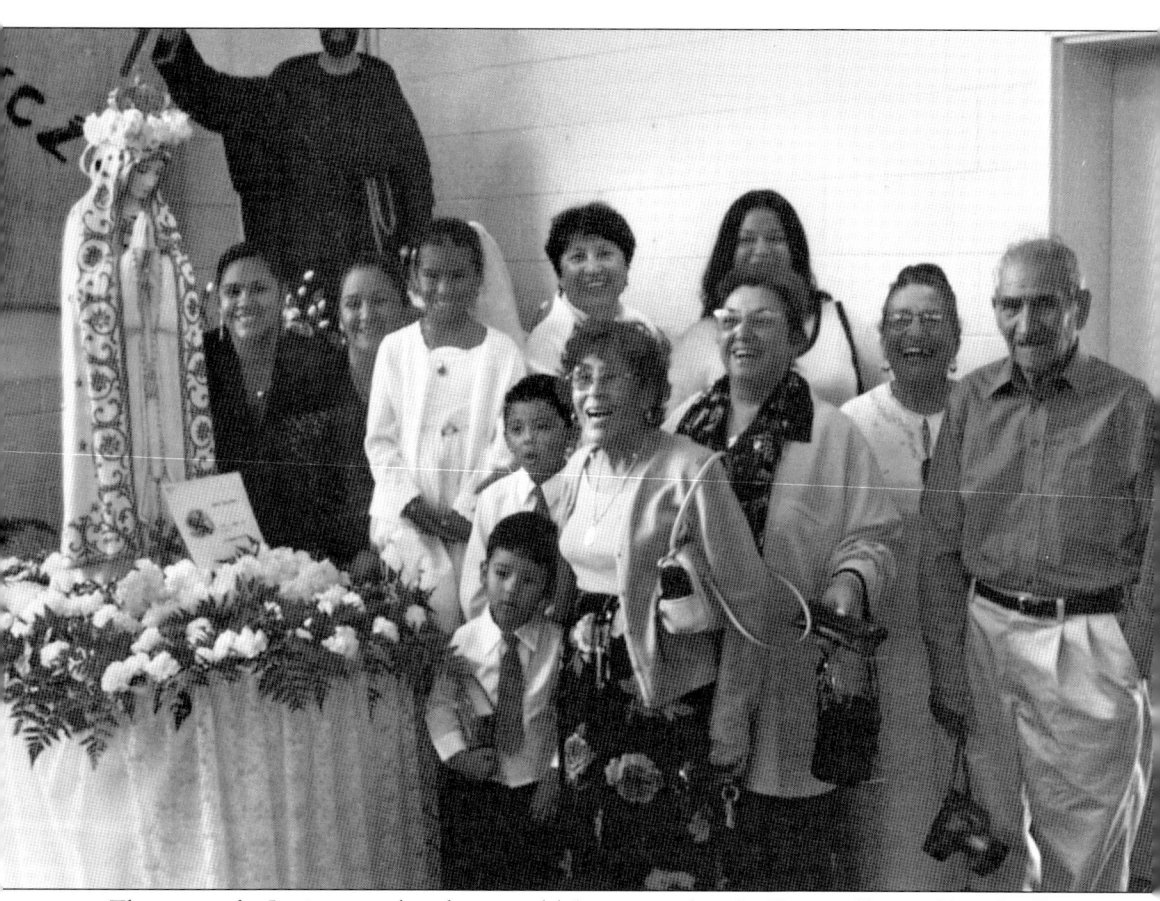

The center for Latino social and spiritual life remained at St. Francis Xavier Church. Shown above is a baptism in the Perez family in May 2004. (Courtesy of the Evangelina Perez Collection, City of Seaside Archive.)

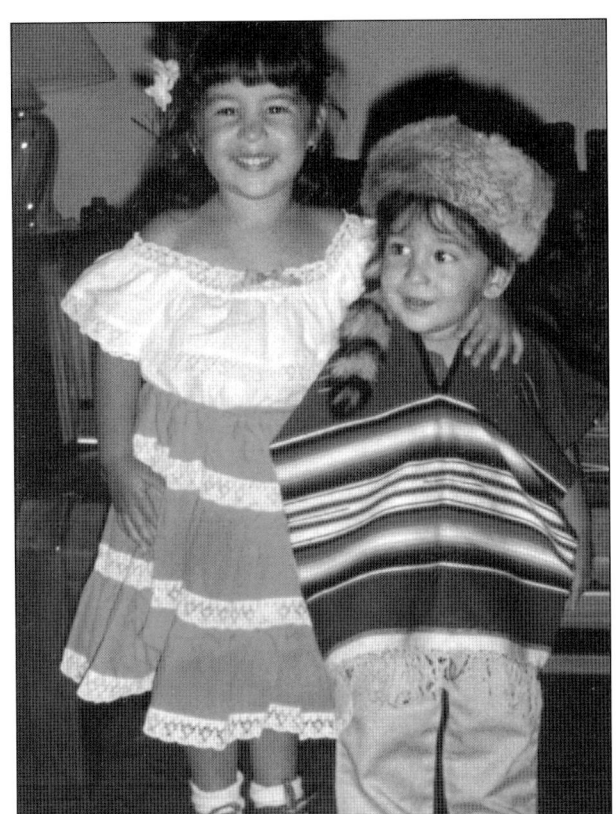

Latinos energetically participated in all aspects of Seaside's social and cultural life. Pictured at left are grandchildren of Evangelina Perez in 1984, and below are, from left to right, Scott, Phillip, and Julian Perez, and Alex Gomez in 1979. (Both, courtesy of the Evangelina Perez Collection, City of Seaside Archive.)

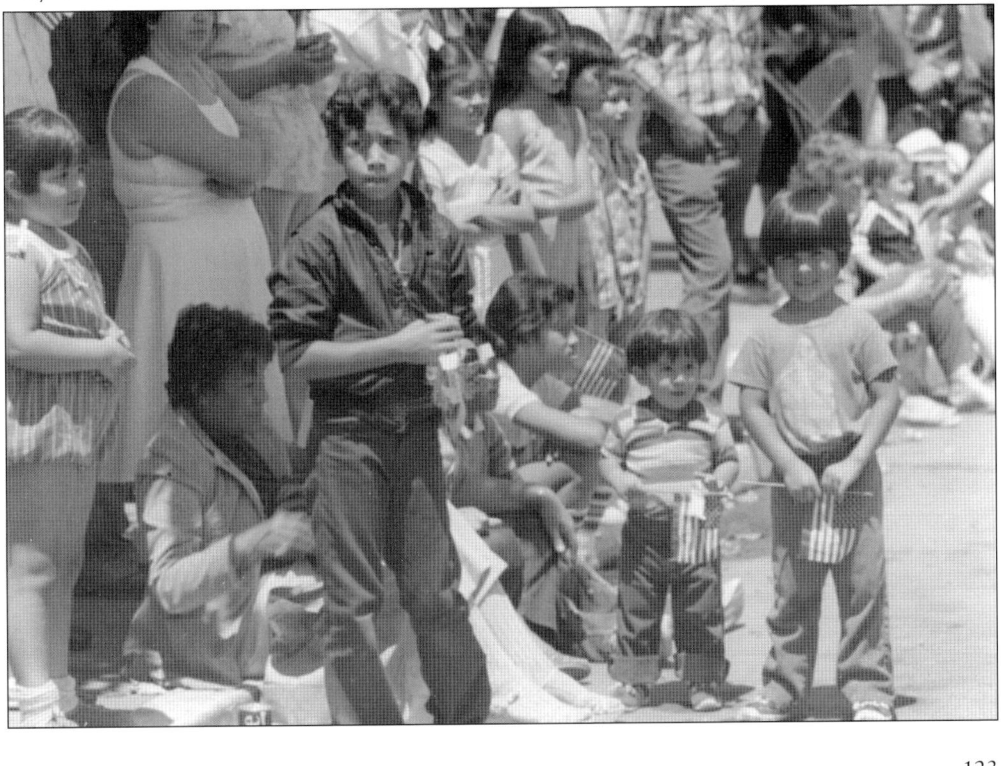

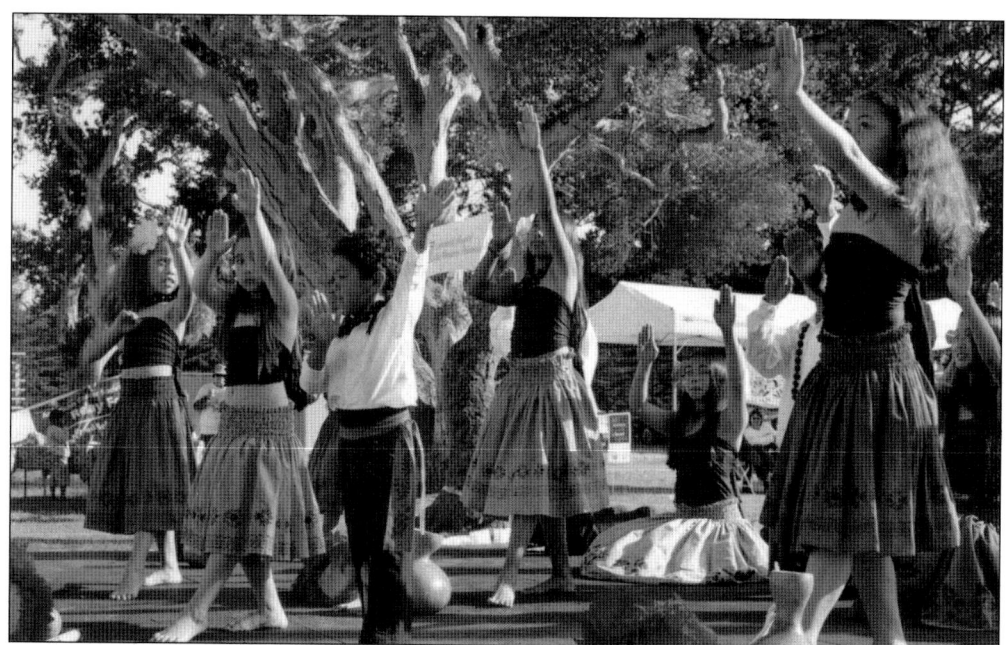

Seaside in 2001 remained a quintessentially diverse suburb that has been a model for California cities undergoing similar population shifts. Although the African American population has shrunk in recent years, the legacy of coalition building, community spirit, and civil rights that was a hallmark of Seaside in the middle decades of the 20th century lives on. Above is the Hawaiian Club in 2005; below is Elijah Hughes (wearing a hat) in May 2004 at a celebration of Pacific Islander culture. Pacific Islanders form an important community in 21st-century Seaside. (Both, courtesy of the Perez Collection, City of Seaside Archive.)

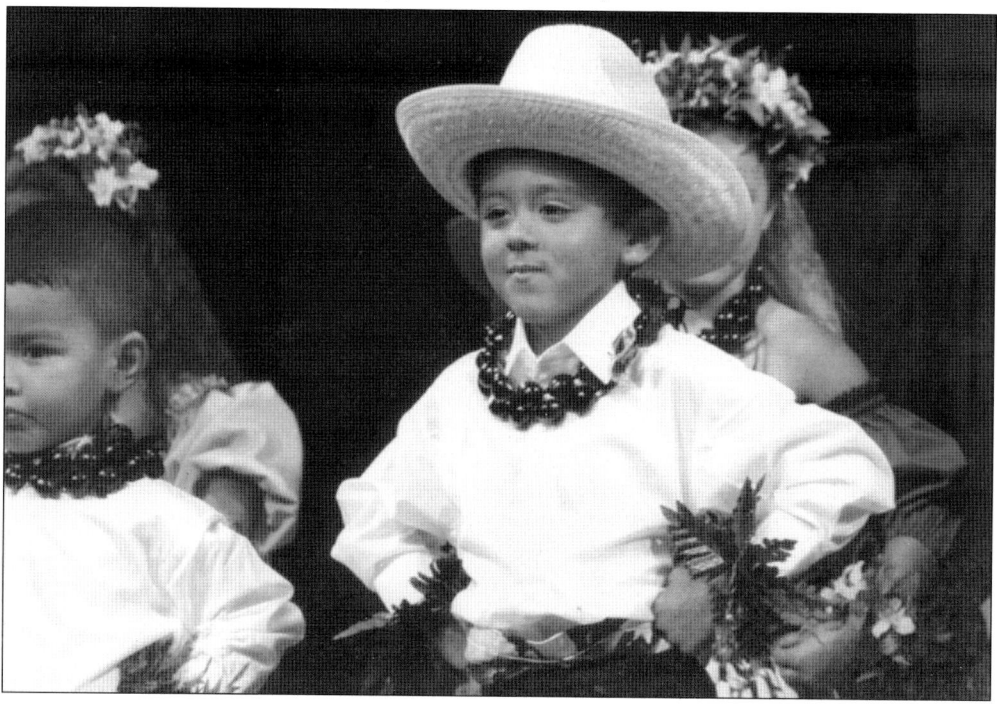

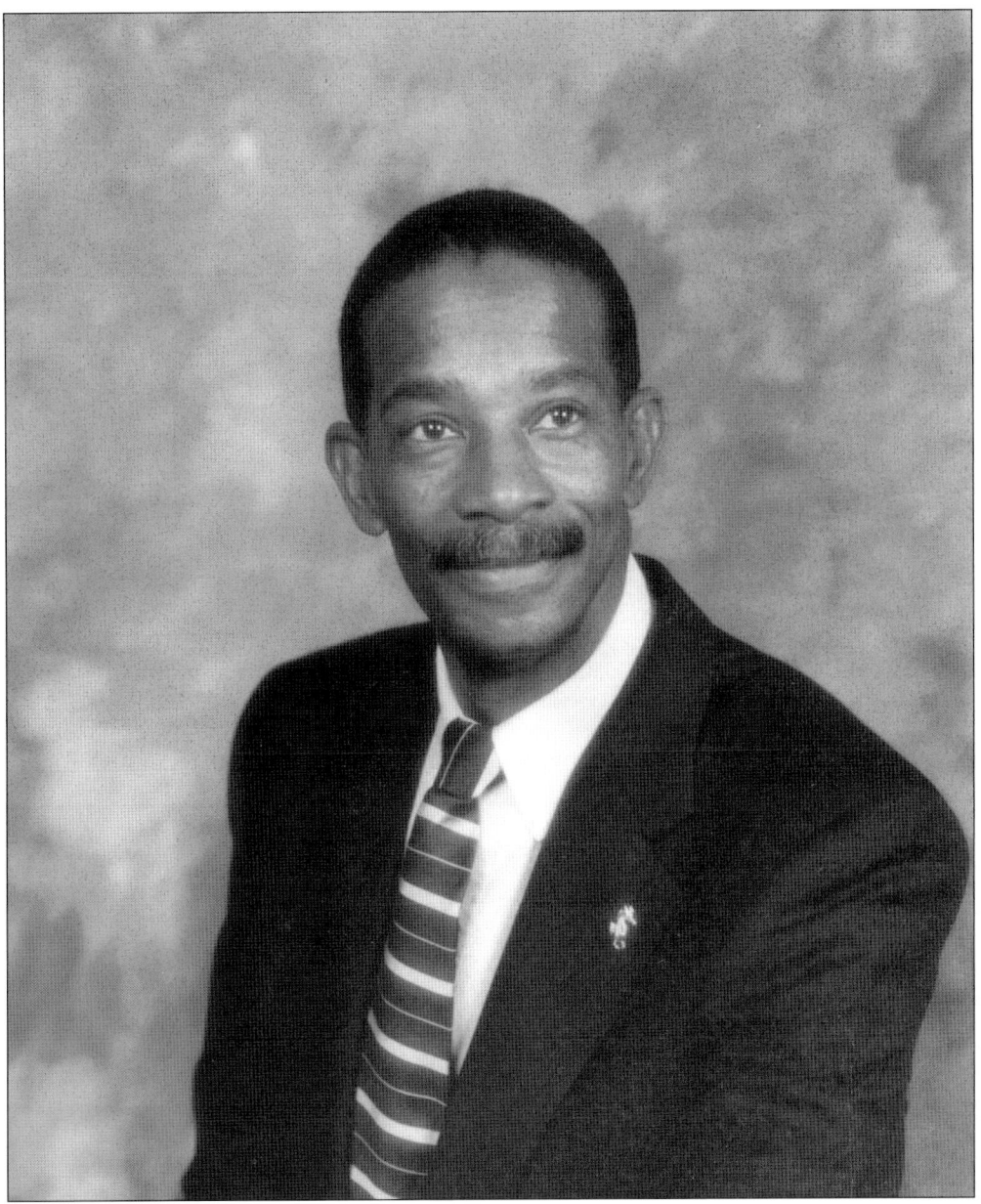

By the election of 1998, a new political coalition led by Jerry Smith had emerged, which included Ralph Rubio, Steve Bloomer, Tom Mancini, and Darryle Choate. Smith easily won reelection as mayor in 2000 with 100 percent of the vote. No one ran against him except a last-minute write-in candidate. Ralph Rubio was elected to the city council, becoming the first Latino to hold public office in Seaside. Smith and the new city council vigorously worked to redefine the city as a resort destination first and foremost. (Courtesy of the City of Seaside Archive.)

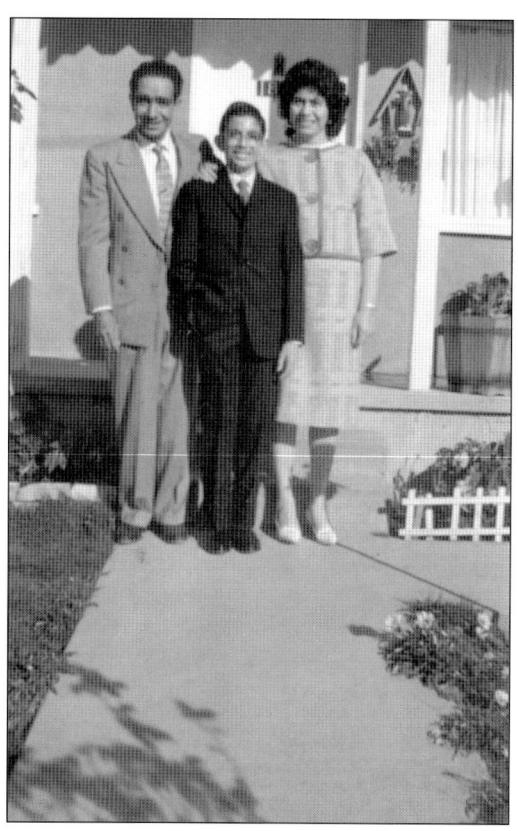

In November 2004, Jerry Smith ran successfully for a position representing the Fourth District on the Board of Supervisors, opening the way for his friend and colleague Ralph Rubio to become Seaside's first Latino mayor. Ralph Rubio's family had lived on the Monterey Peninsula for more than 100 years. A leader in the Carpenter's Union, Rubio shared Smith's vision of a new Seaside that had moved beyond its military identity. The photograph at left shows Ralph Rubio (center) with his father, Salvador, and his mother, Lupe. Shown below are, from left to right, Mary Louise Rubio, Mayor Ralph Rubio, and Lupe Rubio just after the mayor's election in 2004. (Both, courtesy of the Lupe Rubio Collection, City of Seaside Archive.)

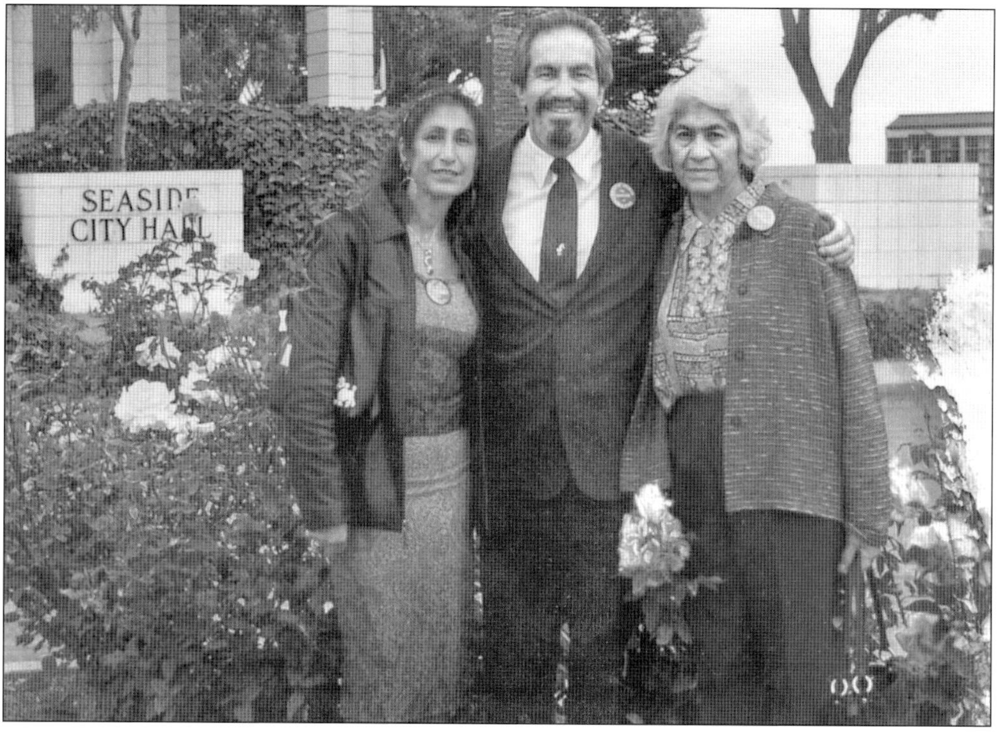

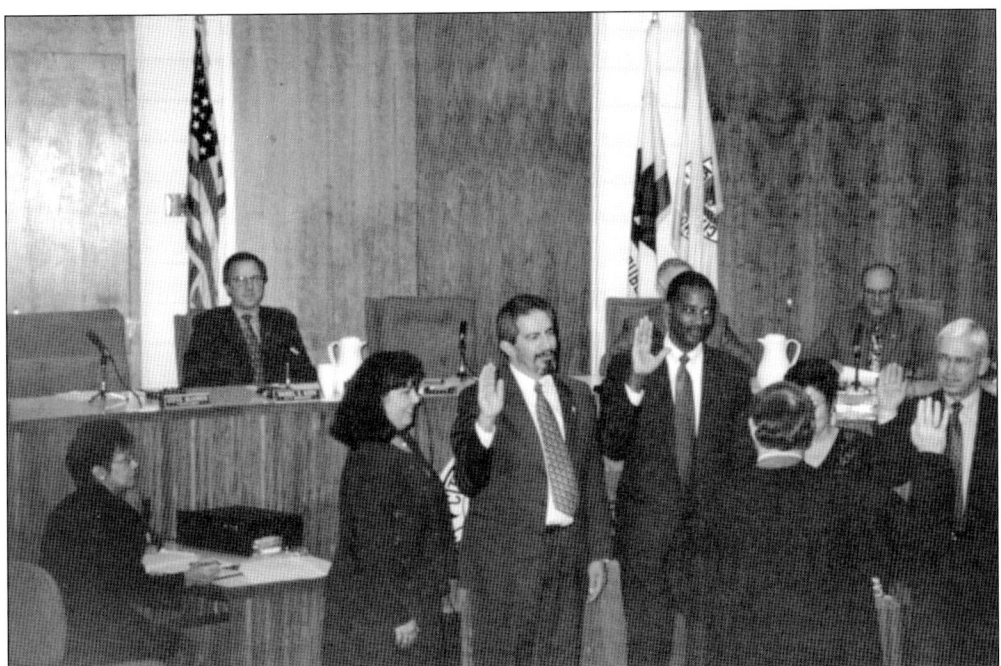

The 21st-century Seaside City Council carries on the coalition building, community spirit, and civil rights that were the legacy of African American political activism and social life, and the hallmark of Seaside in the middle decades of the 20th century. The image above shows Ralph Rubio being sworn in for his first term as mayor. The mayor's wife, Gracie Rubio, is pictured standing on the left. The photograph below is part of the birthday celebration of Martin Luther King Jr. in 2006. (Both, courtesy of the City of Seaside Archive.)

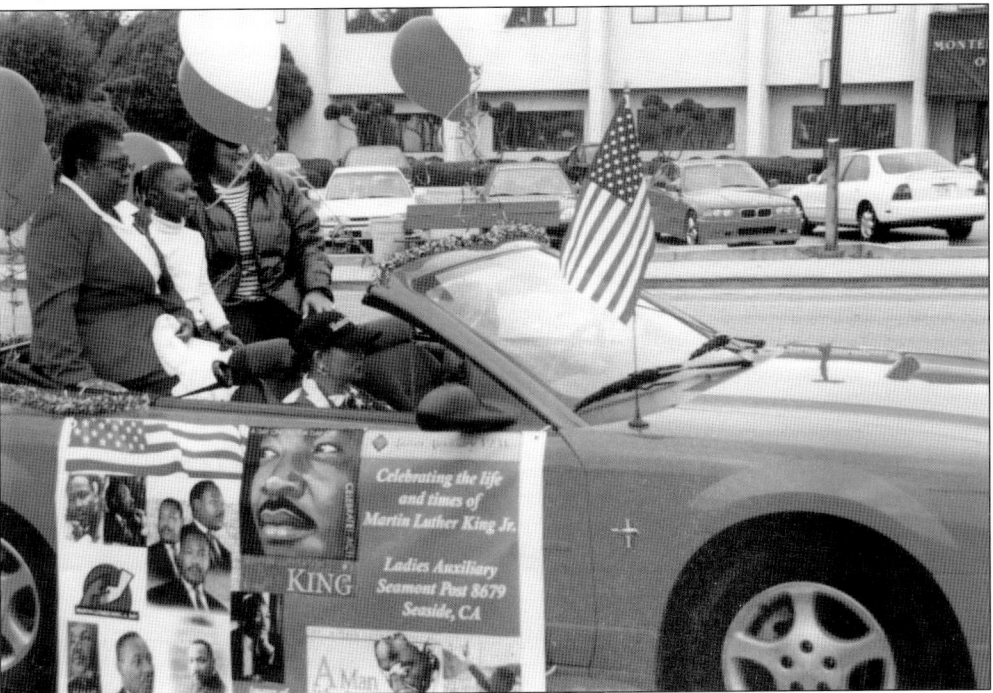

Across America, People are Discovering Something Wonderful. Their Heritage.

Arcadia Publishing is the leading local history publisher in the United States. With more than 5,000 titles in print and hundreds of new titles released every year, Arcadia has extensive specialized experience chronicling the history of communities and celebrating America's hidden stories, bringing to life the people, places, and events from the past. To discover the history of other communities across the nation, please visit:

www.arcadiapublishing.com

Customized search tools allow you to find regional history books about the town where you grew up, the cities where your friends and family live, the town where your parents met, or even that retirement spot you've been dreaming about.

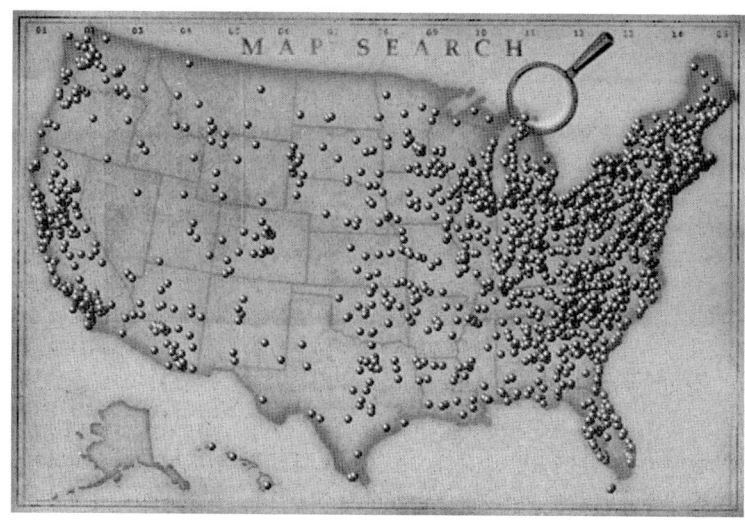